European Monographs in Social Psychology

Social representations of intelligence

European Monographs in Social Psychology
Executive Editors:
J. RICHARD EISER and KLAUS R. SCHERER
Sponsored by the European Association of Experimental Social Psychology

This series, first published by Academic Press (who will continue to distribute the numbered volumes), appeared under the joint imprint of Cambridge University Press and the Maison des Sciences de l'Homme in 1985 as an amalgamation of the Academic Press series and the European Studies in Social Psychology, published by Cambridge and the Maison in collaboration with the Laboratoire Européen de Psychologie Sociale of the Maison.

The original aims of the two series still very much applies today: to provide a forum for the best European research in different fields of social psychology and to foster the interchange of ideas between different developments and different traditions. The Executive Editors also expect that it will have an important role to play as a European forum for international work.

Other titles in this series:

Unemployment by Peter Kelvin and Joanna E. Jarrett
National characteristics by Dean Peabody
Experiencing emotion by Klaus R. Scherer, Harald G. Wallbott and Angela B. Summerfield
Levels of explanation in social psychology by Willem Doise
Understanding attitudes to the European Community: a social-psychological study in four member states by Miles Hewstone
Arguing and thinking: a rhetorical approach to social psychology by Michael Billig

Social representations of intelligence

Gabriel Mugny
Department of Psychology, University of Geneva

and

Felice Carugati
Institute of Psychology, University of Parma

Translated by Ian Patterson

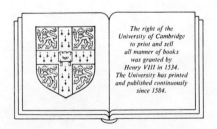

The right of the University of Cambridge to print and sell all manner of books was granted by Henry VIII in 1534. The University has printed and published continuously since 1584.

Cambridge University Press
Cambridge
New York   Port Chester   Melbourne   Sydney

Published by the Press Syndicate of the University of Cambridge
The Pitt Building, Trumpington Street, Cambridge CB2 1RP
40 West 20th Street, New York, NY 10011, USA
10 Stamford Road, Oakleigh, Melbourne 3166, Australia
and Editions de la Maison des Sciences de l'Homme
54 Boulevard Raspail, 75270 Paris Cedex 06

First published 1989

Printed in Great Britain at the University Press, Cambridge

British Library cataloguing in publication data

Mugny, Gabriel
Social representations of intelligence. –
(European monographs in social psychology)
1. Man. Intelligence. Social factors
I. Title II. Carugati, Felice
III. Series
153.9′2

Library of Congress cataloguing in publication data

[Intelligence au pluriel. English]
Social representations of intelligence / Gabriel Mugny and Felice Carugati: translated by Ian Patterson.
p. cm. – (European monographs in social psychology)
Translation of: L'intelligence au pluriel.
Bibliography.
Includes index.
ISBN 0-521-33348-2
1. Intellect – Social aspects. I. Carugati, Felice. II. Title.
III. Series.
BF431.M7813 1989
153.9′2 – dc 19 88-34829
CIP

ISBN 0 521 33348 2
ISBN 2 7351 0260 2 (France only)

UP

Contents

Tables

Preface

Intelligence, if such a thing exists, is the historical creation of a particular culture, analogous to the notion of childhood (Ariès, 1973; Chombart de Lauwe, 1979). The old idea that it is a singular entity is no longer tenable: we have to recognise the plurality of the concept (Château, 1983; Verolié and Castello, 1984). This acknowledgement that intelligence is polysemous, and obviously social in origin, leads naturally on to studying the social representations of intelligence. In fact, as Goodnow (1984) has emphasised, a change in our perspective today is essential: we need to stop thinking of intelligence as a quality possessed by individuals, in varying degrees, and recognise it for what it actually is: a value-judgement, a label, slapped on everybody who happens to have (or not to have) the characteristics regarded as typical of an intelligent person. A semantic change of this sort opens up a new perspective, in which intelligence, instead of being regarded as a quality *per se*, can be seen as an attribute, admittedly socially necessary, which is culturally and historically determined, and therefore as liable to vary between the sub-groups of a single society as from one latitude to another. In short, intelligence needs to be defined socially (Doise and Mugny, 1984) so as to account for the origin of the social issues involved in its measurement, those 'natural' divisions (Moscovici, 1968) which persist even into socialist societies with their claims of classlessness. The 'epistemic subject' of the work of Piaget and the Piagetians appears, perhaps now more than ever, to be a chimera.

How are we to escape from this impasse? Rather than looking for the answer in the development of scientific conceptions of intelligence or of the workings of the intellect (see Sternberg, 1982; Fry, 1984*a*), we have deliberately chosen to investigate the social representations of intelligence, or in other words ordinary, everyday attitudes to intelligence, which are often less naïve than they appear. This approach is fully justified, given a recognition that conceptions of intelligence are actually social constructions, with a multiplicity of significances which, as we shall hope to show, are related to different social integrations. In the end, we should at least be in a better position to distinguish between myth and reality in the notion of intelligence (Salvat, 1976).

The social integrations which determine the social representations of intelligence (and its development, where applicable) are not related primarily, in our analysis, to the weighty sociological variables of age, sex, social class and so on, but derive instead from a socio-psychological approach which owes much to Serge Moscovici's work (1961, 1968) on social representations, defined as appropriate and legitimate objects of social psychology. Thus the trajectory of our research, guided partly by the hypotheses which governed our investigation, and partly by its results, leads us to a consideration of the socio-psychological foundations of representations of intelligence. We shall observe how a representation is constructed, similar to what we are accustomed to think of as the ideology of giftedness, and designed to domesticate the socio-cognitive unfamiliarity created by the differences in intelligence between individuals. It is a process, as we shall see, which implies some kind of information shortage and direct, significant experience of inter-individual differences of a sort typically found among parents (simply by virtue of being parents) and among teachers during the gradual process of socialisation into their chosen function. These are two of the adult socialisations – and we shall be looking at others as well – which have a determining effect on the development of representations of intelligence.

A word of caution is necessary at this point: some of these findings might seem to carry at least an implicit criticism of the socio-cognitive functions at work among both parents and teachers, to mention only those, for their continuing orientation to the ideology of giftedness. And it is certainly no part of our intention to play down this fact, which is self-evident. Nevertheless, one of the most significant aspects of this study is the way its results challenge some of our assumptions about adult psychology, and the forms of bias which govern our representations and our educational practices, especially those of teachers and parents. Our hope is that these results may contribute to a new collective awareness of socio-psychological determinants of adult growth or development which are frequently either overshadowed or unrecognised. We are not accusing either group, both of whom are already quite preoccupied enough with the problems involved in family, occupational and institutional integrations, as well as the daily difficulties of educating children; we want to collaborate in increasing the awareness of socio-cognitive mechanisms which, apparently quite naturally, attend the social representations which we conjure up for the world and for ourselves

Acknowledgements

This study forms part of a research programme currently being carried out at Geneva in collaboration with Willem Doise and Gabrielle Poeschl and is one of a number of additional products of the close international collaboration under the research agreement between the universities of Bologna and Geneva. A preliminary survey of the results was presented to the symposium on 'Le rappresentazioni sociali: campi di indagine teorica ed empirica' at Bologna in December 1983, and to the international conference at Geneva on 'Les répresentations sociales de l'intelligence et de son développement' in June 1984; both these meetings were organised jointly by our respective universities and the Laboratoire Européen de Psychologie Sociale de la Maison des Sciences de l'Homme in Paris. The present book has benefited greatly from the critical discussion stimulated by these meetings. Our analysis was presented and discussed in a more definitive form at the symposium on 'Social and parental representations of intelligence and development' which took place at the 8th Congress of the International Society for the Study of Behavioural Development, in Tours, in July 1985.

This project has been a long one, starting in the summer of 1982, and could not have been completed without the help of a large number of people, the most important of whom are the individuals who agreed to complete the lengthy questionnaire; we are extremely grateful to them for their perseverance. We have been aided in our task in Bologna by Vittorio Biagini, Gabriella Gavelli, Adele Lombardini, Marco Minghetti and Patrizia Selleri, in Neuchâtel by Anne-Nelly Perret-Clermont and Jean-François Perret, and in Geneva by Alessandra Bassetti, Jean-Pierre Gachoud, Simona Grattini, Carmen Roca, Pierre Simond and Marie-Anne Vallet. To all of them we express our thanks.

1 From intelligence to its social representations

Is there such a thing as intelligence? It may seem paradoxical to ask this question after spending more than ten years researching into the social psychology of cognitive development, but the paradox is only superficial: Intelligence, with a capital 'I', is a cultural creation which is central to modern society but which varies according to historical period, latitude and social circumstances. The fact of these variations makes it impermissible to talk about intelligence as a single entity; and yet we use the term every day and are capable of making confident judgements about the intelligence of people we meet, with every appearance that the term is unproblematic. Nevertheless...

Proof of the plurality of meanings of the concept of intelligence is to be found in the variety of definitions provided by intelligence specialists themselves. Sternberg and his fellow-workers (1981) describe a symposium held about sixty years ago at which fourteen experts of considerable standing (such as Thorndike and Terman) were invited to express their views on the nature of intelligence. The conference ended by deciding that there were as many definitions as there were experts, even though there seems to have been a consensus surrounding two, admittedly very general, ideas: namely that intelligence comes down first to the ability to learn from experience, and second to the ability to adapt to the environment. We find an even greater divergence when the views of these English-speaking specialists, the product of a specific scientific culture, are compared with the approach of Piaget and his followers. There is not a great deal in common, therefore, between the definitions of intelligence provided by psychometricians using a variety of tests to assess intelligence quotients (IQ) and Piaget's definition; and although there may occasionally turn out to be a correlation between measurements of IQ and results from a battery of operational tests, this is hardly significant, as the epistemological foundations of the definitions are radically different.

The same is true of the development of intelligence and therefore for different sorts of developmental psychology. Even where there is agreement on how it should be measured (as for instance by a Piagetian operational battery), researchers have differing views on the nature of development and the conditions favourable to it. Some require observation (or in some cases reinforcement) of the correct response, others insist on positive or negative reinforcement (rewards and punishment), while others again will introduce internal conflicts between schemes or patterns of reasoning, or socio-cognitive conflicts between peers, or between adult and child, or will want to reformulate cognitive problems in terms the child can understand, and so on. It seems clear, therefore, that there is no unified theoretical explanation for the development of intelligence either. In addition to this, these different conceptions result in the recommendation of widely divergent educational practices, as witness the heterogeneity of the learning processes and tested experimentally by developmental psychologists (see Strauss, 1972; Strauss and Langer, 1970; Lefebvre-Pinard and Reid, 1980).

If epistemological conceptions of intelligence vary from one researcher to the next, depending on the school of thought they belong to (for historical reasons which could be established, but which we shall not be examining here), just as their theories of development and their more pragmatic approaches to learning processes vary, it must surely be legitimate to assume that a similar heterogeneity, perhaps even more marked, is to be found in the 'common-sense' or 'everyday' conceptions of the man in the street.

It is these social representations of intelligence and its development as recorded at the everyday level, rather than by 'experts', which this book is concerned with. The reasons for studying them are not merely fortuitous, and they stem neither from an attempt to find a way out of an impasse in which we are unable to decide between rival 'expert' positions, nor simply from a temporary, circumstantial interest in social representations because they happen to be fashionable in social psychology. This kind of study is in fact a necessary stage in the development of our own theoretical and experimental approach to cognitive development. This we shall hope to show in the first section of the book, which takes us from the social psychology of cognitive development to the study of representations of intelligence. In the third section we shall tackle the conceptualisation of the socio-cognitive operations implied in the dynamics of these social representations (which will then be illustrated by a broad social psychological study), but before that, in the second section, we shall look at some important issues raised by such a study.

From genetic social psychology to the study of social representations of intelligence

The 'social': a postulate is not enough

There is a solid tradition of thought about the phylogenetic and historical development of the higher cognitive processes which sees them as a consequence of man's interaction with his social, rather than physical, environment. As long ago as 1864 Cattaneo, a precursor of this tradition, believed that new ideas arose from the meeting of different minds, and that they could not be the product either of people working in isolation or of people who agreed among themselves. For Durkheim and Mauss (1969), mental operations involving classification, for instance, were first developed in order to define individuals' membership of social categories such as clan, phratry, tribe and so on. It would therefore be because men grouped themselves, and thought of themselves, in terms of categories that they mentally grouped and classified other beings, until eventually the two sorts of grouping merged into one. Similar arguments have recently been advanced by ethologists (Chance and Larsen, 1976; Humphrey, 1976). In this context, too, intelligence is defined as the individual's capacity to adapt to his environment, but seen initially as a process of adaptation to a social milieu which in turn enables adaptation to the 'physical' milieu, insofar as the species adapts to it. It would thus be through the mediation of social relations that the human being would interact most efficiently with his physical environment. This argument is also implicit in Moscovici's (1968) approach, where he puts forward the idea of studying the human history of nature.

At this very general level of assertion there is (as Doise's historical outline (1985a) shows) a clear consensus among writers otherwise as divergent as Baldwin (1913), Mead (1934), Vygotsky (1962; 1978), Wallon (1969; 1976) and Piaget (1965), to the point where it is possible to conclude that there exists a real postulate of the social (Doise, 1978a) in developmental psychology.

Despite this, psychological research has failed to accomplish the task which Baldwin set specifically for genetic psychology, namely to specify those forms of social interaction which enable individuals to develop. Mead's followers, for instance, moved rapidly into the study of definitions of the self and interiorisation of values within symbolic interactionism (see Carugati, 1979). Vygotsky's pupils, for their part, have not succeeded in clarifying the mediations between social and cultural change and the development of cognitive functioning, only the connections between which have so far been revealed (see, for example, Luria, 1971). As for Piaget, he developed a parallelistic conception (see Doise, 1986) of the connections between social and intellectual development which, by denying any causal relation between them, actually hindered the development of a real socio-psychological explanatory perspective in the Piagetian tradition.

The limitations of this hypothesis of the social therefore become clear from its failure to inspire any studies that set out to define the mechanisms by which the social mediates in the establishment of cognitive processes. Nonetheless, several works have set out over the last ten years or so to try to remedy these omissions, all belonging to the current we refer to as genetic social psychology.

The socio-psychological approach to cognitive development

Genetic social psychology is an expanding subject composed of the various research currents which, for a little over ten years, have been trying to accomplish Baldwin's wish by laying the foundations for a transition from a bi-polar (subject–object) psychology to one that is tri-polar (subject–other–object), to use Moscovici's terminology (1970). Uniting the diversity of approaches, though, there is a characteristically social constructivism, and a similarly social interactionism.

It has to be recognised that the cognitive approaches which adopt the former standpoint, whether they are Piagetian or behaviourist in inspiration, have generally defined intelligence as an individual's adaptation to an environment which is seen in non-social terms. Genetic social psychology asserts a radically divergent viewpoint, defining those psychological factors which are seen as concerned with intelligence as being basically social in nature. The cognitive instruments which the child is induced to work out at the various stages of his development are not primarily reactions to be increasingly both differentiated and integrated into general systems (what Piaget calls logical operations) as a response to a non-social milieu; they should instead be seen as so many mental patternings elaborated by the child in and for social interactions with his peers and with the significant adults in his environment.

The child whose development this new discipline sets out to understand is not any longer, therefore, the idealised *epistemic subject* of Piagetian theory, but a socially integrated child who works out his cognitive instruments in and through his integration into multiple social relationships, at family and peer-group level, and through his experience of school. In this perspective the social is not merely epiphenomenal, brought in as an additional factor which may alter the course of development from time to time, but – in the form of the child's specific social experiences – is actually constitutive of his social and cognitive ontogenesis (Mugny, 1985b).

In this approach the main problem is thus to describe the multiple dynamics at work in these experiences, and to explain how they induce, counteract, modify and in fact provide the main outlines of the child's development up to adulthood. This sort of socio-psychological study of individual development, as the recent collection edited by Doise and Palmonari shows (1984), looks at the development of interaction between young children, patterns of interaction and family lifestyles, control techniques in different models of socialisation, the modalities of interaction in nurseries, the modes of language acquisition and the development of communication, the collective building-up of cognitive instruments and social awareness, the processes of socialisation and the development of identity in adolescence up to and including the changes that accompany the entry into work and citizenship. Another collective work (Mugny, 1985a) focusses more specifically on the development of the child's cognitive processes, and includes several studies which clarify the theoretical foundations of genetic social psychology and pull together the various different approaches to social learning by looking at the collective processes of interaction, communication and working out the meaning of cognitive tasks, the effects of which are not only studied experimentally in the laboratory situation but also set in the context of a new approach to teaching processes. In the following section, therefore, we shall outline the main features of genetic social psychology.

The social construction of intelligence

We can now outline the main features of our socio-psychological approach to cognitive development, which is founded upon a significant amount of experimental research (see Doise and Mugny, 1984; Perret-Clermont, 1980), and which views cognitive instruments (in the broad sense of the term, but particularly the operations described in the Piagetian tradition) as the gradually constructed product of the child's social interaction with peers or adults. This conception goes further than Piagetian parallelism because it assumes a causal connection between social development and cognitive development. This connection, however, has to take the form of a spiral, a sequence of causality moving from one to the other and back again. Our postulate is therefore that participation in social interactions ensures the formation of new, more balanced, cognitive instruments, which enable the child to participate in further, more complex, interactions, which in turn enable new cognitive formulations to be made, and so on. The child's intellectual or cognitive level is thus no more than an abstraction, since a 'transverse' analysis only allows us to define a sort of state, or stage, which is simultaneously a consequence of earlier social experiences and the source of new socio-cognitive experiences.

Moreover, although social interactions play a structuring role, the degree of structuration varies between different moments in the formulation of a notion or of a particular cognitive instrument; their role is most evident, and therefore directly observable, in the initial moment of a formulation. In fact before this initial stage, and as a precondition of its occurrence, the child has to work out what we regard as 'prerequisites' (thus, for instance, for conservation of number to be possible, the child must be able to establish correspondences between terms, and must know his numbers), and these in turn will be the product of earlier social formulations. Once this initial phase of development has been achieved, children are capable of working out these new cognitive instruments on their own. The interdependence necessary to the first stage of the co-elaboration of a new cognitive instrument is, in fact, followed by a gradual process of becoming self-reliant, based upon that earlier interdependence. This sequential model of the effects of a structuring interdependence (for an experimental illustration of which see Mugny and Doise, 1979), takes account of the difficulty sometimes experienced in showing the superiority of collective work over individual work; for this to be done, the prerequisites must already have been formulated, but a moment of self-reliance not yet have been reached. This view has the further advantage that it does not result in a simplistic opposition (of a sort still widespread) between individual and collective work, because it links the two together; its efficacity is based on the already existing cognitive and social abilities of the partners in the interaction, and ensures the subsequent efficacity of the individual work.

Social interaction does, therefore, have structuring power at certain stages in the development of a notion: but what is the alchemy by which it is achieved? We can dispose at the outset of one 'easy' explanation: the child does not progress simply because it is shown the correct model for solving a problem or by positive reinforcement (or negative reinforcement of wrong answers), or at least not solely. The child would, anyway, still have to possess the prerequisites enabling him to grasp the logic of the problem, which is not always clear (Kuhn, 1972). We can thus ignore behavioural or behaviourist explanations (see Bandura, 1971, 1977; Rosenthal and Zimmerman, 1978; Staats, 1975). Even in the most recent versions of social learning theory (for a review of which, see Mugny, Lévy and Doise, 1978) the dominant idea is still that interaction with the correct model (or simply observation of it) is what lies at the source of development. This view is not unproblematic, however: at the ontogenetic level it is difficult to understand how, in these terms, peers could progress without assuming that there is always a partner who is already aware of the correct model; it is a conception which is hard to sustain at the phylogenetic level, too, because it does not take into account the historical evolution of the cognitive instruments that the human race has had to develop at one point or another in the course of its evolution, except by assuming an apriorism, or reinforcement of random changes which turn out to be adaptive, which is the kind of explanation which nowadays seems less and less conceivable in any serious sense. In our view, in short, the child does not simply interiorise a ready-made cognitive instrument or a new way of thinking: he can only formulate these through social interactions.

If, therefore, the structuring powers of social interaction are not derived from observation of the correct model, nor from reinforcement, their dynamic must, as we have shown elsewhere (see Carugati and Mugny, 1985) be socio-cognitive conflict.

The notion of socio-cognitive conflict does, of course, figure in individualist theories of genetic psychology. To take only one example, Inhelder, Sinclair and Bovet (1974) interpreted the learning of cognitive structures as the result of a re-establishment of internal equilibrium following cognitive conflicts caused by a simultaneous confrontation with cognitive schemes or ways of thinking which were contradictory because they were different in kind. The writers then formulated an ingenious set of learning procedures which provided children with an opportunity to confront these contradictory ways of thinking and thereby integrate them into more elaborate cognitive instruments. Here, though, the notion of disequilibrium, like that of re-equilibration, derived from a view of dynamics as strictly internal to the individual subject, whereas everything in fact points to their being fundamentally social in origin.

We have therefore adopted the notion of conflict, but this time placed it within interpersonal relations; hence the term socio-cognitive conflict. The central idea of our model is this, that social interaction structures individual development through the conflicts of response, or the conflicts of communication (the term is Smedslund's, 1966), which it is capable of giving rise to. Cognitive development is therefore regarded as a gradual, step-by-step, social construction of cognitive instruments in response to the confrontation, in social interactions, of contradictory schemas or ways of thinking which are each at first defended by one of the participants. Cognitive progress thus consists of a gradual co-ordination between the child's own schemas or ways of thinking and those of others, which are then integrated into general systems, which can integrate the initially contradictory viewpoints in an increasingly logical way, just as perspective enables different views of the same object to be integrated into one general system.

We have illustrated at some length elsewhere the conditions in which these interactions (between peers, or between child and adult) are capable of inducing this sort of socio-cognitive conflict (Doise and Mugny, 1984; see also Carugati, De Paolis and Mugny, 1980–81); it occurs essentially when the participants at first deploy strategies of response which stem from different cognitive levels relative to the particular task governing the interaction, or when the participants, even though they may be of the same level, present different concentrations, or when, for example in a task involving spatial transformation, the participants have different standpoints. In the case of adults, he or she can also induce socio-cognitive conflict by recourse to a process of questioning (see Lévy, 1981) similar to the socratic method. But whatever the particular dynamic governing any socio-cognitive conflict, the results of the whole set of experiments demonstrate quite clearly that some socio-cognitive conflict must take place if a social interaction is to give rise to cognitive progress by one or both of the participants, during or after the interaction. Socio-cognitive conflict therefore constitutes a necessary – though, as we shall see in the next section, not the sufficient – condition for a social interaction having a structuring role.

There are several reasons why cognitive progress should be conditional upon this confrontational social dynamic, and they may briefly be enumerated at this point. First of all, such conflicts ensure that the child becomes aware that there are other possible responses than his own. Thus the pre-operational child who, until the age of seven or so, is not aware of his own internal contradictions (and so passes unembarrassedly and easily from one response to another) can, as a result of a social conflict taking place here and now, prepare the way for a de-centring. Then, by his contradictory responses the other participant provides information about other response models. On this point, it should be noted that our theory does not require the contradictory response to be a correct one: children are capable of formulating new ways of thinking out of confrontations with incorrect models (something which constituted the main principle of our experimental demonstrations) by taking their and the other child's errors as a starting point. It is also here that our conceptualisation differs radically from theories of social learning based on observation of or interaction with a correct model. This may of course create a standpoint which is favourable to new socio-cognitive construction, but it cannot ever be considered a *sine qua non*. Nor can that kind of approach, unless it alters its fundamental premisses, explain the positive effect of incorrect models that are at the same level as the child's initial cognitive level, or even lower (Mugny, Lévy and Doise, 1978). The effect of a correct model, on the other hand, fits perfectly well with our conception, as it assumes, in any particular case, a socio-cognitive conflict in which the information needed for the correct answer is nonetheless available.

There are two other aspects. First, social interaction may make the child particularly active, and the Piagetian school has frequently stressed the self-regulatory nature of this activity. But the most important point, and this we shall return to in the next section, is that socio-cognitive conflict always challenges the social relations between the participants; although the conflict is also cognitive, it is primarily social, setting up an opposition between the participants. Resolution of a socio-cognitive conflict is therefore also the resolution of a directly interpersonal one.

Things are not as simple as that, however. It is not enough for a conflict of communication between participants to emerge from an interaction: the way the conflict is resolved must also ensure a new cognitive formulation. Obviously this does not always happen. So the argument needs to be taken a step further.

Ways of resolving socio-cognitive conflict

A socio-cognitive conflict does not automatically guarantee cognitive progress on the part of the individuals concerned. The way it is resolved, the modality of its resolution, must consist of a new cognitive formulation. But there are also other possible modalities of resolution, as other dynamics are capable of counteracting this potential progress. We therefore have to take into consideration two major types of modality of resolving socio-cognitive conflict (De Paolis and Mugny, 1985; Mugny, De Paolis and Carugati, 1984), which are to be found even in adult education systems (see Monteil, 1985).

Relational regulations, to begin with the negative side, express dynamics of direct dependence *vis-à-vis* the other, with no modification of the cognitive response. According to this type of regulation, resolution of the conflict aims at solving it from within with the least effort. In asymmetrical social relations, such as with an adult, the child is thus in danger of being limited to behaviour which accommodates to the adult, something we have frequently observed. Admittedly the child may justifiably expect the adult to show greater competence, and therefore should not ignore his responses, but this kind of regulation may be thwarted by the adult himself, particularly by proper use of systematic questioning of his own response as much as that of the child (Lévy, 1981).

Relational regulations of this type are, moreover, not the sole prerogative of the adult. They can also be observed in peer-group interactions, either as a result of asymmetrical sociometric relations, or where there is too great a disparity in cognitive level (in which case a higher level of logical thinking will confer a greater degree of necessity on the answers, and thus ensure a stronger behavioural consistency which may result in unilateral domination (see Emler and Glachan, 1985)). We have also frequently noted that progress in peer-group relations happens more often when the structure of decision is bilateral or reciprocal than when it is unilateral or strongly asymmetrical. Finally, it seems that children sometimes just juxtapose their contradictory responses, without making any attempt to integrate them into a single, collectively thought-out resolution. In all these instances, the relational regulations work against the co-formulation of a level of reasoning higher than that which the children showed themselves capable of in pre-tests.

On the other side of the coin, we define as socio-cognitive the regulations of socio-cognitive conflict which consist of the working out (by both participants, or by one or the other) of a new response model which integrates the initially divergent centrations without, however, denying them. Thus two children judging two lines of equal length to be unequal because they are staggered spatially (each choosing a different one to be longer, by each centring on opposite overshoots) can successfully construct the conservation of length and consequently give the (correct) response – that they are of equal length – as soon as they realise, for instance, that the displacements are complementary, and the compensation therefore reciprocal. Here we can say that there is a cognitive regulation, to the extent that no relational dynamic (unilaterality of decision, socio-cognitive asymmetry, etc.) or situational dynamic (asymmetry of status) counteracts it. Collective elaboration therefore takes place within a tissue of complex social relations which extend well beyond the narrowly cognitive framework of the task. And there can be no doubt that developmental psychology has seriously underemphasised, not to say ignored, these dynamics, which are just as much a part of the child's social world as intra-individual cognitive dynamics. In order to grasp these and incorporate them into a theory, we use the notion of social marking.

To begin by defining it (see Mugny and Doise, 1983): social marking defines any socio-cognitive situation in which can be made salient, to some degree, an existing (or potential) correspondence between responses derived from social regulations (governing a symmetrical inter-personal relation between peers, or a relationship between positions in a social structure, as in child–adult relations) and responses derived from the organisation of the cognitive schemas the child has at a given moment of his development. In order to allow or prevent development, as the case may be, this correspondence has to be made salient and the child must be brought to the point where he describes and confronts simultaneously the responses that derive from his cognitive system and those that derive from his system of social awareness. The mechanism which ensures cognitive progress is once again socio-cognitive conflict, because new responses reflecting cognitive progress can only arise out of the confrontation of contradictory responses.

Socio-cognitive conflict can therefore turn out differently, depending on whether the child makes an abstract division or is directly involved in a division between adult and child, or between peers. Similarly a division will be made differently according to whether the children have deserved the same thing or not, in a task involving the conservation of liquid or of number. And a spatial transformation has different meanings depending on whether the task represents a village (material which lacks specific meaning) or a school classroom (where certain spatial relations have to be conserved because they are regulated by hierarchical relationships governing the class-group). Here social marking introduces social meaning outside the direct social interaction, apart from with the person asking the child the questions (a purely symbolic intervention of the social). But that is enough of examples (for further details, see De Paolis, Doise and Mugny, 1987). The important thing to remember is that children have several registers of response at their disposal, as much 'social' as more specifically 'cognitive' (in the current usage), and that these organise their representations of the social world, and are involved to a considerable extent in the course of social interactions and in the modalities of resolution of socio-cognitive conflicts. And it is probably the fact that they are so diverse which, to a great extent, accounts for the complexity of the links between social interaction and cognitive development, or even perhaps for inter-individual differences. But in any case, an understanding of the dynamic of intellectual development requires a complex approach of a sort that genetic social psychology has only just started to employ. Let us look, therefore, at some possible developments of it as a prelude to our own investigations.

Prologue to the study of social representations of intelligence

As we have seen, then, social interaction is not necessarily an opportunity for intellectual development. Even if it arouses a conflict of communication, it is only effective given certain conditions, the greater number of which involve the meanings implied on the one hand by the task itself (its social marking) and on the other by the course of the interaction itself (particularly the type of regulation). So in order to understand the development of a notion we must understand the representations which the child himself constructs of these interactional episodes, in relation to his cognitive level, his social awareness, and the specific concrete circumstances of the interaction. No meaning, in fact, is ever completely constructed in advance; it also derives from the concrete relations which take place during the interaction.

These brief points take us directly to the central question of this book, that of the social representations of intelligence. Our model of the social development of intelligence does not just involve social interactions but also, and perhaps more importantly, their representation, their reconstruction at the mental level by the individuals in interaction. We have seen this happening from the point of view of the child who, in some situations, is led to formulate one meaning or another from the task and his relationship with the other participant, and in some instances to construct, or fail to construct, more elaborate cognitive instruments. Yet even at this level there is still important work to be done, as we are not yet sufficiently well informed about the social awareness children formulate *vis-à-vis* the social interactions they participate in, nor indeed about the method of formulation itself.

There is another viewpoint in this constant work of formulating meanings, which also needs to be examined, that of the adult who, whether as parent, educator, or in some other role, intervenes to initiate or manage social interactions with the child. Here we may, indeed should, assume that the adult is also involved in interpreting, and so in creating representations of, the socio-cognitive situations with which the child is constantly confronted and, as part of this search for meaning, putting forward 'strategies' to help the child. The way this is done will vary, particularly in relation to the adult's general conception of intelligence and development, his value system, his assessment of the child, and his interpretation of the task itself. In these terms, any cognitive task will always be social, and its outcome (especially in terms of whether cognitive progress takes place or not) will inevitably depend on the coming together of the child's and the adult's representations. But this sort of mutual, reciprocal formulation does not happen automatically. As we shall see later in this chapter, the adult's interpretation and the child's do not necessarily coincide, and the adult is very often far from fully aware of the way the child mentally constructs the cognitive tasks that are presented to him. In short, they are both likely to be subject to biases of interpretation, and these will affect the course of the interaction.

The collective dynamic is complex in a way which has often been underestimated: the educator (to remain at the general level) constructs his or her own representation of development in general and of specific tasks in particular. Depending on the representation, he will become involved in one particular type of interaction with the child (which may be more, or less, conflictual, may or may not involve a model, may or may not be one in which he can have the correct answer). The child also approaches the task with his own representations, by definition distinct from those of the adult, and becomes particularly involved in some kind of relational or socio-cognitive resolution of whatever socio-cognitive conflict that may occur. The way the subsequent interaction unfolds may therefore be hybrid, and the more impenetrable for the participants' mutual ignorance of each other's 'pre-constructs'.

In our view, it is because developmental psychology has no way of grasping this complex of transformations of meaning in its totality that it is still incapable of understanding the mechanisms that govern the differences between individuals in the same sub-group as well as individuals belonging to distinct social groups. It ought to be possible to explain differences in mental capability, which fuel the age-old debate about nature and environment – the nature–nurture argument – and which are used to justify the continual resurgence (which we shall encounter elsewhere in our study) of a particular psychology, or ideology, of giftedness, as long as one takes account of the whole range of elements in the chain which links child, adult and cognitive tasks, via their representations.

Genetic social psychology may perhaps provide the answer to the impasse the developmental disciplines are in. It may, in the end, succeed in articulating the various problematics involved in this complex question. But it will obviously not be an easy matter; and one of the issues which needs to be clarified first is the question of social representations of intelligence among adults, the forgotten figures of child psychology. To grasp the socio-cognitive dynamics which govern adults' socio-cognitive interactions with children, we need first to be aware of the main ways in which they categorise intelligence and intellectual development. Although this is a fairly specialised area, it is an essential step in our understanding of cognitive phenomena and their development. But before we look at it in more detail, it is worth looking at the other, less theoretical, issues involved in it.

Issues involved in studying social representations of intelligence

Why study the social representations of intelligence? As social psychologists, it is impossible for us not be curious about social representations, and have some interest in them, given the current vogue for studying them. Social psychology has turned away from large-scale, general theories (which were always in fact partial, anyway, as they only related to the 'formal' aspects of socio-cognitive processes) and rediscovered content, and with it, a lost seriousness. This study can claim to make a supplementary contribution to this process (as we shall show in the third section of our introduction). But as social psychologists of cognitive development, it seemed to us that an examination of social representations of intelligence was an essential stage in our approach. It is, furthermore, one which raises a variety of issues.

In the following section we put forward three arguments for the importance of the study of representations of intelligence for the study of cognitive processes and their development. The first is a reminder that for all the diverse ways of speaking about intelligence, it is something which almost everybody agrees in placing a positive value on, such that it is a social value of prime importance. The second concerns the impact that representations of intelligence can have on the actual development of a child's intelligence, through the teaching processes by which an adult engages with a child. We shall look in detail at one example relating to the process of communication (which is central to our own developmental approach). The third issue involves the explanation both of intercultural and intra-cultural differences, including those between sub-groups of the same culture.

One term, one value, and a multiplicity of discourses

We know the term 'intelligence' does not refer to any one concept or single theory. Indeed it can fairly confidently be said that there are as many definitions of intelligence as there are schools of thought claiming to define it scientifically. Intelligence lends itself to a great number of different approaches, and so it is dealt with at a variety of analytical levels (Doise, 1986). Psychologists and sociologists therefore use fundamentally different reading grids and terminologies to analyse it or to talk about it; psychologists describe and explain the organisation (Piaget's operations, for example) and workings which structure the mental activity they regard as relevant to intelligence, whereas sociologists analyse the differences between social groups and the kinds of judgement which accord some of these groups the privilege of being 'more intelligent', and of having children who are 'more intelligent', than others, in a society which tends to reproduce its basic divisions (Bourdieu and Passeron, 1964, 1970; Bourdieu and de Saint-Martin, 1975).

Things then get increasingly complicated, as there are divergent definitions within the same discipline; in fact, as we saw at the beginning of the chapter, there are as many definitions as there are researchers. The same is also true of the development of intelligence which, depending on the school of thought, either creates a fixed, *a priori* view, or else gives rise to genetic conceptions, which themselves break down into empiricist, or interactionist and constructivist theories (see Piaget's analysis, 1956).

It is hardly surprising, therefore, that we should find such heterogeneity in everyday attitudes to intelligence. Sternberg *et al.* (1981) looked at definitions of intelligence given by students, and by people on a station platform and outside a supermarket. Although not experts, they all 'knew' what intelligence was, as they were all able to give definitions of it, albeit very divergent ones. This study concluded that there is a variety of definitions, out of which three main forms of intelligence emerge very clearly: the ability to solve problems, verbal ability, and 'social competence'. So although the man in the street does have a conception of intelligence, it appears in a number of prototypical forms rather than as one single model. These conceptions also vary according to the group questioned, and thus according to their social position, especially as concerns the weighting given to academic and 'everyday' aspects in the overall definition of intelligence. The authors also found that the 'naive' conceptions, while not strictly identical, were broadly similar to those expressed by 'experts' on intelligence, which does not exclude the possibility that popular conceptions may constitute one of the main bases of scientific theories of intelligence, where they are then refined and legitimated. In fact it is this diversity of definitions which enables Sternberg (1980) to conclude that, in the final analysis, almost all theories of intelligence (factorial ones in that case, but the point can be generalised) are correct.

The striking thing, then, aside from the fact that everybody has a theory of intelligence, is that despite the diversity of definitions of this single term there is nevertheless a sort of consensus. To begin with, nobody seriously questions the term 'intelligence' itself. Whatever the differences in emphasis, all the discourses share the belief that they are dealing with the same single word – 'intelligence'. But the reason for this is that, no matter what precise meaning is assigned to the word, intelligence is a recognised social value.

Thus when Anderson (1968) asked subjects to assess the degree of attractiveness of 555 adjectives relating to character traits, being 'intelligent' was one of the most highly rated, coming out in seventh place. Bruner, Shapiro and Tagiuri (1958), to take another example, asked their subjects to describe an intelligent person. Their results were clear: only positive characteristics were associated with the idea, and no negative characteristics appeared at all. Being thought intelligent is therefore a good thing, as our study will confirm, even though we shall be qualifying the 'halo effect' somewhat.

Finally, describing an individual as intelligent not only enables us to evaluate and classify him, it also has a fundamental part to play in the social position (and associated privileges) he can lay claim to, and attain. There is no need to illustrate this point, as it is abundantly evident in a society which is still so largely based on the differentiation between intellectuals and non-intellectuals.

The other side of the coin is equally familiar: educational selection and intelligence tests are value judgements, the consequences of which for those the judgement does not favour are often under-estimated. Failure at school, which still reaches high levels even in Europe, involves more than merely being a year (or several years) behind friends with a 'normal' education. It affects an individual's identity, his self-image, and his view of the word, as recent research has clearly shown (see Deschamps, Lorenzi-Cioldi and Meyer, 1982; Bell and Perret-Clermont, 1985). In fact, failure and the low valuation it implies are to a large extent interiorised by those judged 'unintelligent'.

These two well-known aspects, the existence of a single term covering a variety of different discourses, and the social value conferred by being deemed intelligent along with the personal repercussions of not being so, are in themselves two good reasons for being interested in social representations of intelligence, the ways it is perceived in everyday life.

Impact on the child's development

Our approach regards cognitive development as mediated by actual or symbolic social interactions which result in the gradual construction both of cognitive systems (particularly in the area of logical operations) and of systems of social awareness (of the self, the social world, values, etc.). From the constructivist point of view, which we share, this knowledge is thus formulated, actively constructed, by the child through social interactions. This does not only happen between peers: the adult is an essential participant, whether as parent or teacher, or in whatever other function he occupies in relation to the child. And of course the adult also influences interactions between peers, either by instigating them or by regulating them. Even a 'democratic' leader is still a leader. So, since adults intervene continually over the course of a child's existence, it is surely not unreasonable to assume that their ideas about intelligence and development will have a major influence on their interventions, and thus on the child's actual development.

Let us take as an example the scientific debate on the effectiveness of different methods or techniques of learning. In that context, where things are simplified because, theoretically, the transition from the theory of development to specific learning methods is governed by the same hypothetico-deductive logic, it is quite obvious that the techniques vary according to the general conception. We saw this earlier with the notions of conflict and disequilibrium. If a researcher is convinced that the child only learns through environmental pressure, he will offer him a correct model, provide positive reinforcement of it, and if necessary penalise the incorrect response. A researcher convinced of internal capacities to observe reality will come up with situations in which the child sees his thought patterns challenged or invalidated by his observation of the real. In the Piagetian tradition, belief in a process of self-regulation will lead the researcher to create internal disequilibria which can initiate processes of re-equilibration. In the socio-psychological approach, conditions are created which are likely to give rise to conflicts of communication. It is not important here to decide the relative effectiveness of these different learning procedures or the mechanisms they imply. The important fact is that theoretical systems have consequences for didactic approaches, and therefore for the child's development.

It is also reasonable to assume a link between conceptions of intelligence and the child's cognitive development on the part of non-experts. But we still have to determine how, by what mediations, this happens, which is where the difficulty lies. We start at the outset with the idea that the impact may not be direct, if only because the child himself comes to make a representation of the learning episode in his own particular terms, which in all likelihood are not necessarily those which the educator originally intended.

Therein lies the probable explanation of the particular complexity of the literature on the subject (see the review by Goodnow, 1985; Emiliani and Carugati, 1985). Indeed at first sight it is difficult to establish an unequivocal link between the general opinions expressed by adults and their behaviour in specific circumstances. It is certainly right to assume that there are methodological difficulties, as the choice of experimental tasks may not always be the best indicator of the adult's behaviour in his own environment, nor the units of observation necessarily adequate. However, a theoretically more important reason is that people adapt their behaviour, to a greater or lesser degree, according to the situation they are in, by differentiating between their behaviour and their ideas. This explains why the behaviour of fathers is closer to their ideas than is the case with mothers (Stolz, 1967; McGillicuddy-De Lisi, 1982). In reality, because they have a more limited number of interactions with the child, their systems of reciprocal adaptation in different circumstances will be less differentiated (whence the possibility of seeming more 'dogmatic' in relation to the idea–action connection) than the mothers', who develop more complex, and in some ways more decentred, systems. The difference between the sexes in this case is only circumstantial: the mediating factor is the question of reciprocal adaptation.

The problem therefore is that the impact of ideas is mediated by complex transformation sequences which we not yet fully understand. First there is a transition between general ideas, the educational styles the adult claims to support, and actual practice, in which he or she seems to adapt behaviour to fit in with specific aspects of the situation. Then there is a complementary and potentially fruitful approach which starts by regarding the adult's intentions and behaviour as themselves mentally reconstructed by the child, who then elaborates a particular representation of them. This sort of reciprocal constructivism, unduly neglected by research, is well illustrated in the argument put forward by Cashmore (see Cashmore and Goodnow, 1985). In that study, father and mother were asked to assess the importance of different qualities of an ideal pupil. The children did the same, and they also had to 'guess' what their parents' choice would be. While there was almost no significant correlation between the values expressed by the parents (father or mother) and their children, the correlations between the children's values and those they attributed to their parents were almost always significant. Parents undoubtedly have an impact on their offspring, but the mechanisms by which that influence operates are complex, to say the least, and they too call for interactionist and constructivist analysis.

So far, we have stressed the difficulty of establishing causal connections between the representations or ideas of adults and the actual development of the child. We have therefore argued for a complex model of the relations between ideas, behaviour, and impact on the child's development. But having said this, things are sometimes less complicated, and the connections more easily observable. We shall give a detailed example of this at this point, because it bears upon a nodal point in our own socio-psychological conception of cognitive development, one which also concerns the processes of communication. Both are essential to the initiation of socio-cognitive conflicts, which are equally conflicts of communication.

The importance of communication has led a number of researchers to explore its parameters, particularly in communicative exchanges between peers (see Beaudichon, 1982), as well as to provide a thorough micro-analysis of social interactions between children, especially in relation to Piagetian tests (see Vandenplas-Holper, 1979). Communication has also been shown to be of prime importance in the development of mathematical understanding, of symbolic language and of proof in mathematics teaching (Balacheff and Laborde, 1985; Schubauer-Leoni and Perret-Clermont, 1985).

For our purposes, however, we shall be more concerned with instances of communicative exchanges between children and their parents, and the part these play in the development of the child's communication. For communication develops too. Several partly experimental studies (see Robinson, Silbereisen and Claar, 1985) to do with referential communication (in which the individual has, for example, to give a sufficiently accurate oral description of an object for his partner to be able to identify it from among a number of more or less similar ones) have demonstrated that children up to the age of six or seven experience difficulty in understanding that the ambiguity of their message may be a reason for its failure to communicate, and that for the communication to be 'successful' there must be no more than one referent.

Thus although children of five are capable of describing objects in minute detail, they do not communicate sufficiently to enable their partners to make an unambiguous choice. They think that as soon as their message is compatible with the object they are describing and what they want to say about it, it is adequate: they do not realise that, in order to be effective, communication has to adopt the receptor's viewpoint, and that they should therefore distinguish between their own intention and the message they have to transmit. And when communication breaks down, they cannot recognise that the ambiguity of their message can be removed only by providing the necessary complementary information: they are much more likely to take the view that the listener should think harder! The children, in fact, have not yet developed the notion of 'ambiguous information', a form of social understanding which is essential to their future development, partly as regards their potential to profit, from the cognitive point of view, from co-operative interactions with others, especially socio-cognitive conflicts.

According to these authors, the children remain ignorant of the verbal communication process because of the very way in which adults talk to them and thus communicate with them. An analysis of the protocols of parent–child interaction (at home or at school) shows in fact that when a message is not understood because it is ambiguous the adult generally takes the initiative and tries to work out the answer himself, usually by asking for the missing information. Yet while this sort of strategy can be effective all it can do is solve the task in its most pragmatic aspect, 'finding the right answer'. They do not enable the child to learn to communicate effectively, because he does not realise that the adult only asks him to complete his initial statement because he did not, and could not, understand it (Robinson and Robinson, 1981).

Walper *et al.* (1981) also studied the strategies parents used to help their children in situations where there was a communication problem. The children had to complete a referential communication task, with the father or mother present as observers but also authorised to intervene to help the child. All the parents tried to do this, but the children showed no signs of progress in referential communication as assessed in individual pre- and post-tests. This was because in fact the parents were not responding to the communication problem specifically: they made hardly any use of strategies (of socio-cognitive conflict, in our terminology) that might reveal the child's contradictions, express doubts or even reject the first formulation of the message. Consequently the child is not given the conditions for making progress in the communication process itself.

Why do parents behave like this? These authors claim that it is because they do not realise that the children really are not aware of the causes of the failure, or success, of the communication, and that they do not possess the notion of ambiguity in communication. None of the parents, in fact, pointed out the ambiguity of the messages, nor the fact that the child did not take the receptor into account and therefore did not 'decentre' his message at all. Success or failure as they saw it was merely a matter of 'verbal ability' and the capacity to discriminate between objects (which all these children were theoretically capable of doing). It is therefore the way in which they represent the task to themselves that directs how they interact and what help they give the child. Because they do not recognise that the difficulty lies in the communication itself, they do not help their children progress from that point of view. The parents, in reality, were trying to influence the child's immediate behaviour, not communication (Silbereisen and Claar, 1982), because they interpreted the task as a simple problem-solving one and not as a communication task.

We now turn from the negative to the positive side of the problem. Robinson and Robinson (1981) observe longitudinally how mothers react when faced with the problem of communicative failure. Only a very few mothers told their children they did not understand them or that they did not grasp what they were saying. But at six the children of these 'conflictual' mothers had a more advanced understanding of the role of ambiguity in communication than those of mothers who simply guessed the answer or only asked questions of general explanation, not ones specifically related to the communication process. The same authors also report several further studies, this time experimental ones, in which children made progress with communication when the experimenter explained the ambiguity of the initial statements.

There is another longitudinal study which broadly confirms the effect of the development of communication on the child's general cognitive development. Dickson *et al.* (1979) evaluated the process of referential communication between mothers and four-year-old children, each in turn taking the parts of locutor and auditor, and vice versa. The degree of precision of the communication (assessed by the number of correct choices made by the auditor) turned out to be broadly predictive, even two years later, of a variety of measurements of verbal, conceptual and intellectual aptitude (the latter being measured by IQ on a scale adapted for that age; Wechsler, 1974). The effects of communication thus have repercussions for the whole of cognitive development.

This collection of data illustrates two things. First, it reminds us, if we needed reminding, of the actual role played by strategies of intervention (especially parents') on the course of the development of the child's socio-cognitive 'capacities', by emphasising the need to take account of the modalities of communication, the importance of which is not widely enough acknowledged. (This problematic may also be generalised to cover educational situations in general, where many small dramas stem from 'misunderstandings', one-sided interpretations of initial statements which themselves are not always adequate.) And, second, it demonstrates that although communication difficulties arise from the way the child interprets the task and the success or failure of the communication (depending on his psychogenetic level of communication), they also have their roots in the way parents themselves represent the task and the communicative exchange to themselves, and modify their intervention strategies accordingly. The 'scripts' (Abelson, 1976) or the 'social episodes' (Forgas, 1981) that the parents formulate thus probably mediate the child's cognitive progress. This must surely constitute another good reason for studying social representations of intelligence as well as their usefulness for a putative, real 'parental education'.

Intelligence and social and cultural differences

One central problem remains: the differences between individuals. As Rostand (1965) puts it, 'in the "lottery of heredity" the same number never comes up twice'. The problem is aggravated when intellectual differentiations correspond to intellectual differences between cultures, or between sub-cultures in the same society. To that extent it is true that with history we have in a way moved from biological to social phrenology, with the individual's social origins taking the place of his 'bump of mathematics'.

Thus it is that the results of intelligence tests (in the form of IQ tests, or Piagetian tests) are regularly lower for individuals from so-called 'primitive' or 'traditional' cultures than those obtained on average for individuals from western societies. Although some have seen (and in some cases still see) this as the effect of genetic differences between races (see Lemaine and Matalon, 1985; MacKenzie, 1984), the current debate (at least so far as it impinges on our argument) has moved towards a questioning of the whole notion of intelligence (see Berry and Dasen, 1974). One important argument is that these differences are due to a mismatch between the tests and the cognitive processes elaborated in cultures other than those of the inventors of IQ, and that the tests are not suited to their environmental and social ecology. This view certainly represents an essential step forward and decentring, but it needs to be taken a step further, because it does not rule out a hierarchy of values linked to a dominant conception of intelligence (the thought patterns of traditional societies are less abstract because they are linked to a less complex universe, etc.). The more advanced work in this area therefore takes the view that it is the definitions of intelligence which vary from one culture to another and over different dimensions, so that rational hierarchisation becomes impossible. The recent volume of the *International Journal of Psychology*, edited by Fry (1984a), is exemplary in that respect. And the study conducted by Dasen (1984; see also Dasen *et al.*, 1985) among the Baoulé shows how intelligence is defined as 'social intelligence', comprising obligingness, responsibility within the family and the community, deference towards elders, and certain skills (such as memory) which are integral to this social intelligence. Clearly this conception is a long way removed from western and psychometric definitions, and the degree of difference makes it impossible to continue to talk about 'primitive' societies on a deficit or handicap model derived from an obvious socio-centrism. This recent research means that we have to talk simply in terms of a model of differences between cultures, and differentiations in kind in values and norms.

Comparisons between industrialised civilisations such as the United States and Japan (see Conroy *et al.*, 1980; Hess *et al.*, 1980), also reveal divergent value-systems, which have profound implications, particularly for relations between parents and children. And although these approaches do not rule out the long-term search for a universal psychology of cognitive competence (Berry, 1974, 1984), they do require the rejection of a one-dimensional, and therefore strictly hierarchised, view of cognitive functioning, in favour of treating them on a non-hierarchised matrix.

Differences between social groups are not the same as differences between cultures, even though at that level those differentiations are the most immediately visible and obvious ones. In western society, compulsory education for all (or almost all) might seem to introduce some homogeneity into conceptions of intelligence and the values implied in them. One prototype, mostly transmitted by schools, might seem to have emerged as the dominant model (although not excluding other, less recognised or unrecognised models), and that is abstract intelligence, as symbolised by the computer. Yet despite the 'democratisation of learning', not all social groups have equal access to this intelligence. As the saying goes, we are all equal, but some are more equal than others. And the reason for this is that, in the terminology of Bourdieu and Passeron (1964), we are all broadly the heirs of our original social environment.

It is not necessary to go into the question of intelligence tests here: their primary function is precisely to discriminate and to select (Tort, 1974), and in practice they discriminate according to social origin. Similar differences also appear with Piagetian batteries of tests (see especially Coll Salvador *et al.*, 1974a, 1974b), which are no less subject to the dominant definition of intelligence as 'abstract intelligence' (see Haroche and Pêcheux, 1971). Using a spatial transformation test (Mugny and Doise, 1978) following Piaget and Inhelder (1948), or a test of co-ordination of interdependent motor actions (Mugny and Doise, 1979), we also had to conclude that there were statistically significant differences between 'privileged' and 'underprivileged' backgrounds in a Southern European country, the children from the latter being demonstrably less cognitively advanced than those from the more privileged environment.

The problem, then, is to take the argument beyond these conclusions, which appear to be the only ones which fit the evidence, and try to explain them from a socio-psychological point of view. Our reasoning, which follows on from our 'general' socio-psychology of cognitive development, is this: these tests, from this point of view at least, do not take account of the socio-psychological conditions of origin or logical operations. All they do is evaluate the differences between individuals as if they all benefited, or could all benefit, from the same objective conditions of development. Yet this is obviously not the case. To stop at that formulation would therefore be to accept an abstraction, and in fact to obscure social differentiations in the conditions of development.

In the canons of genetic social psychology these conditions presuppose the existence of social interactions and conflicts of communication in relation to the cognitive tasks whose development we are studying, and it is extremely improbable that these interactions are the same in these contrasting environments. We therefore gave our subjects a second stage of tests in which they had to work alone or in groups of two or three in situations likely to provoke a socio-cognitive conflict. The results of individual post-tests were quite clear: whereas the differences between the two backgrounds persisted through the individual work, they became less marked or disappeared altogether, depending on age, when the subjects had had the benefit of a social interaction. The results of these studies (see Mugny, Perret-Clermont and Doise, 1981) do not demonstrate that these differentiations are due to the intervention of differentiated valuations and representations of intelligence and its development, and thus 'close the circle' in the assumed chain of causalities. But this is an additional reason for further research in this direction.

These experimental conclusions raise at least two questions. First they show that the question of inter-group differentiations takes a radically different form, depending on one's conception of intelligence and its development. We saw this with the intercultural studies, according to which prototype of intelligence was adopted (abstract versus social, for example). We also saw it in the intracultural studies. From an individualist epistemological perspective, things appear simple: they stop at a stage which corresponds to our pre-test, and so go no further than the establishment of differences, which incidentally also coincide with 'popular wisdom' and 'common sense'. From a socio-psychological perspective, however, we can go a step further, and provide children with the conditions of interaction taken to be constitutive of their development. We thus provided the opportunity of conflictual interactions with other children, and therefore of socially constructing cognitive instruments for co-ordinating points of view, which, for reasons to be elucidated, are not provided 'naturally', or in equal quantities, by all environments. The lesson to be learned from this is that we modified, at least within the space of an experiment, some of the dynamics of cognitive differentiation between groups, and did it precisely by virtue of a specific representation or conception of intelligence and its development. Why, therefore, should these representations not also operate, albeit in a more diffused way, in the socio-psychological determinants of these differentiations?

This brings us to the second question, why are there these differences between social backgrounds? Since the differences diminish as a result of social interactions on the tasks in question, we may assume that they are statistical rather than innate (in addition to which, we found a similar pattern of development in both environments, moving from social interdependence to autonomy, but with a time-lag of a year in the progression; see Mugny and Doise, 1979). The probability of children from under-privileged backgrounds interacting over similar cognitive tasks, and thus co-ordinating the mental operations that define these cognitive competences, is less than for those from more privileged backgrounds. But, again, why should this be? It is not enough to assume that one environment is culturally richer than the other. This difference in resources still needs to be defined. This is, however, something we still know too little about, from this point of view. Whatever may be said about Bernstein's ideas (and see Labov, 1970; Cole and Bruner, 1971, for a critique of the notion of 'cultural deprivation'), they are interesting (Bernstein, 1960; 1971); the concept of restricted and elaborated codes in fact refers to particular social structures of communication, and we have seen the importance of these. Lautrey's work (1980) also seems to be convergent here, where he reaches the conclusion that a (social) environment which presents both disturbances capable of arousing disequilibrium and regularities capable of allowing re-equilibration seems more favourable to the process of constructing new mental structures than an environment rich in regularity but poor in disturbances, or rich in disturbances but poor in regularity. These types of family environment, however, are not randomly distributed over different social backgrounds, any more than the value-systems which organise these environments. Taken as a whole, these examples imply the existence of different values, but, perhaps more importantly, they also imply different modes of communication specific to each social environment.

So in this connection, too, a study of the social representations of intelligence and its development becomes indispensable, because these modes of communication may imply particular conceptions of intelligence, references to distinct prototypes with divergent valorisations, influencing or directing the modalities of intervention on the child's education. This is a line of research which has not yet received attention.

Intelligence as social representation

How do conceptions of intelligence emerge, and what makes them change? Apart from our working assumption that they can be dated historically, our approach here is not a historical one; instead, it is an attempt to go beyond definitions of intelligence and locate the socio-psychological determinants which influence them. To do this we need a model which will give us a base for plausible hypotheses, and here Moscovici's work on social representations (1961, 1981; see also Farr and Moscovici, 1984) provides sufficient indications of general significance for us to use them for the main outlines of an approach to the social representations of intelligence. Therefore, before dealing with the methodology of our research, it seems wise to provide a brief overview of the theoretical principles which have had a direct heuristic value for our work. The propositions we adopt will therefore be opportunities for putting forward general or specific hypotheses about the socio-cognitive operations implicit in the representations of intelligence. And these have also largely governed our methodological decisions.

The consensual universe of social representations

Social representations are just processes by which individuals symbolically construct reality, cognitive formulations which are marked by particular collective integrations. It is a concept which occupies an intermediate position between sociology (Durkheim, 1983) and psychology, at that point where the individual and the collective (or the social) intersect or connect, and as such social representation is actually at the heart of social psychology. So what kind of logic does this 'social thought' (Rouquette, 1975) have?

In order to indicate its origins, Moscovici (1961) regards it as operating as in some ways the inverse of scientific thought (which Piaget, with many others, takes to be the highest stage of intellectual development). In its pure, and therefore ideal, form this assumes a 'reified' universe founded on systems of highly differentiated roles and categories, in which not everybody is qualified to pronounce, and where not everybody has access to the truth: only experts have the 'knowledge', according to specific criteria and rigorous rules of reasoning and proof, to distinguish between truth and falsehood. This rigorous logic is symbolised by the computer.

For our purposes it is not important that this ideal is never actually achieved in scientific practice. All that matters is the actual model of hypothetico-deductive formulation of knowledge which is predominant, in obvious contrast to the one that underlies social representations. These develop in the many divergent areas of our lives where the scientific model is not dominant, or in areas where in the end it would not be applicable, or 'economic'. They are to be found, as Moscovici says, in 'consensual' areas, where things are agreed rather than demonstrated, and where the rules of scientific thought are supplanted by conventions which are the product of collective formulations (somewhat like the way rumours are disseminated; Rouquette, 1975; Gritti, 1978) where everybody has a voice and their own share of the truth, and where everybody contributes in greater or lesser degree to the collective view. These collective representations, in fact, fulfil particular functions within social relations (Doise, 1978): by constructing our everyday experience at the symbolic level, they help us to justify our attitudes and actions, as well as to anticipate and influence them. In short, they ensure our socio-cognitive adaptation to the realities of everyday life, which explains why they are concerned with particular issues which vary in relation to social integration and experience (see Jodelet, 1984, for examples of this).

Paradoxically, these socio-cognitive constructions are simultaneously inert and yet capable of motion. But in fact they tend towards a degree of stability, as these socio-cognitive operations stem from a certain 'conservatism' (a striking example of which is that of socio-psychological regulations in systems of orthodoxy; see Deconchy, 1971, 1980), which means that they are more concerned with confirmation than falsification; conclusions are more important than premisses, or, to use a legal image, the verdict takes precedence over the trial. Nevertheless, they can be changed, as we shall demonstrate in relation to intelligence, to adapt to new experiences linked to new social integrations.

Another fundamental aspect of social representations is that they obviously vary according to individuals, groups or social categories, and that this has to do with their history and their particular social integration. It is also the reason why we have to talk about social representations, in the plural, rather than simply about social representation. The difference between this and a scientific approach which claims to study *the* representation of the world, space, etc., is thus very clear. But this is because, as Doise (1985) points out, social representations are 'principles which generate positions linked to specific integrations into a set of social relations, and organise the symbolic processes which intervene in those relations'.

Despite the fact that they vary so much, it is still possible to identify modes of organisation and socio-cognitive mechanisms which they have in common, beneath the apparent and actual diversity of content and position. It is some of these modes of organisation and operation which we shall look at next, assessing their significance for a socio-psychological approach to representations of intelligence.

The components of a representation

Following Moscovici (1961) we shall begin by distinguishing a number of separate but complementary dimensions. The first point concerns the amount of information available about the subject matter of the representation, and its degree of exactness. It is clear that the man in the street, for example, is in no sense an expert on this issue, and derives his information from his own experience and whatever he may happen to read. And even where people (usually parents) do have an exact idea of the age sequence for the acquisition of different notions (particularly Piagetian ones; see Miller, White and Delgado, 1980), their ideas vary depending on the culture (Hess *et al.*, 1980; Goodnow *et al.*, 1984), and also within the same culture, depending on the children in question: their expectations are more optimistic for pre-school children, but become pessimistic, or increasingly realistic, when the children reach school age (Entwisle and Hayduck, 1978), perhaps because these expectations become more 'constraining' (Ponzo, 1977). Here the experience of school, as it is felt by parents, serves as a source of information, and obviously affects the way other information is interpreted.

Where this other information comes from is one of the questions we shall try to answer in this study. Sources may include personal experience (often in practice linked to parental experience, as we have just seen), reading more or less specialised magazines, consulting experts, informal social communication (particularly among parents), as we shall show. But at this level, individuals do not, in our view, have access to an organised synthesis of information, let alone to a scientific approach, and depend on scraps of information picked up here and there as they come across them. We shall see later what this shortage of information implies for the representations which are constructed.

In some cases, though, the information may be more systematic. Teachers, for example, undergo a training which provides them with psychological, educational and sociological models of intellectual development. By looking at this occupational category we can therefore study the development of their representations precisely in relation to their integration into the profession; thus we shall see how confrontation with the practical realities of education, an integration generative of new experiences, gives rise to adaptations and adjustments of their social representations, as information that comes from practical experience is liable to contradict the information provided institutionally during their training. But this is to anticipate.

At this point we need to add that, as Moscovici points out, information is by no means everything. Even given the same information, representations may differ. And conversely the interpretation of experience is likely to vary with experience. Also the explanatory value of different potential sources of information may vary, and a denial (see Moscovici, Mugny and Pérez, 1984–5) of information likely to introduce contradictions can sometimes imply ignorance of it. In fact one can go further and assume the existence of a sort of 'informational anorexia'; it may well be in the nature of social representations that they do not imply a search for new information, which might not fit in with the current representation (which takes us back again to the postulate of the primacy of the conclusion). What matters most is the scope, or the field, of the representation, and attitude.

The field of representation implies a selective focus on the elements of information in question and their structuration. Not all the information is dealt with or, if it is, it is not all used to the same extent. In this connection we shall examine two particular hypotheses. Both are concerned with the school, which should be one of the most important areas around which representations of intelligence crystallise. We shall attempt to demonstrate that for parents the question of the child's adaptation to the demands of the school fundamentally alters the organisation of the field of their representation of intelligence (by becoming its principal determinant), just as integration into the educational institution alters that of teachers. Further hypotheses will be advanced later, at the appropriate point, all taking the view that the component elements and the organisation of social representations of intelligence are concerned with the need to take account of new experiences derived from particular social integrations.

As for attitude, this is an important dimension because it situates individuals or groups in a positive or negative relationship to the different components of the representation. Since these attitudes vary in the different elements which compose them, we shall examine them once the component elements and the way they are organised have been clarified by the analysis of the results of our investigation.

The socio-cognitive functions of representations

Why, though, do we make representations of things, and of intelligence in particular? We have adopted Moscovici's conjecture (1981), which has also found support elsewhere, that the primary function of social representations is to enable people to come to terms with the inexplicable, with material that cannot be integrated from the socio-cognitive point of view, by turning the strange into the familiar. This, for example, is what psycho-analysis does when it 'provokes' an ideological system or a religious ethic (Moscovici, 1961); it is how people cope with ill-health (Herzlich, 1969), or 'cohabitation' with the mentally ill when they are too much like ourselves (Jodelet, 1983).

At the outset it must be remembered that social groups do not all respond to the same sorts of unfamiliarity, nor to the same degree. Thus in the case of intelligence we shall consider parents and teachers as most affected by one particular unfamiliarity bound up with the uneven distribution of intelligence among individuals, as we shall be seeing later. There are in fact a number of convergent factors involved in the feeling that something is unfamiliar.

As Herzlich (1972) argues, one of the main causes is concerned with the accessibility of the subject matter of the representation. As we saw earlier, our information about any particular social subject (for instance, intelligence) is often incomplete and scattered. We very rarely hold all the cards, or – to put it another way – the mosaic is usually incomplete; there is therefore a gap, or *décalage*, between the information available and the information necessary for a full understanding of the subject. We only have to consider the situation of parents getting feed-back (in the form of reports, for example) about their own children, but who are unaware of the total distribution of pupils, the normal average of the school or the region, and most of the time of the real reasons for their child's position. Faced with this shortage of information, all they can do is 'represent' their child, the school, or intelligence, for themselves, as they have no more 'objective' way of 'knowing' them. So even though, as we have said, there is not enough information to account for representations of intelligence, we can put forward the hypothesis that the shortage of information constitutes a determinant cognitive element, a favourable breeding ground for social representations (as it is for rumour; see Mugny, 1980).

But it is not only information that is scattered. The same applies to specific interests and personal preoccupations, which vary according to social integration (which also accounts for the multiplicity of the subject matter of social representations). Different social categories or social groups focus differently on specific subjects in order to formulate their social representations of them, particularly in relation to what are commonly called inferential pressures. As far as intelligence is concerned, two categories of individuals are constantly having to communicate, have opinions, and take action, in relation to it. The position of teachers is obvious, as their primary institutional role is both to develop children's intelligence and also to assess the intelligence of each pupil. The second category is that of parents, who are also constantly being asked to take note of the assessment of their children and to react to it in one way or another.

Our hypothesis is therefore that these two factors must coincide for an organised representation to be created. This representation would then be the joint effect of an unfamiliarity felt under inferential pressure, and of a shortage of information. The demonstration of this will be one of our fundamental tasks.

The evolution of representations of intelligence

The reason representations vary from group to group is obviously because they are socially constructed, and because they are the organising principles behind the mental reconstruction of varied social experiences. Thus when we 'interrogate' a social representation, its discourses are so coherent, often despite appearances, as to seem to present an almost exclusively assimilative way of working.

Everyday events do in fact tend to be interpreted on the basis of what the individual, or the group, already have in the way of pre-constructs, as an anchoring process (Moscovici, 1981). They are made meaningful through images, concepts and language-use common to the group, or 'conventionalised' to use the term introduced earlier. This explains why parents tend not to change their educational values and principles while their children are between the age of three and adolescence (Roberts *et al.*, 1984), and why it is very difficult to change the stereotyped views of parents whose children have gone to a 'new' or 'activity-based' school, and who are more sensitive to the apparent lack of order than to the actual process of structuring new relationships in a new type of classroom (Reiner, 1983, cited in Goodnow, 1985, p. 208).

So the tension between the strange and the familiar tends to be resolved wherever possible in favour of the familiar, by a kind of socio-cognitive economy principle. Social thought therefore does not operate analytically, or on the analysis of variance model (like Kelley's 'rational' individual, 1967), but progresses by analogy, looking to confirm conclusions rather than to validate the premisses of the discourse. And social psychology (see Doise, Deschamps and Mugny, 1978; Moscovici, 1984b) is made up of a vast mosaic of socio-cognitive dynamics which make such an 'operation' possible.

To some extent, the notion of contradiction is not applicable to social representations, or at least not in its logical sense. They do not operate analytically, therefore not according to the scientific model of knowledge, and so they remain beyond its reach. Yet to stop having said that would force us to the conclusion that social representations are inert. And while that is one recognised facet of them, it implies that the social integrations, and the personal experiences, which stem from them are unchanging. But in a developmental approach to adult psychology we have to recognise that social experiences vary and are shaped by the decisive moments of adult socialisation (job entry, marriage, the birth of children, etc.; see Mortimer and Simmons, 1978).

It is essential to locate these turning points when we are dealing with intelligence, because they reshape representations by introducing elements of novelty and unfamiliarity, which the changing configuration enables them to domesticate, and also by introducing what we would regard as conflicts of identity. But we need to look at these one at a time.

These changes are connected, in the first place, to the sense of a socio-cognitive unfamiliarity, the resolution of which becomes central and urgent. So what, in the context of intelligence, is unfamiliarity?

Our intuition, in the light of which this study was largely carried out, is that it resides in the experience of differences of intelligence between individuals, and that these differences constitute a sort of 'hard core' (see Abric, 1976, 1984) around which various social representations are constructed, more or less inclined, to put it briefly, either towards a biological hereditarianism or towards a sociological determinism.

This preoccupation with the differences has a long history. According to anecdote, Aristotle had an opinion on the subject, summed up in the saying 'like father, like son', according to which 'those born of elite forebears have every chance of being members of the elite themselves, because nobility is excellent stock'. In the eighteenth century, Helvetius claimed the opposite: 'we are all born equal in mind and character, only education creates differences'. And Rousseau would certainly not have disagreed with that. In the last century the controversy, decked out in scientific colours, took the form of a debate of a very clearly ideological bent (Lemaine and Matalon, 1985), which resulted in the establishment of intelligence tests designed to measure differences in intelligence. This is not the place to engage with that debate, however: the salient fact is that these differences in intelligence introduce an unfamiliarity because of their apparently inexplicable nature, which in fact has still not been explained in properly scientific terms. The feeling of unfamiliarity is even explicitly admitted, and thus maintained, by scientists themselves.

Thus a sociologist, in a recent discussion of inequality of educational opportunity, acknowledges (Girod, 1984, p. 10) that

> teaching is clearly only one of many factors on which the acquisition of knowledge depends. It draws on a multiplicity of sources. In the final analysis it depends essentially on that mysterious process, learning, or in other words the self-development of the structures of reasoning, and the self-organisation in the memory of a certain quantity of information. Often pupils attending different schools, reputedly of different intellectual levels, will nevertheless achieve the same results. Within the same school, and the same class, on the other hand, the level of results varies a great deal from one pupil to another. We do not need a formal investigation to convince us that this is true.

In other words, the recognition of the differences is visible, palpable, immediately accessible to perception, and, in the end, requires no analysing. It is this direct awareness of differences, which is often in fact an awareness of exceptions, to judge by the extract above, which should, in our view, make these differences the core around which representations of intelligence are organised. The same goes for popular views of intelligence. Thus Shipstone and Burt (1973) replicated Flugel's study (1947) in order to assess the changes undergone by the man in the street's conception of intelligence in the intervening twenty-five years. There had clearly been some changes: intelligence was now seen as multi-factorial rather than one-dimensional, there was more criticism of intelligence tests, and there was less divergence between the intelligence attributed to men and to women. Yet the problem of the differences between individuals persisted. To the question: 'Are some people more intelligent than others?', almost 100% of the answers were affirmative. As to why this should be, the answer, 'Because they were born with better brains', was still accepted by 63% of subjects (against 69% twenty-five years earlier). Even though more environmental reasons are also advanced these days, it is still the issue of differences of intelligence which is the most – perhaps the only! – universally recognised aspect, one which is still largely explained in terms of giftedness; our own study provides confirmation of this.

Our next problem is to identify the social groups most preoccupied with the issue. In the terms of our analysis of the representations, these should be the groups which are predisposed to focus on inter-individual differences, or to be professionally concerned with them, as a result of their social integrations. There are at least two categories of individual who experience these differences as part of their everyday lives, namely parents and teachers; and we shall compare their representations with those of other groups who should be less concerned with this issue (with non-parents and students training to be teachers, respectively). We shall not clarify this hypothesis any further at this point, as the whole problematic will be developed in detail when we look at the results of our study.

A number of studies have already been conducted on what may be regarded as parental psychology or the psychology of parents (for a review, see Goodnow, 1985; Sigel, 1985). Yet these have seldom dealt with the representations of intelligence themselves, tending instead to focus on issues related particularly to general educational values or styles of education. These are of major importance for the progress of genetic social psychology, which will have to take account of them. The fact is, though, that they tend either to compare parents from different nations or different cultures (see for example Hess *et al.*, 1980; Conroy *et al.*, 1980), or else to propose a kind of differential psychology of parents, or more precisely of families and styles of education. Our approach, which is complementary, places particular emphasis on the general characteristics which tend to differentiate parents from non-parents, in a generic way.

Finally, there is one other sort of experience which should ensure a change of representation, the conflict of identification (which we have studied for the most part in relation to processes of change in situations of social influence; see Mugny, Kaiser and Papastamou, 1983; Mugny and Pérez, 1985). We assume, in effect, that several social integrations can be in mutual contradiction. No individual belongs only to a single group or category. Instead, he occupies a position within a field of intersecting categorisations (Deschamps, 1977), and his identity is consequently multi-dimensional rather than one-dimensional. Moreover, these intersections can create contradictions between the elements of representation invoked by the different identities, and require particular adjustments to the representation. We shall be examining two instances of this, at least, in detail and we shall come across other examples as well. The first is the case of teachers (expected to 'defend' the educational institution as well to justify their own practice) who are also parents (in which position they may also have to 'defend' their children 'against' the school, or even 'against' themselves), as these integrations may sometimes not be compatible from a socio-cognitive point of view. The second instance is that of mothers who also go to work outside the family, in which case, as we know (Lamb, Chase-Lansdale and Owen, 1979), their occupational integration can come into conflict with the specifically familial roles which are still largely, if not predominantly, the woman's preserve. We may therefore expect, in both cases, some adjustments in the social representation, aimed at resolving these contradictions.

Two comments need to be made on these complementary hypotheses. The first is that, while we can thus envisage some evolution of social representations, this cannot, in theory, come from 'within'. Just as in the case of socio-cognitive development (see Doise and Mugny, 1984), and social innovation in general (Moscovici, 1976; Mugny, 1982; Mugny and Pérez, 1986), change must be induced from outside, or from social conflict, like a 'socialised Gödel theorem'.

The second aspect has perhaps not been made sufficiently clear so far: social representations do not simply have a cognitive function, they are not just a response to a desire to understand and explain things. Their function is also to situate individuals and groups within the social field. In this, they make it possible for individuals and groups to assign themselves their own, distinct, position, which differentiates them from other social entities. They also play a part in the dynamics of identification and identity (see Carugati, 1979). Briefly – and this is another central hypothesis – social representations are also constitutive of socio-psychological identity.

The prototypes of intelligence

Our argument is that intellectual differences (and the interpretation of them) are broadly responsible for organising the social representations of intelligence. This means that one can recognise an individual's degree of intelligence, and thus classify and order individuals according to their intelligence, which presumes a single continuum that can be symbolised by the famous normal curve of the intelligence quotient.

To be able to do this, therefore, implies that we all have a matrix of identities to which every event or individual can be referred, so they can be placed and then classified and named. So whatever conception of intelligence the man in the street may have, or even the expert (since their conceptions are, in the end, very similar; see Sternberg *et al.*, 1981), we are all capable of describing an intelligent or an unintelligent person, as our study will show. This categorisation is also essential because, by a process of deduction (Tajfel, 1972), it implies that other stereotyped characteristics are 'officially' assigned to intelligent individuals (or to unintelligent ones: Bruner *et al.*, 1958, adequately demonstrated the evaluative benefits of being considered intelligent; see also Cantor, 1978, for the prototype of the brilliant person), and it also influences the behaviour (especially, but not solely, educational behaviour) of others towards the individual thus classified.

At this point a new notion has to be introduced, that of the prototype. As we have seen, social representations work analogically, rather than analytically. Individuals therefore are not classified and labelled 'intelligent' or 'stupid' simply to the extent that they correspond at every point with a series of behavioural requirements or particular cognitive attitudes, as specified by an explicitly invoked model of intelligence (operational level in Piagetian tests, for example) which exclusively defines the members of these classes. Even in scientific tests individuals are actually assessed not on these criteria but by their similarity to a prototype of an intelligent person, and thus in terms of parameters derived from the analogy. IQ is a typical example of this because it boils down to the ratio MA/RA, in which mental age (assessed according to specific responses) is related to real age, on the basis of the extent to which the individual in question conforms to, or differs from the main tendency of the age in question. And in similar vein the Piagetian use of operational investigation comes down to assessing the child's distance (albeit in terms of organisations specific to each level) from the normal level on the one hand (for example, 75% of children of a given age have attained a particular level), and on the other hand, and perhaps more fundamentally, from the ideal stage of mastery of logical structures, at the highest formal level of logical abstraction. The same goes for educational institutions, as they define the goals to be reached and the criteria by which children succeed or fail, and which determine whether or not they are 'intelligent' enough to follow this or that course. Given, therefore, that there can be different prototypes, we have had to provide ways of identifying them, particularly because they are all actually conceptions of intelligence.

Even if it were possible, this sort of classification is not analytical when it occurs in social thought, either. Neisser (1979) argues that the intelligent person is a concept organised according to a prototypical model (Rosch, 1977). The fact of being recognised as intelligent thus also depends on the individual's similarity to the imaginary prototype, which does not exclude the possibility that this may itself have been largely defined by extreme examples, from genius (Bach, Mozart and Einstein are names frequently associated with the epithet 'intelligent') at one end of the scale, to 'idiots' or 'imbeciles', to use the popular terminology, at the other. This is surely Thorndike's standpoint, when he defines intellect as the quality which set Plato and Aristotle apart from the idiots of their period. And if the prototype is defined by its rarity (since the extremes are assumed in theory to be uncommon), the question of intelligence is very likely to be posed in terms of a contrast between bright children and mediocre children, the latter thus becoming failures, especially in relation to the demands of the educational institution. In this way, the prototype itself becomes a familiar part of the central core of representations created by differences in intelligence.

On the other hand, the dominant prototype ought in all probability (even if only by implication) to be that of logic and mathematics. Indeed we must assume that the computer has supplanted Plato and Aristotle, and that the specialisation it entails has replaced the openness of humanism (or the breadth of vision of a Leonardo). We shall try to show that, in the last analysis, it is educational success in the realms of logic and mathematics which constitutes the prime parameter for assessing intelligent individuals.

It will also be necessary, and this we shall try to do, to reconstruct the way such a prototype is adopted and the conditions in which this happens. Once again, our assumption is that the reasons are to do with parental experience and identity, and with teaching experience, in exact proportion to the way those experiences render salient an increasing dependence on the school and the modern prototype it propagates. We already know that these prototypes change as children grow older. Thus, as development progresses, adults judge intelligence less and less in perceptual and motor terms, and increasingly in terms of cognitive abilities (Siegler and Richards, 1982). Similarly, teachers in upper schools tend to value the strictly cognitive aspects more exclusively than teachers of the lower grades, who place an equal value on the social aspects (Fry, 1984b).

It is important to recognise these prototypes, because they operate normatively, through parameters for judgements about, and assessments of, the intelligence of a child or a school-pupil, parameters which are liable moreover to vary from one environment to another without the change being made explicit or even impinging on the collective consciousness. Gilly (1980, 1981) in particular has revealed the gap or mismatch which exists between the ideologies teachers claim to espouse and the actual criteria they use for assessing pupils, which are governed more by institutional goals than by avowed intentions.

Because these conceptions of intelligence, and of its prototypes, or – to put it briefly – these social representations of intelligence, often operate without our being aware of them, clarification and explanation of them is essential; they clearly govern our judgements and our behaviour as individuals, and particularly as parents or teachers. Now that this introductory chapter has provided us with a few ideas about them, we are ready to tackle a direct study.

2 Research methodology

By way of preamble

As our examination of the literature has revealed, studies of the representations of intelligence, especially experimental studies, are frequently limited to looking at one particular aspect of the topic (for example, the assessment aspect). We, by contrast, have been concerned to deal with the widest possible range of aspects which may be connected with the representation. We therefore questioned our subjects on the following issues:

- definitions of intelligence
- the development of intelligence
- teaching methods considered appropriate for children in difficulty
- images of the intelligent child
- the relative importance of school subjects in assessing intelligence
- the place of the notion of intelligence within the field of scientific subjects
- normative and informed sources of influence

The method we chose (for an overall view of methods in social science, see Grawitz, 1974) was a questionnaire-based investigation (see Ghiglione and Matalon, 1978). This may sometimes seem a restrictive method, it is true, as it limits the subject to a specific mode of response; it may also seem too suggestive, as it gives the subject ready-made answers which just have to be assessed; and it can also seem not to involve the subject very much, as he or she is, in a sense, reduced to a dialogue with a pile of paper. And, finally, the questionnaire can suffer from another, very serious weakness: its method may be subjective, to the extent that a researcher may draft it in a way that reflects his own representation of the subject.

So why did we select this approach? First of all, by a process of exclusion. We rejected interviews, mainly on account of the problems involved in analysing content (see particularly D'Unrug, 1974), as that obviously reflects the subjectivity of the researcher more than other methods. Nevertheless, we did think the interview method was indicated for the preliminary survey we carried out, which enabled us to orient our formulation of the questionnaire towards the topics which were more-or-less spontaneously broached in the interviews. We carried out a number of interviews in this preliminary stage, and followed them up with an open questionnaire which was answered by about a hundred subjects (Poeschl, Doise and Mugny, 1986). Finally, free associations with the word 'intelligence' were obtained from some forty first-year students as part of our practical work. In other words, we used a variety of methods to ensure that the questionnaire included a range of propositions (which we shall refer to subsequently as *items*) wide enough to provide the maximum coverage of all the different ideas we were thus able to note. We also included some items deriving from articles we came across in the press, particularly in 'specialised' parents' magazines.

In our view, this heterogeneity of opinions was the only possible way of minimising the risks of subjectivity and suggestibility noted above, and of ensuring some kind of representative spread of the different possible positions, even though we cannot claim to have been completely exhaustive. So we quite deliberately drew up a much-longer-than-usual questionnaire (300 questions), which had the additional advantage of motivating the respondents by virtue of the fact that it took nearly two hours to complete.

But the rationale for choosing a 'closed', and therefore restrictive, method (which in practice forces the subjects to respond within the framework of the questions dealt with in the questionnaire, rather than letting them express themselves 'freely') is actually to be found in our theoretical approach to representations, which is based on experimental work, from which we have also taken our methodological data (Doise, Deschamps and Mugny, 1978). This consists of observing the reactions of subjects in strictly defined observation conditions, in accordance with general preliminary hypotheses and more specific predictions derived from the theoretical model which the experiment is designed to validate (see Grisez, 1975). In this context, an open observation methodology (such as the interview) would certainly, indeed necessarily, have produced results. But without a common set of responses for all the interviewees it would have been impossible to make any real comparison, and one which covered the whole range of questions, between the different samples making up our population. Such a comparison was essential for us, precisely because we did not want to observe 'what happens' *a posteriori* (and for an attentive observer there is always something happening), we also wanted to foresee it, *a priori*. In fact, we also wanted to predict it, wherever this was possible by virtue of the knowledge we had already accumulated about social representations in general, and the hypotheses we had formulated (see chapter 1) about the socio-cognitive processes underlying the social representations connected with the notion of intelligence in particular.

To conclude this preamble, it should also be noted that part of the questionnaire gave rise to a genuine experiment in which the subjects responded randomly to one part of the questionnaire which was formulated differently according to two variables, which we shall discuss later on. This experimental approach will also help to validate certain postulates, as well as to confirm, in the context of more rigorous conditions of observation, certain results revealed in the non-experimental section of the questionnaire.

We now turn to the details of procedure and of the questionnaire itself.

The sample

More than 1,000 questionnaires were distributed in and around Bologna and Geneva. Out of the 800 or so which were returned, we were able to use 728, properly filled in, for our analysis (462 from Bologna, 266 from Geneva). These subjects (506 women and 222 men) were drawn from all walks of life: students (292), some of whom (123) were trainee teachers; teachers, most but not all of whom were working in primary schools (216); as well as people who can be characterised as neither students nor teachers, but who came from a variety of occupational groups (manual workers and junior employees, middle-class, managerial class and professional people, as well as housewives). Particular attention was also given to obtaining responses from non-parents (436, almost all of them students) and from parents (292). It is important to make clear that this was thus not a random sample (which would anyway have been impracticable, because of the length of the questionnaire), but a more systematic sampling of contrasting populations, selected to test certain hypotheses. Thus, for instance, it was not by chance that we used teachers and future teachers, as we had a particular interest in assessing the impact of that type of 'socialisation' on representations of intelligence. The same goes for the choice of parents and non-parents, etc. Finally, and as part of a genuine experiment, the subjects were also identified in terms of the relevance (or irrelevance, as we shall see in the case of the students) the notion studied (in this case, intelligence) is supposed to have for them.

The subjects were approached either individually (as acquaintances or associates) or collectively, for example through the medium of parents' or teachers' associations. The students were mostly questioned in the context of courses or practical work. The others normally filled in the questionnaire at home (it was emphasised that for the answers to be valid they had to be done alone), and then returned by post. All the instructions were in writing, and were sufficiently detailed to enable the subjects to answer the whole of the questionnaire on their own and – we stressed this point – in the order given. The questionnaire was anonymous, and confidentiality was guaranteed. Lastly, the subjects were warned at the outset of the length of the questionnaires, and of the fact that it would probably take them two hours. Those who expressed a wish to be informed of the results of the research were later sent an *ad hoc* publication (Mugny, 1985c).

Structure of the questionnaire

On the first page of the questionnaire were the following: the request for the subject's collaboration, an assurance of the purely scientific context and purpose of the research, the length of time it would take, and the reason for this, along with the names and university affiliations of the researchers.

The second page contained a personal questionnaire which asked for the subject's age and sex, their occupation and their position within it, their highest academic qualification, and the numbers of children, brothers, and/or sisters they had. There were explicitly optional questions about the subject's political opinions and membership of trade unions or other associations. These were the only questions which subjects systematically refused to answer, which in fact prevented us from taking them into account in our analysis.

The questionnaire itself actually consisted of seven sub-questionnaires spread over the thirty-two pages of the booklet given to the subjects (the full list of items in their original formulation is given as an appendix). We shall deal with them in the order in which they appeared in the booklet, although the number they have been given for the purposes of our analysis is sometimes different (with the aim of making the presentation of the results more intuitive).

Questionnaires 1 and 2: intelligence and its development

The first two questionnaires, which relate to intelligence (questionnaire 1: Q1) and its development (Q2) were in fact interwoven (in the appendixes, the two have been separated, but the numbering of the items is that of their original order of appearance). The subjects responded to each item, which comprised one simple proposition, by indicating the extent of agreement or disagreement, in their personal opinion, by ringing one (and only one) of seven figures on a seven-point scale (1 = do not agree: 7 = agree: the significance of each figure was explained fully, just once, at the outset, and was expressed as follows: 1 = I disagree absolutely, 2 = I disagree, 3 = I do not really agree, 4 = I neither agree nor disagree, I cannot decide, 5 = I agree on the whole, 6 = I agree, 7 = I agree absolutely).

The items, as we explained above, were formulated so as to represent a sufficiently broad spectrum of the views and positions we had identified in the preliminary phase of the research. The main themes dealt with in questionnaire 1 (though not every item) will now be presented in 'telegraphic' form, many of them as pairs of opposites, and in random order, to provide at least an overall idea of the questionnaire (the sub-questionnaires have not been separated, as the same topic may appear in both):

abstract/concrete intelligence
different modes of adaptation to environment, school and society
relations of autonomy/heteronomy with the adult
affective and personality aspects
attitudes to school and to intelligence
unicity and pluralism in definitions of intelligence
giftedness/development in definitions of intelligence
differentiating status of the school
status and role of error
assessment, punishment
linguistic expression
family
heredity versus 'the heirs'
parallelism/causality between the social and the cognitive
reference to the teacher
collective/individual work
tutoring (child teaching child)
the effect of cognitive models
nature of occupation
physical concomitants, cerebral localisation
educational institution and curricula
prototypes of intelligence
coaching, homework
practical ability
intelligence tests
the mass media, etc.

The range of topics covered is thus clearly very broad. In order to facilitate analysis, the items were sub-divided into two groups. The sixty-six items relating to intelligence 'in general' make up questionnaire 1 (see appendix 1), while the fifty-seven items dealing explicitly with the development of intelligence make up questionnaire 2 (see appendix 2).

Questionnaire 6: the contribution of the scientific disciplines

The third questionnaire (here referred to as Q6: see appendix 6) which the subjects answered (which was inserted in the middle of the long preceding questionnaire, to break the 'monotony') was formulated as follows:

> To what extent, in your opinion, are the following disciplines or subject areas important (especially in the training of teachers) for a better understanding of the development of intelligence? (If you are unable to answer, underline 'I don't know'.)

Twenty-two disciplines were selected, equal weight being given to the different axes of opposition: social sciences versus 'exact' sciences, centration on the individual or on society, culturalist versus differential approaches, normality versus pathology, theory versus practice, methodologies versus techniques, etc. The disciplines selected, in more detail, related to depth psychology (personality, motivation, psycho-analysis), general psychology (social psychology, linguistic psychology, reinforcement), medicine (pediatrics, clinical psychopathology, child neuro-psychiatry, biological maturation), comparative sciences (differences between cultures, sociology of education), teaching models and techniques (pedagogy, ideologies of education, programmed teaching, group dynamics, teaching techniques, sociometrics), and humanist subjects (mathematical logic, philosophy, history of science).

For each discipline, the subjects responded by ringing one of the seven points on a scale of importance (1 = not important, 7 = important). Or they could underline the phrase 'I don't know', which, as we shall see, enabled us to calculate a 'relative shortage of information' index.

Questionnaire 5: the importance of school subjects

The fourth questionnaire to be filled in (which we shall refer to as Q5) was concerned with the centrality of various school subjects for the definition of intelligence. The subjects had to judge how far a child's success or failure in sixteen subjects, the details of which are given in appendix 5, was important in determining the extent of his or her intelligence (again, using a seven-point scale, 1 = not important, 7 = important).

The exact wording of the question was as follows:

> A child may have an aptitude for some subjects and encounter difficulties in others. In your view, how important are the following subjects for determining a child's degree of intelligence?

Questionnaire 4: images of the child, and experimental variations

The fifth questionnaire to be filled in (Q4), like a semantic differentiator (Osgood, Suci and Tannenbaum, 1957), comprised sixty-two seven-point bipolar scales (the subjects ringing one number only) relating to the various characteristics capable of being applied to the intelligent – or unintelligent – child. An important part of these items was derived from the preliminary investigations we undertook before the research, which we mentioned above. We shall not comment in detail on the content of these items, which are to be found in appendix 4, but it is worth indicating some of the principal dimensions underlying them: general attitude, motivation, sociability, integration, tension, relations with the teacher and the family, cognitive aspects, obedience, etc.

One of the interesting aspects of this questionnaire is that it enabled us to carry out a twofold experiment. First, the subjects had to decide what were the characteristics either of a bright child or of a child described as mediocre. This is important for assessing the differentiations, or the perceived gap, between the gifted and the ungifted child.

The second experiment is concerned with the school subject at which the child is bright or mediocre: mathematics, language (French or Italian, depending on the sample), or drawing. The problem here is to see whether the differentiations between intelligent and less intelligent children are independent of the subject in question, or whether, as we suppose, these are accentuated in direct relation to their value or importance for the child's school career.

There are therefore six experimental conditions, produced by crossing two variables (bright, mediocre) and the three school subjects (mathematics, language, drawing). Each subject of course, only received one of the six possible versions of the questionnaire, which were distributed on an entirely random basis among the various sub-groups (Bologna and Geneva, parents and non-parents, teachers and student teachers, etc.).

Questionnaire 3: the effectiveness of teaching procedures

The penultimate questionnaire 3 concerned which teaching methods they judged appropriate for children who had consistent difficulties with mathematics, language, or drawing. The questionnaires were arranged in such a way that each subject was asked to assess their effectiveness for a child having difficulties in the same academic area (mathematics, language, or drawing) as they had had to consider in relation to bright or mediocre children.

The precise formulation of the question was as follows:

> Given a child who has consistent difficulties with mathematics (or language, or drawing) there are various possible reactions, and various different ways of dealing with the problem. Below, you will find several attitudes which might plausibly be adopted towards a child having problems with mathematics (or language, or drawing). Regardless of how acceptable or unacceptable you think these are, we want you to say to what extent you think they are *effective*, or not, in helping the child's development in mathematics (or language, or drawing).

The attitudes and teaching methods proposed cover an equally broad range of solutions which we sum up here to give an idea of the questionnaire's main components (for a detailed list of the fifty-seven items in Q3, see appendix 3):

arousing cognitive activity
assessment, reports, punishment
free and easy, *laissez-faire* attitude
role of the teacher
motivation of the child
correct or incorrect models
work and peer-group relations
changing the school curriculum
reference to parents, to the inspector
coaching, homework
questioning, socio-cognitive conflict
medical and psychological diagnostics
verification, reformulation, etc.

Judgements about the relative effectiveness of the different educational solutions proposed were made on seven-point scales (1 = not effective, 7 = effective).

Questionnaire 7: sources of information

The final questionnaire (Q7, see appendix 7) asked subjects to assess the importance (on a scale from 1 = not important, to 7 = important) of different sources of information which they might plausibly have had recourse to in forming their own ideas about the development of intelligence in children. The possible sources ranged from mass communications (books, magazines and newspapers) to informal communication (discussions with colleagues at work, or with friends, or with other parents), by way of consultation with specialists (psychologists, doctors, pediatricians, welfare workers), personal experience, and professional training. For parents, there was the additional choice of discussion with their child's (or children's) teacher, difficulties encountered with their own children, and discussions with them.

Treatment of the data

When it came to analysing the data, we faced the obvious problem of a very large quantity of information (more than 200,000 items of raw data altogether) which had to be 'summarised'. The decision we made was to submit the data from each questionnaire to a multivariate analysis (SPSS programme, factor analysis, varimax rotation). To begin with, in the next chapter, we shall use the seven factor analyses of the seven questionnaires we have described, to define the dimensions of the representations of intelligence, thus demonstrating their depth and their complexity.

After that, we shall compare the factorial scores corresponding to that analysis for different sub-groups of subjects. Our intention, as we emphasised earlier, is not to provide an exhaustive analysis of all the factors connected with the subjects which are likely to account for variations in the social representations of intelligence (which would have involved segmentation analyses based on the intersection of different sociological attributes), but to verify our various hypotheses about the socio-cognitive functioning of social representations. We therefore deliberately limited our analyses to these demonstrations by comparing, for example, parents and non-parents, or teachers and student teachers, in accordance with our hypothesis about the relevance for the subject of his or her actual experience of differences in intelligence between individuals. These analyses have an undeniable heuristic value, for which we provide more rigorous support in chapter 8, using a strictly experimental approach.

This means that the chapters that follow do not say everything there is to be said. The data can be used for other analyses, and can be approached in other ways. The approach we have adopted is a resolutely socio-psychological one.

3 The dimensions of intelligence: results of the factor analysis

A few preliminary comments are necessary before we tackle the interpretation of the factors. The items, it will be recalled, were partly ordered so as to express a position in generally positive terms, and to express one idea at a time, to protect the overall interpretation from ambiguity. To make the presentation of these results less arduous and more intuitive, we deliberately decided to interpret the factors as if they represented complete acceptance of the views expressed in each item (at least when the saturation of the items was positive: in the case of negative saturations we logically enough considered the items rejected). This in fact facilitates interpretation. However, the reader should not think that the subjects of our study actually accepted the different propositions so completely. Two things ought to be borne in mind.

The first is that the items were standardised before any factor analysis and the mean of all the items was thus reduced to zero (with a standard deviation of one), regardless of the actual mean on the seven-point scale. So, for example, the main factor in questionnaire 1 is what we have called the theory of giftedness, a long-established form of popular thinking about intelligence. That does not mean that our subjects accept that idea as it stands. The reverse, in fact, since an examination of the means in the different items making up the principal factor underlines a general rejection of that conception of intelligence. Yet this factor is the principal one, and the one which explains the plus variance, precisely because that old debate obviously still organises people's positions *vis-à-vis* intelligence. Nowadays, however, perhaps also for reasons of social desirability (there being some opinions which it is socially desirable not to hold), it is not the extent of *agreement* with the theory of giftedness which is at issue, so much as the extent of *disagreement*. Whatever the case, though, it will become clear that the debate is still far from dead, even though in general it seems to be 'overtly' rejected.

The other aspect to remember is that this analysis is a general one, concerned with the intrinsic meaning of the factors, the dimensions around which social representations of intelligence are organised: we shall be seeing at a later point how acceptance or rejection of these different aspects of intelligence is distributed among the sub-populations of our sample. To enable the reader to obtain a more precise idea of the tendencies of the responses, appendices 1–7 show, for different sub-groups of subjects, the mean of each item on the seven-point scale (of agreement or disagreement, for example). Thus both these means and the results of the variance analysis are given, for information, first for parents and non-parents, then for student teachers and teachers with or without children, and finally for parents who are not teachers, from Bologna and Geneva.

Finally, it should be noted that as a general rule comparisons between sub-samples for the different factorial scores were controlled on the basis of univariate statistics (variance analyses) relating to the most saturated items of each factor, which are the ones which play the greatest part in determining their significance. For obvious reasons of space, however, only a few of the most theoretically important comparisons (particularly those relating to parental and teaching experience) are detailed fully, item by item (in appendices 1–7).

So let us look now at the dimensions of intelligence as ordinary people represent them. We shall give the saturation or correlation between each item and the factor under consideration in brackets. The number of the item refers to the corresponding appendix, where the full content will be found.

General aspects of intelligence

A factor analysis was conducted on the sixty-six questions relating to intelligence in general, with the purpose of identifying its main dimensions. Of the factors which emerged, we have retained nine: the six whose eigen-value (after varimax rotation) was greater than 1, and factors 7, 8, and 10, the interpretation of which is both clear, and important for subsequent theoretical demonstrations. The six factors account altogether for 29.7% of the variance, or 10.2%, 6.6%, 3.9%, 3.3%, 2.9% and 2.8% respectively (before rotation; the nine factors considered total 36.5%, the last three accounting for 2.5%, 2.2% and 2.1% respectively). Given the deliberate heterogeneity of the items, as regards dimensions tackled and positions put forward for each dimension, the section of the variance accounted for may be regarded as considerable.

Factor 1: the theory of natural inequalities and giftedness

As we have just pointed out, the first factor is concerned with an old debate about intelligence, which ought really to be settled by now, but which appears to persist in our society (a 'progressive' magazine recently drew attention to the fact that it is still a live issue even at the scientific level; see

Autrement, 1984). But the factor has multiple aspects, and these we shall look at now, always remembering that we are presenting the factor from the viewpoint of the people who most fully accept (or least reject) the various items composing it (whose saturation on the factor is in theory at least .20).

One primary characteristic is the recognition of the 'astonishing' or not easily explicable existence of differences of intelligence between individuals. In fact:

> the existence of differences of intelligence between individuals is a mysterious problem which science has been unable to solve (Q1, item 56; .48);
>
> some people are born with more intelligence, others with less (Q1, item 109; .27).

The issue of differences between individuals, within the same culture, which reappears implicitly in other items linked with this factor, is, however, more than just a stated fact. It is combined with the adoption of a discriminatory attitude which is both elitist and segregationist, as it involves the belief that:

> there must be more advanced curricula for intelligent children than for less intelligent ones (Q1, item 122; .48);
>
> basing curricula on the child of average intelligence results in the impoverishment of the most intelligent (Q1, item 27; .36).

But what is intelligence, from this viewpoint? The theory of natural inequalities rests on a sort of psychology of abilities, and various items accepted from that perspective relate to a notion of capacity of aptitude, whether it be mental or social. Thus:

> intelligence is the child's capacity to understand the meaning that the teacher gives to a question (Q1, item 82; .44);
>
> intelligence is gauged by the capacity for abstract thought (Q1, item 20; .32);
>
> being intelligent means knowing how to take advantage of an opportunity (Q1, item 53; .31);
>
> being intelligent means agreeing to disagree with other people (Q1, item 29; .33).

The tolerance of contradiction emphasised by that last item none the less seems to merge into a degree of social conformity, as:

> an intelligent person is one who can adapt to the dominant ideology (Q1, item 78, .21).

And this 'dominant ideology' has a single definition of intelligence, which in fact is based on educational achievement in the logical and mathematical subjects which have major educational importance (or a high educational 'valency'):

> there can only be one definition of what intelligence is Q1, item 74; .19);
> you have to be intelligent to do well at school (Q1, item 62; .19)
> logic and mathematics are the prototypes of intelligence (Q1, item 7; .22).

Furthermore, these mental and social capacities or aptitudes imply specific attributes, because:

> intelligence is primarily a rigorous attitude in thinking and in action (Q1, item 47; .34);
> a child who does not value intelligence will never be intelligent (Q1, item 46; .27).

This therefore introduces a new theme, because these are attitudes which are developed within the family:

> intelligent children come from families where the parents value intelligence (Q1, item 73; .22);
> if parents do not valorise a particular subject, efforts to teach it will be in vain (Q1, item 103; .23).

Although this indirectly affirms the role of the school, a greater emphasis is placed on the family's mediating role between the child and school. Thus:

> homework is important because it enables a relationship to be established between the parents and the school (Q1, item 23; .41).

Finally, this conception of intelligence merges into a belief in the biological determination of intelligence, almost in the literal incarnation of intelligence, stemming from a degree of belief in phrenology:

> the brain is the birthplace of intelligence (Q1, item 35; .35);
> intelligence can be measured by the shape and size of a person's cranium (Q1, item 57; .21).

This 'belief', if we can call it that, is reminiscent of the pioneering work of Galton (see Lemaine and Matalon, 1985; Thuillier, 1984).

To sum up, this factor touches on a number of aspects of intelligence, and relies on a widely used form of popular thought, used particularly to justify failure at school within the framework of the dominant ideology (see the GFEN report, 1976). It is based essentially on the theory of natural inequality and giftedness; genetic inheritance seems to play an important part in it, but so also do the attitudes to intelligence developed within the family. The concept can thus be defined by the following synthesis:

intelligence is a gift which is divided unequally among the population;
intelligence needs to be protected by a policy of discrimination, particularly in schools (which is where, it seems to us, this concept establishes itself as ideology);
intelligence is defined as a sum total of mental and social aptitudes which enable the child to succeed at school, especially in subjects with a high educational valency (like mathematics);
these aptitudes develop through the attitudes to intelligence which obtain within the family;
intelligence, finally, is largely a question of biology, or even morphobiology.

Factor 2: conformity, or social intelligence

The second factor is concerned with a form of intelligence defined socially as adaptation – conformity – to the dominant social norms of western, bureaucratised society. The most saturated items on this factor refer primarily to the idea of adaptation:

being intelligent means conforming to the norms of a society which has become bureaucratic (Q1, item 88; .59);
an intelligent person is one who can adapt to the dominant ideology (Q1, item 78; .52);
intelligence is the individual's capacity to adapt to the society in which he lives (Q1, item 69; .29);
intelligence means managing to get on with other people despite initial differences of outlook (Q1, item 89; .22).

Here conformity is treated positively, without criticism or ridicule. It is also conformity in response to a well-defined society (western society), and the school seems to be the main site of this adaptation, or socialisation as one might perhaps call it:

western culture is the prototype of intelligence (Q1, item 99; .31);
being intelligent means adapting to school (Q1, item 104; .54);
intelligence is the child's capacity to understand the meaning that the teacher gives to a question (Q1, item 82; .21).

Lastly, this conformity to the ambient norms is expressed in terms of the *savoir-faire* and self-presentation which embody it:

> being intelligent means knowing how to present yourself in the best light (Q1, item 96; .50);
> being intelligent means having good manners (Q1, item 64; .49);
> being intelligent means knowing how to look after yourself in life (Q1, item 87; .32);
> being intelligent means knowing how to take advantage of an opportunity (Q1, item 53; .21).

Unlike the first factor, which was concerned particularly with the biological or innatist aspects of intelligence, this second factor relates to a definition of intelligence which is fundamentally social. In fact, it seems to stem from a social ability, the capacity to conform to social norms. Intelligence therefore implies a kind of decentration of one's own viewpoint in order to adapt to the norm: intelligence becomes a sort of management, albeit conformist, of conflicts. This aptitude for – or attitude towards – conformity involves a *savoir-faire*, a resourcefulness, which is frequently evoked to define intelligence. But we are not dealing here with 'practical' or 'manual' intelligence (as opposed to abstract intelligence), but with social intelligence.

Factor 3: the definitional relativism of intelligence

This factor raises the question of the unicity or multiplicity of definitions of intelligence and, as a corollary, of the origins of the definition or definitions. From the viewpoint of those who acknowledge what we call the 'definitional relativism of intelligence', the position is summed up by the most saturated item on the factor:

> if certain social categories seem to be more intelligent, this is because they define what intelligence is themselves and impose their definition on others (Q1, item 113; .62).

So who, precisely, does 'decide' which definition of intelligence will be the dominant one? In this relativist perspective, that depends on the culture. In fact:

> every culture has its own definition of intelligence (Q1, item 119; .47).

But it also, and more crucially, depends on social differentiations within cultures. Thus the position on the debate about differences in intelligence between the sexes is that:

> if men are seen as more intelligent than women this is because men define intelligence to their own advantage (Q1, item 100; .49).

Another important and relevant differentiation is that between social classes:

> the rich invented the notion of intelligence to justify their wealth and power (Q1, item 91; .44);
> intelligence sanctions social injustice: when it comes to intelligence, it is the rich who get that, too (Q1, item 59; .33).

This socially created inequality of intelligence is, moreover, to some extent 'circumstantial' (even though the circumstances may continue into the future), since

> intelligence is an invention of our society for the purpose of adapting to new economic demands and current technological conditions (Q1, item 10; .32).

The definitional relativism of intelligence therefore implies a historical dimension in which intelligence appears as a creation of our own time. In this relativist perspective, intelligence tests are, understandably, not very popular:

> intelligence tests are misleading: all they do is measure the differences (particularly the economic differences) that exist between different social categories (Q1, item 32; .44).

This idea is confirmed by another item whose negative saturation this time indicates that those who adopt this viewpoint tend to reject the idea that:

> intelligence tests enable the intellectual capacities of children to be measured with precision (Q1, item 8; −.20).

As for the item:

> intelligence is simultaneously a question of biology, psychology and sociology (Q1, item 58; .29),

we assume that it is connected with this factor essentially for the sociological side of this very general assertion.

This third factor, then, concerns a critical attitude towards the notion of intelligence. It is an attitude that claims a relativism in the definition of intelligence, in both inter-cultural and intra-cultural dimensions. Intelligence thus appears as defined, through an asymmetrical relationship of differentiation, by the dominant social entity; and this entails a rejection of psychometrics as they can only 'measure' – or justify – those asymmetrical differentiations, which are in some ways similar to Bourdieu's homologies (see Bourdieu and De Saint-Martin, 1975).

Factor 4: the cybernetic prototype of intelligence

The fourth factor relates to a more or less computer-based model of intelligence which, for simplicity, we shall call cybernetic. According to this model:

> the computer is the perfect model of what intelligence is (Q1, item 17; .54); and
> logic and mathematics are the prototype of intelligence (Q1, item 7; .48).

This conception of intelligence thus has to do with higher cognitive activities, with formal thought, or 'operations on operations', to paraphrase Piaget (1956). Briefly,

> intelligence is gauged by the capacity for abstract thought (Q1, item 20; .35).

This conception, logically enough, gives science (the epistemological model of which would be entirely homologous with the definition of intelligence) the task – or the right – of defining and assessing intelligence:

> only science can define what intelligence is (Q1, item 60; .44);
> intelligence tests enable the intellectual capacities of children to be measured with precision (Q1, item 8; .34).

On this factor, intelligence is therefore defined by the higher cognitive processes (the abstractions of logic and mathematics), symbolised by (fifth-generation) computers as artificial intelligence, and established as a legitimate subject of scientific study. It can be summed up, synthetically, under the label of the cybernetic prototype (or model) of intelligence.

Factor 5: the adaptive function of intelligence

The fifth factor, unlike the preceding ones, does not appear to be concerned with attitudes to intelligence as such, like the theory of giftedness, the vision of social conformity, definitional relativism, or the cybernetic model of intelligence. It 'quite simply' concerns intelligence as an adaptive function, regardless of the actual object of this adaptation. Thus:

> intelligence is the individual's capacity to adapt to the society in which he lives (Q1, item 69; .60);

but the adaptation is not merely a social one, as:

intelligence defines the individual's adaptation to his physical environment (Q1, item 120; .59).

This kind of adaptation implies resourcefulness:

being intelligent means knowing how to look after yourself in life (Q1, item 87; .33)
being intelligent means knowing how to take advantage of an opportunity (Q1, item 53; .32).

It also includes adaptation in an academic context:

being intelligent means adapting to school (Q1, item 104; .25).

Finally, the idea of adaptation is closely allied to the idea according to which:

intelligence means managing to get on with other people despite initial differences of outlook (Q1, item 89; .21).

All the saturated items on this factor refer to the adaptive function of intelligence in all its relations to milieu, whether physical environment, interpersonal relations, or educational or social background. To put it briefly, this factor concerns the individual's adaptation to the various situations in which he exists, a capacity here called intelligence.

Factor 6: intelligence as family heritage

This factor is concerned with the origin, not the definition, of intelligence. This origin is restricted to the family, or rather, perhaps, to the family background.

First, the family seems to be a good indication of intelligence, to go by the familiar saying:

'like father, like son': this is equally true for intelligence (Q1, item 55; .44).

This transmission, is however, not a genetic one (as was the case with the first factor), but is a product of family attitudes:

intelligent children come from families where the parents value intelligence (Q1, item 73; .50).

Any family, in other words, is a potential source of intellectual development: the family link between child and intelligence depends basically on socio-economic or socio-cultural level, as measured by the parents' occupation:

'tell me the parents' occupation and I will tell you the child's intelligence' (Q1, item 95; .53).

These three items, which are the only ones we retained, thus relate to intelligence as family heritage. The family is seen as the site of socialisation into intelligence. But this 'capacity for socialisation' depends on the parents' social and occupational level. The family appears to be valorised (in relation to intelligence) when it coincides with a fairly elevated social status.

Three other factors (7, 8, and 10) also merit interpretation for their theoretical pertinence, despite having an eigenvalue of less than 1 after rotation.

Factor 7: the differentiating function of the school

Here, again, we only retained the three items most clearly associated with this seventh factor. As we analyse them, they are concerned with a 'discriminating' function of the school, which seems simultaneously to reveal, accentuate and produce differences of intelligence between individuals.

First there is the fact that:

> school further accentuates the differences of intelligence that exist between individuals (Q1, item 123; .61).

But this accentuation merely reproduces sociological differences, in the manner of the 'inheritors' of Bourdieu and Passeron (1964):

> the school only reveals differences of intelligence which already exist by virtue of different social backgrounds (Q1, item 75; .51).

This revelatory function should in fact qualify the relatively 'extreme' nature of the next assertion:

> it is the school which creates intellectual differences between children (Q1, item 14; .41).

In short, whether the school reveals, accentuates or creates differences in intelligence, what is significant is the school's differentiating function, which is clearly associated with pre-differentiations of a sociological order.

Factor 8: intelligence and personality

The eighth factor really takes its meaning from two items:

> intelligence is above all a question of character (Q1, item 11; .64);
>
> intelligence is a problem of personality (Q1, item 36; .50).

Although the reference to character types is clear, as is the reference to a theory of personality, there is insufficient data at this level for us to form a more precise idea of the theory of personality involved. So we shall only retain the principle underlying this factor: that intelligence is a question of personality or character.

Factor 10: teachers and failure

This factor is a very useful one, as it concerns the teacher's responsibility for failure at school. Let us look first at the two items on which it is based:

> failure is generally due to the teacher's lack of understanding of the child (Q1, item 48; .64);
> failure could generally be avoided, given more patience on the part of the teacher (Q1, item 66; .57).

This factor is distinct from factor 7. There it was the educational institution itself which was accused of creating, or at least accentuating, sociological differences. This tenth factor, on the other hand, puts the blame squarely on the teacher personally, who is seen as the source of failure though a lack of understanding or impatience towards the child. This highly personalised factor ought therefore – this is to anticipate, but it will turn out to be the case – to offer a direct challenge to the social identity of professional teachers. The label we have given this factor – teachers and failure – seems to us to make clear the direct responsibility attributed to teachers.

Summary

The factor analysis of general opinions about intelligence has revealed several complementary dimensions. Having labelled them all, we shall now briefly recapitulate them. Because these labels tend to synthesise the meaning of each factor, they obviously run the risk of simplifying them or sometimes truncating them slightly. It may therefore be helpful to take the opportunity of going back over the actual detail of the original propositions which make up the factors.

The first factor concerns the extent of agreement with the theory of natural inequalities, which we sum up as the theory, or ideology, of giftedness. It recognises the existence of differences in intelligence between individuals. But it also argues for an elitist and discriminatory educational policy.

The second factor advances a definition of intelligence as conformity to the dominant social norms of our western, bureaucratic society, and this conformity is, in fact, given a positive value.

The third factor reveals an approach which is critical of intelligence, and which gives salience to the social and cultural relativism of the actual definition of intelligence, as one put forward by the dominant social entities within an asymmetrical social relationship.

The fourth factor proposes a definition of intelligence based on the higher cognitive processes. Its prototype is logical and mathematical abstraction and its symbol is the computer.

The fifth factor concerns the functional aspects of intelligence. Its main function is adaptation and accommodation to its environment, both physical, interpersonal and educational as well as more broadly social.

In the sixth factor, intelligence seems to be mediated to some extent by the family, the social and occupational status of which is central and ensures the transmission of positive attitudes to intelligence. This therefore appears as a family heritage.

The seventh factor is also concerned with the origin of intelligence, but here it is the school which passes it on, accentuating, revealing or producing differences between individuals on the basis of pre-existent sociological differentiations.

The eighth factor refers to the dependence of intelligence on character and personality, although there is admittedly some ambiguity about the nature of these characteristics.

Finally, the tenth factor attributes direct responsibility for failure at school to the teacher. This responsibility is a direct, personal one – not institutional – and is due to impatience with, or incomprehension of, the child.

How intelligence develops

A factor analysis was conducted on a further fifty-seven questions, this time those relating to the developmental aspects of intelligence. We shall be making use of ten factors, totalling 38.3% of the variance, namely 8.7%, 5.7%, 4%, 3.4%, 3.2%, 3%, 2.8%, 2.7% 2.5%, and 2.3%, respectively, before rotation. Although only the first six of these had an eigenvalue greater than 1 after rotation, the other four have again been retained for their theoretical implications.

We turn now to these various dimensions of the development of intelligence which we found among our subjects. As before, our interpretation will be founded on the viewpoints of those who accept the positively (in theory, at least .20) saturated items on the factors.

Factor 1: learning social rules

This factor is in some ways reminiscent of the conception advanced by Durkheim and Mauss (1969) at the beginning of the century, according to which the first logical categories in human history were social categories.

Here, however, this historic thesis about the sociogenesis of cognitive operations is transposed to the level of their ontogenesis.

Thus:

> the child is capable of understanding logic because he understands the rules of social life (Q2, item 101; .62);
> The development of intelligence is the gradual learning of the rules of social life (Q2, item 71; .51);
> the child first of all learns the logic of human relationships, and only later generalises this to natural phenomena (Q2, item 85; .26);

however, the opposite was also regarded as possible, although to a lesser degree:

> in order to understand the workings of society, the child must first have a grasp of logic and mathematics (Q2, item 117; .24).

Several points need to be stressed at this point. First, a close involvement between social awareness and awareness of logic and mathematics is asserted. But this position goes beyond mere analogy, or Piaget-style parallelism (Piaget, 1965, for example). If we take the two most saturated items (Q2, items 101 and 71), two complementary elements in fact appear: first, the idea that social awareness is anterior to logical awareness, and next and perhaps even more important, the idea of a causality going from the social to the logical (even though the opposite is also seen as a possibility, to a lesser degree (see Q2, item 117)).

However, this causality does not operate without assumptions about a certain amount of authority or coercion being exercised over the child, so that he interiorises social rules:

> the child learns to respect the social rules of logical knowledge by learning respect for adult authority (Q2, item 43; .53);
> punishment is a spur to progress (Q2, item 26; .21).

Finally, the school is perhaps a privileged location for this socialisation of intelligence, as:

> school curricula are the basic instruments for the development of children's intelligence (Q2, item 54; .24).

So we may sum up this factor as concerned with the learning of social rules, insofar as they stem from logical and mathematical awareness.

Factor 2: socio-cognitive conflict

The label of this factor is, admittedly, slightly 'egocentric'. But the various items do in fact tend to agree with a number of the positions we have developed in our work on the social psychology of cognitive development (Doise and Mugny, 1984; Mugny, 1985a; Mugny and Carugati, 1987). This view of development is essentially based on the notion of socio-cognitive conflict as the motive force for development, and on the utilisation of error (the child's or other people's) in social interaction. According to this representation, a non-scientific one this time:

> you have to use the child's mistakes to help him make progress (Q2, item 68; .62);
> mistakes are a source of progress for the child (Q2, item 84; .54).

Mistakes must, on the other hand, be used in a 'conflictual' way:

> it is by contradicting the child when he makes mistakes that you help him develop his intelligence (Q2, item 3; .37).

We take the following to mean the same:

> the child needs negative assessments of his work in order to understand the necessity for improvement (Q2, item 16; .38).

In this perspective:

> permissive education is all very well, but it is not effective when it comes to developing children's intelligence (Q2, item 38; .20).

As we see it, this 'permissiveness' relates to an 'empathetic' view of the relationship with the child, whereas the perspective articulated here tends to argue the need for conflict, understood as a sort of 'contradictory debate'. For this, there has to be a heterogeneity of response (or of intellectual level) between children, as is attested by the rejection (because the saturation is negative) of the idea that:

> for group work to be effective the children need to be at the same intellectual level (Q2, item 107; −.20).

Furthermore, interaction with a child at a lower level, somewhat after the manner of the work on the 'tutoring effect' (see Allen and Feldman, 1973; Gartner, Kohler and Riessman, 1971), appears as a source of cognitive progress:

> the child develops his intelligence when he has to explain problems to a child less advanced than himself (Q2, item 111; .24).

To summarise, this factor is concerned with a sociogenesis of intelligence through conflictual interactions in which the child learns from his, or someone else's, mistakes. To simplify, we shall call it the dynamic effect of socio-cognitive conflict on the development of intelligence.

Factor 3: relational equilibrium

This factor is concerned with the idea that development requires a good socio-affective equilibrium, both within the family and at school. This means above all that:

> a friendly relationship with the teacher is the best teaching technique for developing intelligence (Q2, item 72; .58);
> the development of intelligence requires a balanced affective development (Q2, item 70; .46).

This relational equilibrium plays a role at the level of family background, as:

> the parents are the child's main model for the development of his own intelligence (Q2, item 80; .37)

and, more generally:

> it is essential to the development of the child's intelligence that he should be able to establish good communication with his friends and with adults (Q2, item 105; .35).

This equilibrium also applies to 'horizontal' relationships, between peers, as this next proposition confirms:

> it is reciprocity in relationships with other children which enables intelligence to develop (Q2, item 81; .24).

This factor is therefore in contrast with the preceding one, in which the salient point was cognitive or socio-cognitive conflict. Here, in a relational and affective context, intelligence seems to be connected to the development of good communication and good relationships between the child and adults or his peers, or what we have described as relational equilibrium. It is interesting to note that factors 2 and 3 are – by definition – orthogonal, and that they are not just two opposite poles of the same attitude, tending either towards conflict or towards friendship. The socio-cognitive conflict we saw in factor 2 does not therefore necessarily imply the negation of a relational equilibrium in the relations between individuals.

Factor 4: the effect of the mass media

The meaning of factor 4 is derived from two very heavily saturated items relating to the positive influence of the mass media on the development of intelligence. The first concerns the use of television:

> television encourages the child's intellectual development (Q2, item 34; .77).

The second item specifies the reasons for its effectiveness:

> the use of audio-visual means (TV etc.) enables use to be made of a situation familiar to the child to stimulate his intellectual development (Q2, item 24; .61).

That this factor relates to a positive view of the influence of the mass media in general, and not just of audio-visual ones, seems to be borne out by the rejection (the saturation being negative) of the idea that:

> comics hinder the development of intelligence (Q2, item 45; −.18).

We regard this factor as relating to the impact of the mass media.

Factor 5: revelatory error

For the interpretation of this factor we have only used the two most highly saturated items, both of which correspond to a single idea. It is concerned with error again, but without giving it the dynamic status we saw in factor 2. Here mistakes are simply seen as an indication of the failure of the child's thinking to measure up to the ideal, and therefore correct, model:

> the child's errors are evidence of the level of his intelligence (Q2, item 42; .59);
> the child's errors reflect the inadequacy of his thinking (Q2, item 6; .50).

The small number of other items which are less strongly associated with this factor do not provide any coherence from this perspective, so we have restricted ourselves to these two items, emphasising that error appears as revelatory of a form of thinking (of the child's cognitive level) and thus as a parameter for the diagnosis of an inadequacy in it, in relation to an 'ideal' model of intelligence.

Factor 6: heteronomy: obstacle to intellectual development

This factor sees the convergence of three items towards a single idea, the rejection of coercion as a source of development: this follows Piaget (1965) who saw heteronomy as an obstacle to cognitive development (and we have also provided experimental illustration of a similar idea (see Mugny, De Paolis and Carugati, 1984), namely that a coercive relational regulation is generally hostile to cognitive development). As in Piaget, the items in this sixth factor regard heteronomy as an attribute of relations between the child and the adult. Thus:

> a hierarchical relationship can never be the source of genuine intellectual progress (Q2, item 77; .56).

> coercion is never a source of intellectual development (Q2, item 61; .54)
>
> the child's habitual compliance towards the adult does not allow him to develop his intelligence (Q2, item 116; .37)

To use the terminology of our own work on this subject (see Mugny and Doise, 1983; Mugny, De Paolis and Carugati, 1984), we regard this factor as concerned with the idea that relational regulations (in this case, but not exclusively, relations of heteronomy between adult and child) are obstacles to intellectual development.

This factor is the last to present an eigenvalue greater than 1 after rotation. However, the following four are worth considering, insofar as they are relevant to the next stage of our analysis, in which we make comparisons between them and our various sub-samples.

Factor 7: the negation of the idea of development

This factor seems to be concerned with the refutation of the whole idea of development, or of any real change in the cognitive processes. Instead of development there is giftedness (which implies the preservation of differences between individuals) and the simple realisation of a programme fixed at birth. That is the sense in which we see it as a negation of development. The items supporting this interpretation were the following:

> the development of intelligence progresses according to a biological programme fixed at birth (Q2, item 9; 63);
>
> the child spontaneously develops his innate capacity for intelligence (Q2, item 28; .29).

The negation of the whole idea of intelligence which seems to us to underlie this view is made clear in two further items. First:

> intelligence does not develop; it is a hereditary gift (Q2, item 31; .45).

Then the same idea is summed up, in more popular language, in:

> you can teach a child good manners, but not intelligence (Q2, item 18; .35).

Factor 8: the competence of teachers

This factor really rests on a single item, which states that:

> the competence of teachers is the best guarantee of the development of children's intelligence (Q2, item 110; .66).

Competence also has an institutional aspect, to judge by another item according to which:

> school curricula are the basic instruments for the development of children's intelligence (Q2, item 54; .66).

With the appropriate degree of caution, we take this factor to relate to the competence of teachers.

Factor 9: autonomy
This factor also raises some problems of interpretation, but enables us to see the way different sub-samples give differing weight to the idea of the child's autonomy. The idea of autonomy is explicitly present in the most heavily saturated item of this factor:

> in order to develop his intelligence the child must be autonomous, and particularly be able to resist the suggestions of adults (Q2, item 65; .54).

By implication, it also underlies the two other items that make up this factor. First:

> when a child makes a mistake in generalising a new rule to a situation where it is inadequate, it shows that he is making progress (Q2, item 22; .37).

One can also, more simply, consider the child making progress as autonomous in relation to the response stemming from the correct model.

Finally:

> the child develops his intelligence when he has to explain problems to a child less advanced than himself (Q2, item 111; .33).

Here autonomy is expressed by the possibility of envisaging progress outside a privileged relationship with the adult.

Although this factor can, in our view, be accounted for in terms of autonomy (an autonomy of peers *vis-à-vis* adults, and *vis-à-vis* a correct model solution) we nonetheless need to be very cautious about it when we look at the question of the differences between samples.

Factor 10: strict assessment
Unlike the two preceding factors, the interpretation of the last factor is quite clear. It is basically concerned with the problem of assessing a child's cognitive performance by means of reports. One of the two items on which this factor principally rests makes the position quite clear:

> the best stimulus to development is assessment, especially by means of reports (Q2, item 112; .46).

The word 'especially' in this item may be entirely incidental, as is implied by the second item, which would be rejected by those who accept the preceding idea (because the saturation is a negative one):

> judgements of the child's work are more valuable than reports for the development of intelligence (Q2, item 108; −.49).

This favourable attitude towards reports – and against other kinds of judgements – stems, moreover, from a degree of strictness in regard to the child, exercised, of course, for his own good and the benefit of his intellectual development, in this perspective, as is confirmed by two other saturated, albeit comparatively weaker, items on this factor:

> punishment is a spur to progress (Q2, item 26; .21);
> permissive education is all very well, but it is not effective when it comes to developing children's intelligence (Q2, item 38; .21).

To make clear the strict nature of the assessment recommended by this factor, we refer to it as strict assessment.

Summary

The analysis concluded, let us recapitulate the dimensions around which the representations of the development of intelligence are organised.

The first factor follows Durkheim and Mauss in regarding intellectual development as a gradual process of learning social rules and norms.

The second factor also relates to a social conception of cognitive development, but this time in terms of socio-cognitive conflict, in the course of which the child comes to benefit from his mistakes and those of others.

The third factor is also social, because it makes intellectual development conditional on a good social and affective equilibrium in the child's relationships with adults and peers.

The fourth factor considers the beneficial effects of the mass media, particularly audio-visual techniques.

In the fifth factor, the child's errors are regarded as indicative of the inadequacy of his thinking, and thus as revelatory of his intellectual level. Error here has a diagnostic, rather than a developmental, value.

Factor 6 expresses the idea that the relational regulations in the child's relationship with an adult can only be obstacles to intellectual development. In short, complying with adult coercion appears as counter-productive.

Factor 7 simply negates the whole idea of development, since it appears to be no more than the activation or realisation of a biological programme fixed at birth.

We have said above that caution needs to be exercised in the interpretation of factors 8 and 9. The eighth factor seems to relate to the importance of teachers' competence, as the guarantee of children's intellectual development, while the ninth seems to concern the positive effect of a degree of autonomy on the part of the child (or children, among themselves) *vis-à-vis* the adult.

The interpretation of factor 10, finally, is unambiguous, and concerns the positive effects of strict assessment of the child's intellectual performance, in the shape of reports.

Teaching methods

The questionnaire therefore involved judgements about the effectiveness (or ineffectiveness) of various teaching methods or classroom procedures which might be considered in the case of a child having systematic difficulties (in mathematics, language or drawing). How then did the response to the fifty-seven propositions that made up this questionnaire organise themselves? The factor analysis revealed six factors with an eigenvalue greater than 1 after rotation, totalling 40.3% of the variance (15.3%, 11.0%, 4.7%, 3.4%, 3.2% and 2.7% respectively, before rotation). We shall, however, also interpret the next four factors, for their potential interest; they account for 8.9% of the variance (2.4%, 2.2%, 2.2% and 2.1% respectively). Considering the large number of items and the heterogeneity of the 'teaching solutions' advanced, the responses to this questionnaire are particularly highly organised. And taking account of the saturations on the various factors, the threshold of the saturations we have retained is normally .40, although we do also make some reference to items which, although less heavily saturated, are no less useful for clarifying the general orientation of a factor. Now let us look at the factors themselves.

Factor 1: pressures on the child

This factor, along with the second, is the most important from the point of view of the variance it explains, but it is not easy to analyse. So before making our synthesis, we should look at its various components. A central and dominant teaching concern appears in two guises: the importance of repetition, and presentation of the correct model answer. These two aspects are profoundly complementary, even if only because it is hard (from the viewpoint we are presenting) to imagine the repetition of a way of solving a problem having a beneficial effect on development if it was not the correct one. The ideas that relate to this dual aspect are as follows, in order of importance (the ideas concern what to do with a child who is having difficulties):

make him repeat the correct answer several times (Q3, item 55; .64);
make him repeat the exercise several times (Q3, item 36; .56);
make him observe a friend who gives the right answer (Q3, item 33; .51)
show him that the correct solution means everybody can be in agreement (Q3, item 57; .49);

although very 'normative', this solution nonetheless stresses one of the virtues of a correct model;

tell the parents he should have private tuition (Q3, item 32; .42);

(a solution relating to the self-explanatory notion of 'coaching').

And, with a less marked saturation:

make him do other problems of the same kind (Q3, item 22; .33).

We would also want to add to this list some other, more general, solutions, involving the parents directly:

give the child extra homework in the area where he has difficulty (Q3, item 34; .53);
advise the parents that the child should have extra tuition or stay down a year (Q3, item 25; .32).

This dual aspect, of repetition (with its distant overtones of behaviourism?) and of insistence on the correct form of answer, is paralleled by the use of methods of coercion in the form of rewards and punishments, or threats, even if they are only carrot-and-stick arguments:

ask him to respect the rules as he respects the teacher (Q3, item 50; .56)

(admittedly this item may seem somewhat marginal);

show him that he is falling behind the others (Q3, item 37; .52).

This reciprocally competitive strategy is complemented by the following proposals:

make him compete with other children (Q3, item 26; .52);
warn him that you will tell his parents (Q3, item 47; .51);
give him a bad report (Q3, item 23; .43);
promise him a reward if he does better (Q3, item 20; .42).

Further on we also find:

give him a punishment (Q3, item 9; .28)

This attitude of severity towards the child who fails is also expressed institutionally in various ways (as we have already seen in the case of staying down – see item 29), some relating to parents, but more to do with the educational hierarchy:

> refer the child to the inspector or the head teacher (Q3, item 8; .30)
> talk to the parents about the child's difficulties (Q3, item 7; .28).

The latter items seem, in the perspective, to entail shifting the problem either to the top (the inspector) or to the bottom (the parents) of the educational hierarchy.

To sum up then, this factor turns upon two main points:

1. the importance of repeating an exercise, associated with an explanation of the correct model;
2. the use of methods of coercion, going from reward to punishment by way of ridicule, the carrot-and-stick argument.

On 'average' therefore – supposing there could be an average in this context – it would seem that the educational solution envisaged comes down to putting some kind of pressure on the child (this refers particularly to children with intellectual problems: but then 'bright' children do not really present problems, except in very extreme cases). That is, therefore, how we have summed up this factor, although it is important to keep its various component elements in mind.

Factor 2: reformulating problems

This factor also involves a form of repetition, but this time with a fundamentally different educational significance:

> practise different problems which will help him find the right answer (Q3, item 52; .61);
> make him do other problems of the same kind (Q3, item 22; .43).

Repetition, if that is what this is, is here aimed at clarifying the dimensions involved in the problems set, and involves formulating them in ways that are capable of producing a correct understanding and, if necessary, reformulating them in ways more appropriate to the child's understanding:

> give a concrete example of the question (Q3, item 54; .57);
> suggest games which involve the problem that needs solving (Q3, item 16; .54);
> check that he really understands the data of the problem (Q3, item 12; .50);
> ground the examples in the child's everyday life (Q3, item 6; .47);

show him how the question often arises in relations with other people (Q3, item 11; .42).

These attempts to reformulate problems so that they become intelligible to the child can also involve:

make him explain his reasoning (Q3, item 38; .41);
make the children work in small groups (Q3, item 53; .43).

This factor, therefore, is clear: it brings into play the idea that the task of the educator (who, in this case, seems to be the teacher), faced with a child who is failing, is to change the way he asks the child questions, so as to make them 'socially intelligible' (Finn, 1985). In this set of ideas, repeating the problem is designed to ensure that it is intelligible, by using concrete examples, especially ones drawn from the child's everyday experience. This is why it seems legitimate to refer to this factor as the need to reformulate cognitive problems given to the child.

Factor 3: improving the 'psychological atmosphere'

This factor involves five propositions, relating to the psychological atmosphere surrounding the child with intellectual difficulties. In order of saturation, the five items are:

give the child responsibilities (Q3, item 19; .63);
help the child regain self-confidence (Q3, item 18; .61);
be more patient with him (Q3, item 21; .55);
find out whether the child has family problems (Q3, item 28; .52);
improve the classroom atmosphere (Q3, item 27; .49).

One of the other items, less saturated on this factor, is also worth noting, as it supports the interpretation above:

help to dispel the child's psychological resistance to the subject in which he has failed (Q3, item 41; .32).

This factor thus stems from what we have called an 'empathetic' attitude to the child, an attitude which aims to cope with the psychological problems encountered by the child. So it is necessary to be patient with a child whose problems may derive from his family situation (see Q3, item 28), to give evidence of patience towards him (Q3, item 21), but above all, to help him regain his self-confidence (Q3, item 18) by giving him responsibilities (Q3, item 19). This attitude derives from a 'popular' conception of psychology, which endows it with the ability to create a psychological atmosphere in which the child's intellect will be able to blossom (especially in the classroom, see Q3, item 27). To simplify the interpretation of this factor we refer to it as the necessity of improving the psychological atmosphere within which the child will develop his intellectual abilities.

Factor 4: motivational diagnosis

The fourth factor concerns a twofold attitude to a child having cognitive difficulties – verifying what the child knows, and thereby motivating him. The verification function, which is to some extent a diagnostic one, comes first:

check the vocabulary he knows (Q3, item 40; .58);
determine the level of his understanding before trying anything else (Q3, item 44; .55).

However, the diagnostic function also has a positive, motivational purpose, as the other saturated items on this factor indicate:

teach him to be rigorous in his work (Q3, item 42; .55);
interest him in the problem posed (Q3, item 43; .51);
try to make him attentive (Q3, item 39; .48);
help to dispel his psychological resistance to the subject in which he has failed (Q3, item 41; .46).

Since this set of solutions is organised around these two ideas – verification of the child's knowledge, and his motivation, we refer to this factor as a motivational diagnosis of the child.

Factor 5: severity

The fifth factor is concerned with a strict attitude to the child, symbolised by some kind of punishment, as the three most saturated items indicate. Accordingly, there is a need to:

give him a punishment (Q3, item 9; .53);
spur him on by making fun of him in front of his friends (Q3, item 5; .52);
give him a bad report (Q3, item 23; .44).

The small number of less saturated items on this factor also confirm this severity of attitude:

warn him that you will tell his parents (Q3, item 47; .37);
refer the child to the inspector or the head teacher (Q3, item 8; .34);
ignore him, if the majority of the class does the task correctly (Q3, item 45; .34)
show him that he is falling behind the others (Q3, item 37; .30).

The attitude advanced on this factor, then (which was almost entirely for the teachers), is one of severity towards the 'problem' child. This severity has various facets:

1. punishment or negative assessment;
2. ignoring the child, by marginalising him;
3. reference to authority outside the classroom, whether to parents or to higher levels of the educational hierarchy.

For the sake of simplicity, though, and without denying the varieties of meaning in the factor, we refer to it as severity towards the child.

Factor 6: wait-and-see and laissez-faire

This factor is equally unambiguous, and concerns policies of wait-and-see and non-intervention. According to this approach, the need is:

> not to force him, things will come with time (Q3, item 35; .61);
> not to worry him, let him go at his own pace (Q3, item 2; .59);
> do not tell him he is wrong (Q3, item 48; .45).

But alongside this apparently laid-back benevolence towards the child, there is also a kind of defeatism:

> do not intervene, as intelligence is a gift that cannot be altered (Q3, item 56; .37).

This can even be used to justify neglecting a difficult child:

> ignore him if the majority of the class does the task correctly (Q3, item 45; .21).

To summarise, the attitude advanced here is one of wait-and-see coupled with *laissez-faire*. We have named the factor accordingly.

There are four other factors deserving interpretation.

Factor 7: medical and psychological expertise

Here the solution of the child's difficulties is left to the 'specialists'. The solution advanced is to:

> ask for the child to be given a psychological examination (Q3, item 49; .67);

and to

> ask for a consultation with a psychiatrist (Q3, item 30; .66).

Of course it is difficult to be certain that this factor constitutes evidence of a naturalisation of failure. Yet the situation is seen as sufficiently serious to warrant recourse to doctors, after consultation with the school authorities:

refer the child to the inspector or the head teacher (Q3, item 8; .30).

Parents are also consulted, and counselled:

> talk to the parents about the child's difficulties (Q3, item 7; .25);
> tell the parents he should have private tuition (Q3, item 32; .24);
> advise the parents that the child should have extra tuition, or stay down a year (Q3, item 25; .23).

Medical and psychological expertise – the salient feature of this factor – thus seems to be envisaged, perhaps as a last resort, against a rather gloomy and pessimistic background.

Factor 8: 'tutoring' (children teaching children)

This factor is clearly concerned with the 'tutoring' approach, in which children teach other children (see the work of Allen and Feldman, 1973):

> make him work with a child who is less advanced than himself (Q3, item 4; .59);
> show him a solution which is even less correct than his own (Q3, item 10; .49);
> make him work with a child who makes the same mistakes as he does (Q3, item 24; .48);
> make him play the role of teacher to a younger child (Q3, item 51; .38).

Here, therefore, effectiveness is attributed to social interaction between peers, none of whom have the correct answer, and who are thus meant to construct their intellectual instruments socially. This therefore appears as a social constructivism (implying conflict and the efficacity of making mistakes) which, unlike the first factor, is not based on the transmission of the correct model, as this other item confirms:

> tell him he is wrong without giving him the solution (Q3, item 15; .19).

This social constructivism we regard as a 'tutoring' factor, as that teaching approach is the most pronounced.

Factor 9: repetition

This factor places importance on various different aspects of repetition. First, as extra work as an aid to combating the child's 'handicap':

> tell the parents he should have private tuition (Q3, item 32; .54);
> make him repeat the exercise several times (Q3, item 36; .42)

give the child extra homework in the area where he has difficulty (Q3, item 34; .29).

But besides extra work for the mediocre child, repetition relates to a complementary solution which has consequences for the disposition of the child's time, in that it ensures actual repetition in cases where the first attempt has resulted in failure:

advise the parents that the child should have extra tuition or stay down a year (Q3, item 25; .49).

This factor is, therefore, considered to concern repetition in the form of extra work, the need for the child in difficulties to practise the activities that present problems for him more frequently, either as extra homework or as private tuition. If these measures are unsuccessful, then a more radical solution, which seems to lie at the heart of this factor, is that the child should repeat the school year.

Factor 10: modifying the curriculum

There is only one salient item in this factor, and that envisages modifying school curricula:

modify the school curriculum so as to adapt it to the child's intelligence (Q3, item 13; .70).

Two other items, though they present lesser saturations, manifest the same viewpoint, first:

check that he really understands the data of the problem (Q3, item 12; .21).

The other suggests a way of revising the curriculum:

use more stimulating methods, such as television (Q3, item 14; .36).

The salient fact, though, is the questioning of the school curriculum.

Summary

Having completed this analysis, let us look again at the main outlines of each factor.

The first set of solutions envisages some sort of pressure on the child. One of the most important kinds involves making the child repeat the exercise, but providing him with the correct model for solving the problem. Complementary to this 'normal' cognitive activity, psychological pressures on the child are proposed (competition, threats, punishment, reward, etc).

The second set proposes, on the other hand, that problems should be reformulated so that they become intelligible to the child.

The third factor turns on a psychological atmosphere of confidence and responsibility likely to foster intellectual progress.

Factor 4 concerns verification of the level of the child's knowledge and understanding and, in addition to diagnosis, has the aim of stimulating the child's abilities and aptitudes.

The fifth factor, in contrast, to do with severity, especially punishment and marginalisation of the mediocre child.

The sixth factor stems from a kind of defeatism, and argues for a wait-and-see approach (things will take their natural course), accompanied by a clear non-interventionism.

Factor 7 proposes, as a last resort, appeal to the expertise of child psychology and psychiatry.

The solution advanced in factor 8 is close to the teaching technique known as 'tutoring', in which children teach other children. It therefore envisages interaction between peers, without the aid of the correct answer, which is designed to be constructed socially.

Factor 9 lays the emphasis on repetition, either as extra homework or private tuition, or, if necessary, as the child staying down and repeating a school year.

Finally, the last factor puts forward the idea that the curriculum should be modified at the institutional level.

Models of the child

For this questionnaire the subjects had to use sixty-two scales to describe children who were bright or mediocre in mathematics, language (French or Italian) and drawing. The factor analysis here includes the totality of subjects, without reference to the experimental circumstances whose effects we shall be looking at later. This analysis revealed seven factors with an eigenvalue greater than 1 after varimax rotation, all of which are interpreted below. Altogether they account for 48.3% of the variance (23.8%, 6.7%, 5.0%, 4.0%, 3.4%, 2.9% and 2.5% respectively, before rotation). The following are the 'models of children' identified by the analysis, in which we have normally used the items presenting a saturation of at least .40.

Factor 1: the gifted child

The first model is the gifted, one might almost say the model, child, who somewhat ironically prefigures the ideal managerial whizz-kid. The child is described in terms of the extent to which he tallies with perfection in social, educational and family life.

One important 'dimension', if we can call it that, of this factor relates to the child's motivational capacity. According to the ideal model, he is attentive (.74), reserved (−.72: note that we have, of course, adjusted our interpretation to fit the plus or minus sign of the saturation, by taking the positively connoted pole of the scale as our base), studious (.64), motivated (−.69), interested (−.63) and untiring (.42).

From the cognitive point of view, this model child is quick to understand (−.75), is capable of synthesis (.73), has a good memory (.64), is profound (−.62), and cultured (.53), and so does well at school (.54). He is meticulous (.44), and reads a lot (.46).

He also has the advantage of being creative (.45). He is curious (of course) (.69), and asks questions (.68). He is critical (.58) and does not copy his schoolmates (.51).

He is mature (.63) beyond his years, because he is precocious (.59), privileged (.55), self-confident (−.57), and well-balanced (.42). He tends to dominate (.51), he is clever (−.44), and can express himself well (.45). For some reason, clearly random, he also has a good teacher (.43). A truly model child (the sort we would all like to have?)

Factor 2: the sociable child

Very different from the model child; only the sociability dimension is taken into account here. On that dimension, the child is pleasant (.58), has a sense of humour (.50), likes to play (.47), especially with his schoolmates (.47). He is also talkative (.44) and communicative (.42). Here, then, the important thing is that the child should be happy (.42).

Factor 3: the well-behaved child

The third dimension on which the child was assessed was that of discipline. To keep to the positive pole of this factor we describe him as well behaved. He is disciplined (.69), obedient (.66), and respectful (−.59). He also goes to bed early (.51)!

Factor 4: the child with no problems

This factor describes the degree of tension in the child. From the 'good point of view', he is relaxed (−.73), calm (.57), serene (−.55) and happy (−.46). He also has the advantage of not being jealous (−.42). In short, the serene, unproblematic child.

Factor 5: the communicative child

This factor concerns the child with a rich vocabulary (.65) and a facility for expressing himself (.60). He is, in short, 'communicative' (.37). His ability to communicate is probably not unconnected with the fact that he reads a lot (.63).

Factor 6: 'Agnan'

'Agnan' is a well-known figure in the 'petit Nicolas' stories. He is always right (.63), he is smug (.48) and, sad to say, he tells tales (.42).

Factor 7: the inheritors

Basically the same as Bourdieu's usage, the child being the child of intellectual (.60) and rich (.54) parents.

Summary

The summary is as clear as the factors. On the first factor, the child is judged on the extent to which he is – or is not – a gifted child, a model child, wide-awake, intelligent and creative. The second factor concerns his sociability, the third his discipline, while the fourth relates to the child with – or without – 'psychological' problems. The fifth concerns the child's communicativeness, and the sixth the popular image of the teacher's pet. The seventh and last factor treats the child as inheritor of his parents' social and cultural baggage.

Intelligence and school subjects

In the questionnaire on school subjects, the respondents had to judge the relative importance of sixteen subjects, currently offered in schools, for assessing a child's intelligence. The factor analysis of the answers revealed three groups of subjects which accounted for a total of 58.7% of the variance (40.6%, 9.9% and 8.2% respectively, before rotation).

Factor 1: subjects with a high educational valency

Examination of the saturations on the first factor shows that almost all subject areas are connected with this general factor (on the statistical criterion $p < .05$). In order to grasp its specific qualities, however, we shall interpret it on the basis of saturations of at least .40.

The most important subjects are the following: mathematics (.79) and geometry (.71) score most highly, both representative of the logical and mathematical sciences whose educational valency (for example, their importance for entry into a new class) is obvious. A second group concerns other subjects of high educational valency, and relates to language-learning: mother tongue (French or Italian: .61), grammar (.56), reading (.47) and composition (.47). Finally, there are the subjects which involve the acquisition of different kinds of knowledge: natural sciences (.58) and history (.46). We may also mention geography which, with a saturation of .38, only just falls outside our criterion.

To sum up, the most important subjects for this first grouping have a high educational valency, and have to do with learning logic and mathematics, language and its rules, as well as acquiring knowledge and understanding.

Factor 2: subjects with a weak educational valency

We might have called this second group of subjects out-of-school activities, were it not for the fact that they are normally offered in school as well. But although they are recognised as important in the teaching of young children, it is equally clear that as the children grow older, these subjects are given less and less educational valency. The subjects in question are drawing (.68), gymnastics (.67), handicraft (.66) and music (.64); only history, with a saturation of .40, surprised us slightly.

The least that can be said, in the current state of our teaching systems, anyway, is that these areas are complementary 'activities' to teaching, rather than subjects in their own right, based on the transmission of a particular area of knowledge within an established and restrictive curriculum. We therefore refer to this group of more expressive activities as activities with a low educational valency.

Factor 3: language activities

The third factor is concerned with language activities: poetry (.61), reading (.44) and grammar (.44). Religion also appears, but this is probably because of the verbal elements it entails. But it is spelling which presents the greatest saturation (.80), and which governs our interpretation of this factor. Thus the linguistic knowledge implied in the first factor seems to emphasise the formal aspects of language (such as knowledge of the rules of grammar), whereas here, in contrast, the accent seems to be more on language activity aimed at understanding the content of language, as the two strongest saturations suggest: spelling (with its plethora of exceptions?) and poetry, both of which imply the repetitive exercise of a linguistic activity. For the sake of simplicity we shall refer to this group of subjects as linguistic activities.

The contribution of scientific disciplines

This questionnaire was concerned with the importance the subjects attributed to twenty-two scientific disciplines, particularly in the training of teachers, for understanding the development of intelligence. The factor analysis revealed five factors (the first two of which had an eigenvalue greater than 1 after rotation) totalling 52.5% of the variance (26.7%, 8.4%, 6.8%, 5.6% and 5.0% respectively, before rotation). For the most part, again, we have only used the items with a saturation of at least .40.

Factor 1: social sciences

This factor relates to an eclectic approach to the relations between the individual and society. On the individual pole, we find theories of personality (.63), theories of motivation (.44) and psychology of language (.46). On the social side, at the macrosocial level, are the sociology of education (.48) and comparisons between culture or cultural anthropology (.40), and at the microsocial level, group dynamics (.54). Given this eclecticism, is social psychology (.66) supposed to create the socio-psychological articulation which seems to be its role (see Doise, 1986)? Whatever the answer, and without going into the detailed content of this factor, we regard it as being concerned with the importance of the social sciences for understanding the development of intelligence.

Factor 2: clinical disciplines

The second factor is concerned with the importance of the clinical disciplines which have developed in the medical sector. The two most important are clinical psychopathology (.70) and child neuropsychiatry (.66), in both of which doctors bring their expertise to bear on the understanding of intellectual development. Psychoanalysis also figures here (.47), not surprisingly as it generally concerns a clinical and mental pathology, and also as it presupposes medical training on the part of its practitioners. There is only minor difficulty, the proximity of sociometrics (.40), which could be taken as a discipline permitting access to mental disturbances which are either social in origin or in their salient features. We refer to this group of disciplines as clinical disciplines.

Factor 3: teaching and teaching methods

This factor is only concerned with these disciplines as they relate to teaching and teaching methods. In order better to understand intelligence and its development (and perhaps thereby contribute more effectively towards it), pedagogy (.45) as a whole, and teaching methods (.54) in particular (for instance, programmed teaching (.39)), need to be developed, as also do more socially oriented disciplines like the sociology of education (.40) and ideologies of education (.40). Taking the factor overall, we have focussed on the dominant didactic concern for an educational approach which seems to us likely to encourage the development of intelligence.

Factor 4: humanism

Only two disciplines, philosophy (.63) and the history of science (.78) present high saturations on this factor. Since they are both concerned with reflection about man and the history of his scientific undertakings within a humanist tradition, we refer to this factor as humanism.

Factor 5: language and biology

This is a sort of 'Chomsky factor' (cf. the famous debate between Chomsky and Piaget edited by Piatelli-Palmarini, 1979), as it is to some extent a simplified version of that position which this factor seems to represent. Linguistic psychology (.45) is linked with biological maturation (.48) and pediatrics (.41) so that it can, if necessary, relate to a biological dimension of language development. This biological conception of language development is referred to as the language and biology factor.

Summary

Five readily interpretable factors thus organise the scientific disciplines designed to clarify our understanding of the development of intelligence. The first relates to the social sciences, the sciences of the individual and society. The second concerns the clinical disciplines such as psychopathology or child neuropsychiatry, while the third groups together the disciplines involved in teacher training. The fourth factor concerns philosophy or the humanist approach. And finally the fifth is characterised by a biological and maturationist approach to language.

Sources of information

The last questionnaire asked the subjects to assess the importance of fifteen sources of information which they might have been influenced by in forming their own ideas about the development of the child's intelligence. The factor analysis of the results revealed five factors (the first two of which presented an eigenvalue greater than 1 after rotation), totalling 65.7% of the variance (29.3%, 12.7%, 8.9%, 7.6% and 7.2% respectively, before rotation). The items with a saturation of at least .40 have been retained.

Factor 1: specialists

This factor assigns greatest importance to consultation with pediatricians (.72) or doctors in general (.71). But it is not only medical specialists who are involved, as contact with welfare workers is also considered important (.57), as is consultation with psychologists (.54). This group of four specialists, whether in medicine, welfare work, or psychology, is very clearly distinct from the importance attributed to other possible sources of information.

Factor 2: parental experience
As we shall see later, this factor is very specific to parents. Importance is given to sources of information which are really only accessible to parents, such as discussions with their children (.86), discussions with their children's teachers (.72), and the difficulties their children encounter (.70). This factor is undeniably concerned with parental experience.

Factor 3: the mass media
Two items saturate this item very strongly: one relates to magazines, newspapers, and radio and television programmes (.71), and the other to reading books (.67). We refer to this factor as the mass media as a source of information.

Factor 4: education
The two saturated items on this factor relate to education in general (.63) and professional training in particular (.59).

Factor 5: informal social communication
Importance here is given to discussion with friends (.69), most of whom will either be other parents (.48) or colleagues (.37). The factor thus concerns the importance of interpersonal communication.

Summary
The sources of information which influenced our subjects' ideas about the development of intelligence are drawn from five clearly distinct spheres:

specialists (doctors, psychologists, welfare workers)
parental experience
the mass media
education
informal social communication

The interest of the different dimensions which this last questionnaire isolated lies in their 'ability' to tell us about possible connections between different representations of intelligence and the origin of the information underlying them. It is this, particularly, that we shall be looking at in the next chapter.

4 The socio-psychological origins of representations of intelligence

Our main interest here will be in specifically socio-psychological, rather than merely sociological, variables. Thus although we shall be distinguishing and comparing various sub-samples (over the totality of factors, with the exception of those connected with the image of the child, as these will be analysed separately in chapter 8, and are thus only referred to occasionally here), we shall not be doing it primarily on the basis of their social origin, as we shall be doing later, but on the basis of the position subjects adopted on questions that stem from specific socio-psychological hypotheses which, furthermore, were introduced *a priori* so that they could be examined. The replies to these questions should, we believe, constitute the organising elements of the different social representations that were outlined in the previous chapter.

We shall be looking at two questions, of which the first is perhaps the more important. On a number of occasions, Moscovici has put forward the idea that social representations are ways of domesticating, or making familiar, what is unfamiliar (Moscovici, 1984a). We shall be trying, first of all, to develop this hypothesis.

Second, we shall be looking at the origin of social representations of intelligence in slightly different terms, though with the same outlook. We shall, therefore, be trying to show that the absence or inadequacy of information – what we refer to as information shortage – particularly in relation to the institutionalised explanations of intelligence and its development put forward by different scientific disciplines, generates particular representations. However, we shall also show that this information shortage is not by itself a sufficient explanation of the emergence of representations.

The familiarisation of the unfamiliar

In order to test the hypothesis that unfamiliarity is actually the organising principle of a given social representation, we considered our subjects' replies to item 56 of the questionnaire on intelligence, according to which 'the existence of differences of intelligence among individuals is a mysterious problem which science has been unable to solve'.

This item, which was deliberately cast in those words, refers to two component elements of unfamiliarity:

1 the existence of unfamiliarity is ensured by the inability of the sciences (which are highly authoritative sources) to provide a rational explanation of a phenomenon;
2 What is unfamiliar is defined: it is the existence of differences between individuals for which there is not really any exhaustive or definitive explanation, even in scientific circles.

On the basis of the replies to this key question, we eliminated 145 subjects, made up of the hundred or more who chose answer 4 (and were therefore in some way undecided), and those who failed to respond to it. The 583 remaining subjects were then divided into two groups, one comprising the 288 subjects who rejected the proposition more or less strongly (answers 1, 2 and 3), the other the 295 subjects who approved of it (answers 5, 6 and 7). The first group, therefore, represents the subjects for whom intelligence does not present an insoluble problem, whereas the second unites those for whom differences in intelligence between individuals are, as they see it, strangely problematic, and insoluble even scientifically.

After that we looked at the differences in factorial scores in relation to the different sub-questionnaires, referring to the subjects for whom differences in intelligence seemed strange as 'STR' subjects, and to those for whom this was not the case as 'NSTR' subjects. Table 4.1 gives the averages of these factorial scores, as well as the results of the variance analysis (and it should be noted here that *the thresholds are always given according to a bilateral hypothesis*).

As for intelligence in general (questionnaire Q1), the most striking fact is the huge difference between STRs and NSTRs in relation to the theory of natural inequalities or giftedness (Q1F1, NSTR $= -.51$, STR $= +.51$, $F = 299.933$ $p = .000$; the degree of freedom, given here once only, is 1/581), given that the item we looked at in order to differentiate STR and NSTR subjects was part of that questionnaire (it should be noted that this problem only occurs in relation to this factor, as this item is not significantly saturated on any of the other factors of Q1, and does not appear in the other questionnaires; and in any case the subjects were divided into STR and NSTR on the basis of their actual response to the key question, before any normalisation).

So the statement of unfamiliarity is part of a very specific representation in which, it will be recalled, the recognition of natural differences is

Table 4.1 *Mean factorial scores of subjects for whom differences of intelligence constitute an unfamiliarity (STR; n = 295) and of those for whom they are not strange (NSTR; n = 288), and analyses of variance (F and p values are only given where p < .20). The sign '+' indicates agreement with the ideas summarised by the label attached to the factors.*

Q1	Intelligence	NSTR	STR	F(1/581)	p
F1	The theory of giftedness	−.51	+.51	299.933	.000
F2	Conformity	−.03	+.03	—	—
F3	Relativism	−.04	+.07	2.441	.119
F4	The cybernetic model	−.02	−.03	—	—
F5	Adaptation	+.06	−.08	4.191	.041
F6	Family heritage	+.16	−.15	23.230	.000
F7	The differentiating school	+.02	−.01	—	—
F8	Personality	+.04	−.02	—	—
F10	Teachers and failure	−.06	+.06	3.812	.051
Q2	Development of intelligence	NSTR	STR	F(1/581)	p
F1	Learning social rules	−.10	+.05	5.017	.025
F2	Socio-cognitive conflict	−.02	+.05	—	—
F3	Relational equilibrium	−.08	+.05	4.255	.040
F4	The effect of mass media	−.03	+.05	—	—
F5	Revelatory error	−.04	+.09	4.225	.040
F6	Heteronomy	+.02	−.06	—	—
F7	Negation of the idea of development	−.12	+.11	13.275	.000
F8	Competence of teachers	−.11	+.12	13.023	.000
F9	Autonomy	−.07	+.09	6.188	.013
F10	Strict assessment	−.13	+.12	17.459	.000
Q3	Teaching methods	NSTR	STR	F(1/581)	p
F1	Pressures on the child	−.18	+.18	23.997	.000
F2	Reformulating problems	.00	+.03	—	—
F3	Improving the 'psychological atmosphere'	−.05	+.01	—	—
F4	Motivational diagnosis	−.10	+.11	9.066	.003
F5	Severity	−.06	+.04	2.488	.115
F6	Wait-and-see and *laissez-faire*	−.05	+.03	—	—
F7	Medical and psychological expertise	−.01	−.05	—	—
F8	Tutoring	+.07	−.05	3.226	.073
F9	Repetition	−.10	+.12	12.345	.000
F10	Modifying the curriculum	+.06	−.02	—	—
Q4	Models of the child	NSTR	STR	F(1/571)	p
F1	The gifted child	+.08	−.05	—	—
F2	The sociable child	+.01	.00	—	—
F3	The well-behaved child	−.02	+.05	—	—
F4	The child with no problems	+.06	−.08	1.745	.187
F5	The communicative child	−.02	.00	—	—
F6	'Agnan'	.00	−.01	—	—
F7	The 'inheritors'	+.01	.00	—	—

Table 4.1 (*cont.*)

Q5	School subjects	NSTR	STR	F(1/581)	p
F1	Subjects with a high educational valency	+.03	+.02	—	—
F2	Subjects with a weak educational valency	+.13	−.14	13.681	.000
F3	Language activities	−.09	+.13	9.618	.002
Q6	Scientific disciplines	NSTR	STR	F(1/581)	p
F1	Social sciences	+.08	−.07	4.288	.039
F2	Clinical disciplines	+.10	−.09	6.914	.009
F3	Teaching and teaching methods	.00	+.01	—	—
F4	Humanism	−.06	+.04	2.006	.157
F5	Language and biology	−.05	+.08	4.278	.039
Q7	Sources of information	NSTR	STR	F(1/581)	p
F1	Specialists	−.10	+.05	4.925	.027
F2	Parental experience	−.19	+.16	21.567	.000
F3	The mass media	+.14	−.09	11.653	.001
F4	Education	+.07	−.06	4.153	.042
F5	Informal social communication	−.04	+.01	—	—

combined with a discriminatory and elitist attitude. The stress on the idea of giftedness as an explanation for the mysterious disparities in the distribution of intelligence has the further corollary that it excludes other explanations, which are anyway likely to be incompatible with the ideology of giftedness. The STR are therefore more likely than the NSTR to reject (or less likely to accept – which, from our point of view, amounts to the same thing: we shall not pursue this) the idea of an adaptive function for intelligence (Q1F5, NSTR = +.06, STR = −.08, F = 4.191 p = .041), just as they are less prepared to concede the influence of family background (Q1F6, NSTR = +.16, STR = −.15, F = 23.230 p = .000). Only one effect of environment does seem to be acknowledged: the personal responsibility of teachers receives greater emphasis from the STR (Q1F10, NSTR = −.06, STR = +.06, F = 3.812 p = .051).

Moving on to the origin of intelligence (questionnaire Q2), we find that systematic differences again appear between STR and NSTR, three of which provide confirmation for what we have just seen. First, the STR are more likely than the NSTR to reject the whole idea of development in favour of explanations to do with giftedness and biological programming (Q2F7, NSTR = −.12, STR = +.11, F = 13.275 p = .000), and to recognise consistently that errors can only be indicative of the cognitive level – one might even say cognitive state – of the child (Q2F5, NSTR = −.04, STR = +.09, F = 4.225 p = .040). STR subjects, again, agree in setting more store by the ability of teachers (Q2F8, NSTR = −.11, STR = +.12, F = 13.023 p = .000). It therefore seems quite clear that, as well as giftedness, the STR acknowledge some influence on the part of the school environment.

Other differences appear too. STR appear to be more prone than NSTR to regard development as essentially a matter of learning social rules (Q2F1, NSTR = −.10, STR = +.05, F = 5.017 p = .025). STR subjects thus seem to differentiate between innate intellectual aptitudes and knowledge which comes from socialisation, which provides a better explanation of the supposed impact of the school. This learning process further assumes a stricter attitude to assessment on the part of the STR (Q2F10, NSTR = −.13, STR = +.12, F = 17.459 p = .000). Yet despite this apparent strictness, STR subjects believe that the best context for development is a good relational equilibrium (Q2F3, NSTR = −.08, STR = +.05, F = 4.255 p = .040). It seems that, once the idea of intellectual giftedness has been 'established', the whole issue of a child's development can be seen in terms of socialisation into social norms.

STR are also more likely to regard particular teaching methods (questionnaire Q3) as more effective. Thus they are more in favour of putting pressure on the child (to counteract the influence of innate gifts? Q3F1, NSTR = −.18, STR = +.18, F = 23.997 p = .000), of motivational diagnosis (Q3F4, NSTR = −.10, STR = +.11, F = 9.066 p = .003), and perhaps also of strictness, although here (Q3F5) the difference does not reach a sufficiently significant threshold. Finally, they are in favour of repetition and staying down (Q3F9, NSTR = −.10, STR = +.12, F = 12.345 p = .000). The STR are on the other hand less in favour of *tutoring* than the NSTR (Q3F8, NSTR = +.07, STR = −.05, F = 3.226 p = .073), as if in their view little positive could emerge from peer-group interaction. STR also tended to disparage the usefulness of modifying the curriculum, which would fit logically with the ideology of giftedness, but the statistical threshold is much too low (Q3F10). As we also saw in connection with the origin of intelligence, then, the central problem – once intellectual giftedness is acknowledged – is one of socialisation, as if there were a gap, though not a contradiction, between intelligence given once and for all, and the child's capacity for development in all other social directions.

Taken together, the results so far indicate that the sense of unfamiliarity which inheres in differences of intellectual aptitude does orient the way the subjects talk about intelligence and its development in their responses to our questionnaire. There is in fact a twofold discourse in operation. The first element is constructed around the theory of natural inequalities and, as we have seen, runs through the various questionnaires on intelligence and its development. Once this aspect is settled, and settled in the context of an ideology of giftedness, a second, parallel, discourse emerges which recognises the existence of development. This, however, is not intelligence 'properly so-called', but a kind of 'social intelligence' defined in terms of awareness of and respect for rules and social norms. This aspect is thus developed through systematic but not necessarily overwhelming pressure on the child, pressure which is applied particularly in the school context, where clear responsibilities are attributed to teachers and their competence.

Bearing this in mind, we now turn to the results of the other questionnaires, noting at the outset that no perceptible difference occurs in the image of the child (questionnaire Q4); this would tend to confirm that the problem is not seen as one intrinsic to the child, so to speak, but lies rather in the question of causal explanations for intellectual differences between individuals, as the models of the child here do not vary.

Differences do appear on the other hand in connection with the school subjects (questionnaire Q5). Thus activities with a low educational valency are less highly regarded by STR (Q5F2, NSTR = +.13, STR = −.14, F = 13.681 p = .000), although they place more importance on language work (Q5F3, NSTR = −.09, STR = +.13, F = 9.618 p = .002), and there is no difference when it comes to the importance attributed to subjects with a high educational valency. That this is not a chance result is confirmed by the tendency to reduce language to a biologically determined process, as we saw with the factor analysis of scientific subjects.

Looking at it from another viewpoint, there are two sets of subjects which STR regard as less useful for telling us about intelligence: the social sciences (Q6F1, NSTR = +.08, STR = −.07, F = 4.288 p = .039) and medical and clinical disciplines (Q6F2, NSTR = +.10, STR = −.09, F = 6.914 p = .009). This dual result to some extent validates our differentiation between STR and NSTR subjects, and thus our 'induction' of unfamiliarity, because the STR cannot find the kind of explanations in scientific subjects which the NSTR can. So the social representation of intelligence which we have seen taking shape among the subjects who experience this sense of unfamiliarity arises out of this lack of understanding and explanation.

The only group of subjects which the STR see as more important than the NSTR is the one concerned with the biological and maturationist approach to language (Q6F5, NSTR = −.05, STR = +.08, F = 4.278 p = .039), which is in fact very much in line with the innatist representation of intellectual giftedness, one of the most significant expressions of which is constituted by language or linguistic work, which as we have just seen is highly regarded by STR.

Finally, what sources of information do the STR (still in comparison with NSTR) draw on for their representation? First, clearly, their own experience as parents (Q7F2, NSTR = −.19, STR = +.16, F = 21.567 p = .000). This result is important, as it will to a considerable extent orient our subsequent analysis: the fact of being a parent seems to have a particularly marked influence on the representation of intelligence. The second source is specialist advice, which itself is likely to be sought as a result of parental experience.

Two other results are interesting for different reasons. The first is that the STR make less use of information drawn from their training than do the NSTR (Q7F4, NSTR = +.07, STR = −.06, F = 4.153 p = .042): unfamiliarity would therefore tend to diminish as professionalisation provides institutionalised explanations (as is the case, as we shall see later, for teachers). The second result is that the STR take less advantage of explanations which stem from reading than those which involve other kinds of mass communication (Q7F3, NSTR = +.14, STR = −.09, F = 11.653 p = .001). It is clear that the STR seem to develop a representation of intelligence marked by a minimum of recourse to external explanation, whether this be institutional (as we saw in the case of scientific subjects) or of a more informal kind. In our view, therefore, the STR's social representation which we have outlined arises from the absence of 'alternative' explanations to latch on to.

This idea of alternative social models, which are subjectively lacking to the STR, seems to us to make an important point. If this interpretation is correct it ought to be possible to show that the (relative) shortage of information implied by the absence of such models, especially scientific ones, to counteract the ideology of giftedness, does in fact have a part to play in the emergence of this social representation. This is what we shall set about demonstrating now.

Shortage of information

Unfamiliarity, in this case created by the differences between individuals, thus creates uncertainty which tends to be solved by constructing a representation of intelligence organised mainly around the idea of giftedness (or at least that is the aspect which we are examining at the moment). Why though, after all, should these differences seem so strange? Our hypothesis argues that they seem so to those who do not have an alternative explanatory model at their disposal. We can in fact assume that, in order to put forward such a model, individuals must have access to specific information, particularly to the scientific disciplines concerned with the question. Moreover, at this level the details of the explanation are unimportant: the only significant factor is a person's belief in the interpretative power, or otherwise, of a given model which, if need be, they can adopt without actually knowing or understanding it.

Clearly, we do not have any direct information, however imprecise, about either the quality or the quantity of our subjects' actual knowledge, with which to answer this question. And, for obvious reasons, we did not want to take the social or educational level of our subjects as a criterion. The question therefore has to be approached very indirectly, on the basis of the subjects' 'admission' of their 'ignorance'. One of the questionnaires (Q6), it will be remembered, concerned the relative importance of various scientific disciplines for understanding the nature of intelligence, and in it, in order to get some indication of the degree of shortage of information the subject felt he had at his disposal, we purposely added an extra answer to the usual seven-point scale, the chance to respond 'I don't know', which otherwise we seldom used. Using the numerous responses which expressed ignorance about one discipline or another, we divided the sample into two: the IGNOR subjects, who ringed more than two 'I don't knows', and who evinced a greater shortage of information, and the NIGNOR subjects who ringed none, one, or two at most, and who are therefore regarded as better acquainted with these competing models.

The main hypothesis, of course, is that a lack of information about alternative explanations ought to give greater salience to the problem of differences between individuals as the nucleus of the representation of intelligence that is organised around the theory of giftedness. But in addition to that we also assume that this information shortage should only have the effect of organising the social representation for those groups who are directly concerned with these differences, that is, where these are psychologically pertinent for the subject. We can take it, especially in the light of the evidence revealed in the previous section, that this pertinence ought to be particularly salient for parents and teachers, who are more likely to encounter these inter-individual differences in the course of their parental and/or professional experience, than for students. It would seem likely that these differences do not constitute a real problem, a real unfamiliarity, for students, or at least not to the same extent, and therefore that we should not find the same incidence of this information shortage in their representation of intelligence. In order to test this hypothesis we therefore compared the IGNOR subjects (those who, by our criteria, were the least well-informed) and the NIGNOR subjects (those who, by our criteria, were the best-informed), first among the students, and then among the non-students, the majority of whom were parents and/or teachers.

The students

An examination of table 4.2 shows first of all the extent of this lack of information. The 143 IGNOR students (the most 'ignorant') were less knowledgeable about and/or less aware of the interpretative capacity of the social sciences than the 149 NIGNOR students (Q6F1, NIGNOR = +.18,

Table 4.2 *Mean factorial scores for the best-informed (NIGNOR; n = 149) and least-informed (IGNOR; n = 143) students, and analyses of variance (the F and p values are only given where p < .20). The sign ' + ' indicates agreement with the ideas summarised by the label attached to the factors.*

Q1	Intelligence	NIGNOR	IGNOR	F(1/290)	p
F1	The theory of giftedness	−.20	−.21	—	—
F2	Conformity	−.04	−.01	—	—
F3	Relativism	+.06	−.05	—	—
F4	The cybernetic model	−.21	−.12	—	—
F5	Adaptation	−.02	−.22	5.601	.019
F6	Family heritage	−.02	−.07	—	—
F7	The differentiating school	+.14	−.11	7.488	.007
F8	Personality	+.05	+.09	—	—
F10	Teachers and failure	+.09	−.08	4.348	.038
Q2	Development of intelligence	NIGNOR	IGNOR	F(1/290)	p
F1	Learning social rules	−.11	−.11	—	—
F2	Socio-cognitive conflict	+.14	+.16	—	—
F3	Relational equilibrium	−.05	−.05	—	—
F4	The effect of mass media	−.02	−.19	3.588	.059
F5	Revelatory error	−.04	+.06	—	—
F6	Heteronomy	+.01	.00	—	—
F7	Negation of the idea of development	−.20	−.03	3.475	.063
F8	Competence of teachers	−.06	+.09	3.265	.072
F9	Autonomy	+.05	−.17	6.207	.013
F10	Strict assessment	−.08	+.01	—	—
Q3	Teaching methods	NIGNOR	IGNOR	F(1/290)	p
F1	Pressures on the child	.−20	−.07	—	—
F2	Reformulating problems	+.08	−.08	2.791	.096
F3	Improving the 'psychological atmosphere'	.00	−.09	—	—
F4	Motivational diagnosis	−.13	−.22	—	—
F5	Severity	+.01	−.05	—	—
F6	Wait-and-see and *laissez-faire*	−.12	−.10	—	—
F7	Medical and psychological expertise	−.04	−.11	—	—
F8	Tutoring	+.19	−.08	8.645	.004
F9	Repetition	−.09	+.03	1.865	.173
F10	Modifying the curriculum	−.02	−.14	1.854	.174
Q4	Models of the child	NIGNOR	IGNOR	F(1/280)	p
F1	The gifted child	+.10	+.17	1.746	.188
F2	The sociable child	+.06	−.02	—	—
F3	The well-behaved child	−.09	−.03	—	—
F4	The child with no problems	−.11	−.20	—	—
F5	The communicative child	−.06	−.01	—	—
F6	'Agnan'	+.02	−.08	—	—
F7	The 'inheritors'	+.09	−.10	3.619	.058

Table 4.2 (*cont.*)

Q5	School subjects	NIGNOR	IGNOR	F(1/290)	p
F1	Subjects with a high educational valency	−.13	−.22	—	—
F2	Subjects with a weak educational valency	+.19	−.03	4.962	.027
F3	Language activities	−.11	−.24	—	—
Q6	Scientific disciplines	NIGNOR	IGNOR	F(1/290)	p
F1	Social sciences	+.18	−.22	14.234	.000
F2	Clinical disciplines	+.05	+.03	—	—
F3	Teaching and teaching methods	−.03	−.22	4.543	.034
F4	Humanism	−.11	+.02	—	—
F5	Language and biology	−.21	−.25	—	—
Q7	Sources of information	NIGNOR	IGNOR	F(1/290)	p
F1	Specialists	−.13	−.30	3.418	.065
F2	Parental experience	−.41	−.36	—	—
F3	The mass media	−.01	−.12	—	—
F4	Education	+.02	−.33	14.849	.000
F5	Informal social communication	+.08	−.10	3.866	.050

IGNOR = −.22, F = 14.234 p = .000; the degree of freedom, given here once for all the results, is 1/290), as also of that of the teaching disciplines (Q6F3, NIGNOR = −.03, IGNOR = −.22, F = 4.543 p = .034).

This failure to perceive that these disciplines can be in competition and can provide 'rational' explanations is paralleled by a similar information shortage at the level of sources of information. Although practically none of the students had any information derived from parental experience, the IGNOR referred to specialists less than the NIGNOR (Q7F1, NIGNOR = −.13, IGNOR = −.30, F = 3.418 p = .065), drew less information from their own education (Q7F4, NIGNOR = +.02, IGNOR = −.33, F = 14.849 p = .000), and from informal social communication about intelligence (Q7F5, NIGNOR = +.08, IGNOR = −.10, F = 3.866 p = .050). It will be seen, and this is important for our argument, that the general shortage of information revealed here clearly validates the *a priori* criterion which we selected for differentiating the NIGNOR and IGNOR subjects.

The dominant fact in the responses of the less well-informed subjects is thus their tendency to respond negatively to a large number of items. They also fail to consider the adaptive function of intelligence (Q1F5, NIGNOR = −.02, IGNOR = −.22, F = 5.601 p = .019), the differentiating function of the school (Q1F7, NIGNOR = +.14, IGNOR = −.11, F = 7.488 p = .007), or the personal responsibility of the teacher (Q1F10, NIGNOR = +.09, IGNOR = −.08, F = 4.348 p = .038).

As far as the development of intelligence is concerned, only the competence attributed to the teacher is accorded greater recognition by the IGNOR students (Q2F8, NIGNOR = −.06, IGNOR = +.09, F = 3.265 p = .072), which is moreover in blatant contradiction of the claims made above. Additionally, these subjects have less confidence in the positive effects of the mass media (Q2F4, NIGNOR = −.02, IGNOR = −.19, F = 3.588 p = .059), and in the usefulness of the child's autonomy for his development (Q2F9, NIGNOR = +.05, IGNOR = −.17, F = 6.207 p = .013). And while they are more accepting of the items on another factor (Q2F7, NIGNOR = −.20, IGNOR = −.03, F = 3.475 p = .063), this is because they quite simply reject the whole notion of development.

We find the same negative tendency in relation to school subjects, as the only effect stems from the fact that the IGNOR subjects valorise the school subjects with a weak valency less than the NIGNOR (Q5F2, NIGNOR = +.19, IGNOR = −.03, F = 4.962 p = .027). The same tendency appears *vis-à-vis* the image of the child, where the only effect is the lesser willingness to regard children as 'inheritors' (Q4F7, NIGNOR = +.09, IGNOR = −.10, F = 3.619, df = 1/280, p = .058); here too the IGNOR do not draw on anything which could indirectly provide an explanation of the differences of intelligence between individuals.

In the case of teaching methods, too, the IGNOR subjects' tendency towards negation (in this case, of their effectiveness) is further borne out by the way they judge 'tutoring' to be less effective than the NIGNOR (Q3F8, NIGNOR = +.19, IGNOR = −.08, F = 8.645 p = .004), as they also do with the reformulation of problems set for the child (Q3F2, NIGNOR = +.08, IGNOR = −.08, F = 2.791 p = .096).

As far as the students are concerned, therefore, we can say that the generalised shortage of information, in relation to scientific disciplines – but also to other possible, and perhaps more informal sources – is not expressed by an organised social representation so much as by a general tendency to respond in a more negative way, or a refusal to take up a position on the notion of intelligence. But, as the complete absence of difference on the subject of the theory of giftedness factor (Q1F1) emphasises, this relative ignorance is not paralleled by an ideology of giftedness, and thus with any preoccupation with the problem of the differences between individuals. Would this be the case with non-students, on the other hand, as the parents among them would have to confront the unfamiliarity (so to speak) of their own children, and the teachers would obviously encounter differences between the pupils in their classes?

The non-students

Table 4.3 gives the mean factorial scores for the 183 most 'ignorant', and for the 253 best-informed, non-students. Let us first of all see whether they confirm the information shortage. This is in fact the case for the social sciences (Q6F1, NIGNOR = +.14, IGNOR = −.17, F = 16.429 p = .000), for medical and psychological disciplines (Q6F2, NIGNOR = +.06, IGNOR = −.14, F = 6.210 p = .013), and for teaching and teaching methods (Q6F3, NIGNOR = +.15, IGNOR = −.01, F = 4.564 p = .033).

This lack of awareness of scientific disciplines is accompanied by a degree of limitation in the available sources of information, whether these derive from reading and the mass media (Q7F3, NIGNOR = +.12, IGNOR = −.07, F = 5.908 p = .015), or from education (Q7F4, NIGNOR = +.24, IGNOR = −.09, F = 20.625 p = .000). Finally (and this will be useful later on), this shortage of information rests on a foundation shared by both these sub-groups, that is, parental experience (cf Q2F7), which is demonstrably claimed as a source of information (although often a subjective one).

So what representation of intelligence do the least-informed individuals develop? It is highly organised, and is defined by three dimensions: the ideology of giftedness, a conformist view of intelligence, and the attribution of responsibility for failure to the teachers.

First, it is the non-student IGNOR subjects who most endorse (or least object to) the theory of natural inequalities (Q1F1, NIGNOR = +.03, IGNOR = +.28, F = 8.852 p = .003), and reject the potentially competing model of definitional relativism (Q1F3, NIGNOR = +.06, IGNOR = −.09, F = 3.417 p = .065) even though they are in favour of the cybernetic model of intelligence (Q1F4, NIGNOR = +.02, IGNOR = +.24, F = 7.930 p = .005). On the other hand, they reject the notion of the development of intelligence in favour of a vision of intelligence as inherited programming (Q2F7, NIGNOR = .00, IGNOR = +.19, F = 6.626 p = .010).

This innatism is coupled, in a paradox which we have already noted earlier, with a conformist view of intelligence, or a view of intelligence as conformity. In fact, the development of intelligence as something social (rather than something logical and mathematical, which is seen as innate) is conceived as a gradual process of learning social rules (Q2F1, NIGNOR = +.01, IGNOR = +.16, F = 3.250 p = .072), which, while requiring special attention to the psychological atmosphere (Q3F3, NIGNOR = −.03, IGNOR = +.11, F = 3.290 p = .070), mainly implies the exercise of pressure on the child (Q3F1, NIGNOR = −.04, IGNOR = +.27, F = 12.572 p = .000).

Finally, the inadequacy of information is expressed by an emphasis on the responsibilities of the teacher as an individual, as failure is attributed more to the teachers (Q1F10 NIGNOR = −.08, IGNOR = +.10, F = 5.059 p = .025), and development is seen as very largely dependent on the teacher's competence (Q2F8, NIGNOR = −.12, IGNOR = +.14, F = 11.705 p = .001). This is of major interest, because the attribution of responsibility

Table 4.3 *Mean factorial scores for the best-informed (NIGNOR; n = 253) and least-informed (IGNOR; n = 183) non-students, and analyses of variance (the F and p values are only given where p < .20). The sign ' + ' indicates agreement with the ideas summarised by the label attached to the factors.*

Q1	Intelligence	NIGNOR	IGNOR	F(1/434)	p
F1	The theory of giftedness	+.03	+.28	8.852	.003
F2	Conformity	−.03	+.08	1.747	.187
F3	Relativism	+.06	−.09	3.417	.065
F4	The cybernetic model	+.02	+.24	7.930	.005
F5	Adaptation	+.05	+.11	—	—
F6	Family heritage	.00	+.07	—	—
F7	The differentiating school	−.04	+.03	—	—
F8	Personality	−.03	−.06	—	—
F10	Teachers and failure	−.08	+.10	5.059	.025
Q2	Development of intelligence	NIGNOR	IGNOR	F(1/434)	p
F1	Learning social rules	+.01	+.16	3.250	.072
F2	Socio-cognitive conflict	−.13	−.06	—	—
F3	Relational equilibrium	.00	+.08	—	—
F4	The effect of mass media	+.10	+.02	—	—
F5	Revelatory error	.00	−.01	—	—
F6	Heteronomy	.00	−.01	—	—
F7	Negation of the idea of development	.00	+.19	6.626	.010
F8	Competence of teachers	−.12	+.14	11.705	.001
F9	Autonomy	+.02	+.06	—	—
F10	Strict assessment	−.02	+.09	2.164	.142
Q3	Teaching methods	NIGNOR	IGNOR	F(1/434)	p
F1	Pressures on the child	−.04	+.27	12.572	.000
F2	Reformulating problems	−.01	.00	—	—
F3	Improving the 'psychological atmosphere'	−.03	+.11	3.290	.070
F4	Motivational diagnosis	+.11	+.13	—	—
F5	Severity	−.02	+.06	—	—
F6	Wait-and-see and *laissez-faire*	+.07	+.09	—	—
F7	Medical and psychological expertise	+.04	+.06	—	—
F8	Tutoring	−.08	+.02	—	—
F9	Repetition	−.03	+.09	2.325	.128
F10	Modifying the curriculum	+.11	−.03	3.335	.069
Q4	Models of the child	NIGNOR	IGNOR	F(1/424)	p
F1	The gifted child	−.05	−.14	—	—
F2	The sociable child	+.02	−.06	—	—
F3	The well-behaved child	+.08	−.02	—	—
F4	The child with no problems	+.14	+.05	—	—
F5	The communicative child	+.05	−.01	—	—
F6	'Agnan'	+.04	.00		
F7	The '*inheritors*'	−.02	+.02	—	—

Table 4.3 (*cont.*)

Q5	School subjects	NIGNOR	IGNOR	F(1/434)	p
F1	Subjects with a high educational valency	+.10	+.13	—	—
F2	Subjects with a weak educational valency	−.01	−.12	1.670	.197
F3	Language activities	+.09	+.15	—	—
Q6	Scientific disciplines	NIGNOR	IGNOR	F(1/434)	p
F1	Social sciences	+.14	−.17	16.429	.000
F2	Clinical disciplines	+.06	−.14	6.210	.013
F3	Teaching and teaching methods	+.15	−.01	4.564	.033
F4	Humanism	+.03	+.03	—	—
F5	Language and biology	+.19	+.11	—	—
Q7	Sources of information	NIGNOR	IGNOR	F(1/434)	p
F1	Specialists	+.20	+.07	2.041	.154
F2	Parental experience	+.23	+.30	—	—
F3	The mass media	+.12	−.07	5.908	.015
F4	Education	+.24	−.09	20.625	.000
F5	Informal social communication	−.02	+.04	—	—

would add further to the IGNOR subjects' cognitive uncertainty: in fact, the attitudes and, to some extent, the competence of a particular teacher are also unpredictable, for the same reason as the differences of intelligence between individuals. So, to put it another way, the imputation does not provide a permanent, predictable explanation of the differences between individuals, but makes explaining them twice as much of a problem. This is obviously why the IGNOR subjects see less clearly than the others the usefulness of modifying the school curricula (Q3F10, NIGNOR +.11, IGNOR = −.03, F = 3.335 p = .069).

In conclusion, it should be pointed out that this representation of intelligence among the less well-informed non-students does not result from a different assessment of the different school subjects, nor of the models of the child.

Conclusions

There are several conclusions which can be advanced about the insufficiency or shortage of information. The first is that it does not result in a specifically organised representation among students, but operates simply as a general ignorance, expressed now and then by some sort of refusal to define intelligence, or a cognitive difficulty in defining it, or adopting a position towards it. One might guess that ignorance fails to create a social representation among students because it has no focal point in general, and no focus on intellectual inequality in particular.

The opposite situation obtains, as we saw, for the non-students. They, in fact, have to face a real problem, which is the more difficult to solve as they do not have a 'rational' explanatory model, and that is the differences of intelligence that they see in their children or their pupils. For them, the shortage of information means the absence of a stable reference, a rationality provided by a scientific approach to the question. The place of this impossible rationality is taken by another rationality, that, which is really socio-psychological, of the ideology of giftedness. Since neither science nor the educational institution can explain the differences between individuals, they become naturalised in the canons of a theory of natural inequality. Then one model of intelligence – the logico-mathematical one – becomes salient, and, as the saying goes, either you have got a gift for mathematics or you haven't. Finally, there is another form of intelligence, in some ways more social and more dynamic, which can be developed by putting pressure on the child, and this is defined in terms of conformity to social rules.

In the final analysis, this social representation of intelligence as these analyses have defined it originates in the conjunction of two fundamental elements, both of which are really socio-psychological in nature: on the one hand, a focus (induced by the actual experience of an unfamiliarity as a result of parental or professional life, as we shall see later) on an unfamiliarity which is pertinent in the individual's relation to the notion of intelligence, or on the other hand a shortage of models that can be seen as explanatory of this unfamiliarity. In the chapters which follow we shall see how various identities (parental, professional and sexual) can intervene in the determination of such a representation.

5 Parental identity

The notion of parental identity is almost neologistic. It is not one of the generally acknowledged aspects of individual social identity, nor is it one of the variables of sociology or social psychology. In one of the most systematic series of research on socio-psychological identity, Zavalloni (1971, 1973, Zavalloni and Louis-Guérin, 1984) lists eight main dimensions, relating to gender, nationality, age, occupation, social class, religion, political sympathies and, lastly, family status – which may sometimes relate to being a parent. But there is no mention of a parental identity in itself.

The study of social representations cannot be reduced simply to analysing sociological differences in discourses except by using a particular methodology to isolate it within a given society. It is concerned with socio-cognitive operations which are not reducible to ponderous sociological variables. The representations, in fact, possess at least a degree of autonomy from the main currents of official thought and the major established ideologies. In the case of intelligence, our hypothesis is that these representations are largely derived from parental experience which, as a socio-psychological variable, has long been undervalued (if not ignored), possibly because it is such a universally obvious characteristic that, although it is implicitly or explicitly acknowledged, there has been very little real investigation of its psychological implications.

In what ways is parental experience likely to be able to influence representations of intelligence? Our answer to this is directly related to the conception of social representations as familiarisations of the unfamiliar, a conception supported by several results in the last chapter. The idea is really very simple, although it also has a great many serious consequences: the child constitutes, in a sense, an element of unfamiliarity within the family nucleus. He is unfamiliar because he is unpredictable. Quite apart from the unpredictability of appearance, there is no way of anticipating personality, character, ways of behaving, or even intelligence, with any degree of certainty. In this chapter we shall try to show the effects of what we regard as a parental identity, which has its own ways of operating, even though, of course, it is liable to be modified by sociological variables, as we shall see later.

Table 5.1 *Mean factorial scores of non-student subjects without children (NPAR; n = 157) or with at least one child (PAR; n = 279), and analyses of variance (F and p values are only given where p < .20). The sign '+' indicates agreement with the ideas summarised by the label attached to the factors.*

Q1	Intelligence	NPAR	PAR	F(1/434)	p
F1	The theory of giftedness	−.13	+.29	24.450	.000
F2	Conformity	−.09	+.08	3.975	.047
F3	Relativism	+.08	−.05	2.338	.127
F4	The cybernetic model	−.01	+.18	5.908	.015
F5	Adaptation	+.12	+.06	—	—
F6	Family heritage	+.15	−.04	6.088	.014
F7	The differentiating school	+.10	−.08	5.435	.020
F8	Personality	−.02	−.06	—	—
F10	Teachers and failure	−.02	+.01	—	—
Q2	Development of intelligence	NPAR	PAR	F(1/434)	p
F1	Learning social rules	−.08	+.16	7.955	.005
F2	Socio-cognitive conflict	−.16	−.07	—	—
F3	Relational equilibrium	−.05	+.08	2.916	.088
F4	The effect of mass media	+.01	+.10	—	—
F5	Revelatory error	−.12	+.05	4.773	.029
F6	Heteronomy	−.01	.00	—	—
F7	Negation of the idea of development	−.12	+.19	16.210	.000
F8	Competence of teachers	−.15	+.07	8.444	.004
F9	Autonomy	+.01	+.05	—	—
F10	Strict assessment	−.14	+.13	12.345	.000
Q3	Teaching methods	NPAR	PAR	F(1/434)	p
F1	Pressures on the child	−.22	+.27	29.630	.000
F2	Reformulating problems	−.07	+.03	—	—
F3	Improving the 'psychological atmosphere'	−.05	+.07	2.268	.133
F4	Motivational diagnosis	−.03	+.20	8.436	.004
F5	Severity	−.01	+.02	—	—
F6	Wait-and-see and *laissez-faire*	−.01	+.12	2.719	.100
F7	Medical and psychological expertise	−.04	+.10	3.040	.082
F8	Tutoring	+.12	−.13	9.359	.002
F9	Repetition	−.06	+.07	2.379	.124
F10	Modifying the curriculum	+.16	−.01	4.474	.035
Q4	Models of the child	NPAR	PAR	F(1/424)	p
F1	The gifted child	−.04	−.12	—	—
F2	The sociable child	−.03	.00	—	—
F3	The well-behaved child	+.06	+.03	—	—
F4	The child with no problems	+.15	+.08	—	—
F5	The communicative child	+.10	−.02	2.044	.154
F6	'Agnan'	+.05	+.01	—	—
F7	The 'inheritors'	−.02	+.01	—	—

Table 5.1 (*cont.*)

		NPAR	PAR	F(1/434)	p
Q5	School subjects	NPAR	PAR	F(1/434)	p
F1	Subjects with a high educational valency	.00	+.18	4.995	.026
F2	Subjects with a weak educational valency	.00	−.09	—	—
F3	Language activities	−.06	+.22	10.266	.001
Q6	Scientific disciplines	NPAR	PAR	F(1/434)	p
F1	Social sciences	+.12	−.05	4.886	.028
F2	Clinical disciplines	+.07	−.08	3.589	.059
F3	Teaching and teaching methods	+.02	+.12	1.906	.168
F4	Humanism	−.16	+.13	11.960	.001
F5	Language and biology	+.05	+.21	5.732	.017
Q7	Sources of information	NPAR	PAR	F(1/434)	p
F1	Specialists	+.01	+.21	4.949	.027
F2	Parental experience	−.31	+.58	122.458	.000
F3	The mass media	+.16	−.02	4.909	.027
F4	Education	+.34	−.03	25.573	.000
F5	Informal social communication	−.02	+.02	—	—

The effects of parental experience

Before taking this new notion of parental identity any further, let us just look at the differences between the 279 parents (PAR) and the 157 non-parents (NPAR) for the various factorial scores, the averages of which are to be found in table 5.1; the mean for each item is also given, for both sub-samples, in appendices 1–7. Note that only non-students are considered here. The analyses will be presented in relation to five separate but complementary problematics.

Do parents have an information shortage?

The experience of being a parent brings into salience the question of what kind of information they have. Parental experience itself is clearly the principal determinant of this (Q7F2, NPAR = −.31, PAR = +.58, F = 122.458 p = .000), and this is very much a personal or interpersonal experience which does not relate to any fixed model. Admittedly the variations in children and in the relations between children and parents do not lend themselves to a single model. This kind of subjective information is the more salient as information derived from professional training is less important to parents (Q7F4, NPAR = +.34. PAR = −.03, F = 25.573 p = .000), as is that derived from reading and the mass media (Q7F3, NPAR

= +.16, PAR = −.02, F = 4.909 p = .027). Children take up a lot of time, of course.

The only information external to parental experience comes from the specialists (Q7F1, NPAR = +.01, PAR = +.21, F = 4.949 p = .027). However, it is doubtful how much real importance can be given to the structuring capacity (for the representation of intelligence) of brief conversations or consultations with a doctor or paediatrician. The figures anyway speak for themselves: parents' information comes essentially from their direct parental experience. So what model of intelligence do they draw from this information?

The giftedness model

According to our analysis, then, parents are confronted with an unfamiliarity constituted by the child or children whose unpredictable characteristics do not necessarily correspond to whatever expectations there may have been. One of the main consequences of this ought to be an accentuation of the tendency to develop the theory of natural inequality, and at a more general level, the ideology of giftedness. A number of results confirm this prediction.

First, the conception of giftedness as an explanation of intellectual differences, as it appears on the first factor of the first questionnaire, seems to be more marked among parents than non-parents (Q1F1, NPAR = −.13, PAR = +.29, F = 24.450 p = .000; the degree of freedom, given here once for all the examples, is 1/434). This is complemented by the fact that the parents are most in agreement with the item which rejects the whole idea of development in favour of a notion of biological programming (Q2F7, NPAR = −.12, PAR = +.19, F = 16.210 p = .000). When we come to school subjects, parents attribute particular importance to linguistic activities (Q5F3, NPAR = −.06, PAR = +.22, F = 10.266 p = .001), the biological nature of which is made clear in connection with scientific subjects where the fifth factor, concerned with a maturationist and innatist conception of language, is the one that finds most approval among parents (Q6F5, NPAR = +.05, PAR = +.21, F = 5.732 p = .017).

In similar vein, parents, who are more prone to see the child's errors as simply revealing the child's cognitive level (Q2F5, NPAR = −.12, PAR = +.05, F = 4.773 p = .029), also tend to be more willing to consider a wait-and-see, *laissez-faire* attitude (Q3F6, NPAR = −.01, PAR = +.12, F = 2.719 p = .100), and to take a more positive view of recourse to medical or psychological expertise (Q3F7, NPAR = −.04, PAR = +.10, F = 3.040 p = .082).

It would seem, from this first set of results, that parents are more likely than non-parents to take a naturalising view of intelligence and its development. Parental experience can thus be seen as one of the main roots of the ideology of giftedness which clearly underlies these different responses.

Heteronomy

A second dimension which emerges from the analysis of these opinions is the tendency of parents to emphasise their agreement with propositions which relate to socialisation into social norms. Thus parents are more ready than non-parents to countenance another form of intelligence, defined as social conformity (Q1F2, NPAR = −.09, PAR = +.08, F = 3.975 p = .047), with the corollary that the development of this intelligence is seen in terms of learning social rules (Q2F1, NPAR = −.08, PAR = +.16, F = 7.955 p = .005). Having adopted this definition, parents argue for stricter assessment (Q2F10, NPAR = −.14, PAR = +.13, F = 12.345 p = .000), and are also more inclined to contemplate strong pressure on the child alongside an example of the correct answer (Q3F1, NPAR = −.22, PAR = +.27, F = 29.630 p = .000).

Thus the fact that parents favour motivational diagnosis (Q3F4, NPAR = −.03, PAR = +.20, F = 8.436 p = .004) but not the 'tutoring' approach, in which the child teaches another child (Q3F8, NPAR = +.12, PASR = −.13, F = 9.359 p = .002), probably arises because this socialisation into social rules is the prerogative of parents and teachers, both of whom are authority figures legitimately able to define such rules, and because this form of social intelligence cannot be produced by autonomous social development, especially within peer-group relationships. This is closer to heteronomy than to the autonomy advanced in Piaget's (early) work.

However, this does not imply a 'war' against children: the pressure can be applied with sufficient flexibility to ensure a socio-cognitive equilibrium favourable to good development (Q2F3, NPAR = −.05, PAR = +.08, F = 2.916 p = .088). One further item would tend to confirm the importance the parents set by improving and ensuring a good psychological atmosphere, if the statistical threshold were not so weak (Q3F3, NPAR = −.05, PAR = +.07, F = 2.268 p = .133).

School is the criterion

There are several ways in which the school career is definitional of intelligence. First of all, the competence of the teachers is a guarantee of development (Q2F8, NPAR = −.15, PAR = +.07, F = 8.444 p = .004). But, more importantly, parents have to consider the existing schools as the best they could be, because they are less persuaded than non-parents of the usefulness of modifying the curriculum (Q3F10, NPAR = +.16, PAR

$= -.01$, $F = 4.474$ $p = .035$). This of course fits in with the logic of heteronomy, which demands that the child adapt to the school, rather than the other way around.

The outlook of the parents may also be regarded as homologous with the effective functioning of the school, since parents measure intelligence in terms of success in subjects with a high educational valency (Q5F1, NPAR $= .00$, PAR $= +.18$, $F = 4.995$ $p = .026$). Moreover, their prototype of intelligence is logical and mathematical (Q1F4, NPAR $= -.01$, PAR $= +.18$, $F = 5.908$ $p = .015$).

So school, which is one of the preoccupations which necessarily concerns all parents, becomes a criterion, or indeed the only criterion, of intelligence (we say 'becomes' as non-parents do not exhibit this tendency). Here, therefore, parental identity concerns a kind of gradual socialisation, but this time on the part of the adult.

The role of the family

It might be supposed that the family, which occupies so much of parents' time and attention, would be seen as playing an important role in the child's intelligence. And, indirectly, that is indeed the case, judging by the heteronomy of the conception of the development of social intelligence. Yet when the question of the family intellectual heritage is explicitly raised, parents tend, oddly, to be more dismissive of it (Q1F6, NPAR $= +.15$, PAR $= -.04$, $F = 6.088$ $p = .014$). Thus parents are less willing than non-parents to agree that intelligent children come from families where intelligence is valued, and where the social and occupational level is higher. Why?

There are two possible, and complementary, explanations. First, as we have seen, parents are more likely to embrace the theory of natural inequality: in that perspective, intelligence is a gift, it is inborn, and cannot have anything to do with the social and cultural level of the parents. So it is a form of innatism which is closer to a genetic lottery than to any systematic genetic filiation of the sort that underlies eugenics. And second, parents may sometimes refuse to blame the family background where it is unvalued or unvalorisable, either because the socio-economic and cultural level is objectively low, or because the children have disappointed their parents in some way. These answers might therefore reflect a way of preserving socio-psychological identity by putting the responsibility for failure elsewhere, when objectively the chances of success, particularly at school, were low. We shall try to find some support for this hypothesis later.

A similar reason seems to lie behind parents' rejection of the idea of the school's differentiating function (Q1F7, NPAR $= +.10$, PAR $= -.08$, $F =$

5.435 $p = .020$), as that is explicitly related to the school's 'revelation' and accentuation of differences which already exist according to social background, and therefore according to the family. In protecting the family, then, parents are ultimately defending their own socio-psychological identity, which happens to be parental.

Summary

The notion of parental identity seems to rest on characteristics specific to various psychological aspects of parental experience. All things being equal (but are they?), the fact of being a parent gives rise to the representations (and also to behaviour, which is outside the scope of our methodology) which create parental identity. We have identified several clearly organised aspects of these. First of all, the model of giftedness or of natural differences would seem to stem from parental experience; or, at the very least, we can say that parental experience provides a particularly fruitful ground for the development of that ideology. Our explanation, for which we shall be providing support in the course of the analysis, has to do with the unfamiliarity, the mixture of uncertainty and unpredictability, that surrounds the personal and physical future of the neonate. This cognitive disquiet can also be observed at the pre-natal stage, where it is expressed particularly in the desire to discover the sex of the child, and also associated with the use of pre-natal screening to detect and (often distressingly) prevent anomalies, especially genetic defects such as Down's syndrome. Thus the 'shock of birth' is a shock for the parents, too. Moreover, the uncertainty continues throughout the child's development, or at least until adolescence, one assumes.

In fact, once they have got over the initial shock (if such it is: one does not want to dramatise), parents are faced with the need to socialise the child, especially in preparation for and in the course of his schooling. The representation of intelligence is thus completed by a somewhat conformist view of intellectual and social development, which is based on a largely heteronomous initiation into the elementary rules of social life. In this context intelligence is defined by success in the important subjects at school, particularly those to do with the cybernetic prototype of intelligence. From the point of view of the psychological significance of parental experience, it has to be borne in mind that parents' relationships with their children gradually become more dependent on the child's integration into the school (the degree of success of which can also be a major influence on the amount of uncertainty).

Finally, one last aspect emerges: the marked refusal by the parents to acknowledge the importance of the family for the development of intelligence, perhaps insofar as the subjects do not all, by any means, belong to a social or occupational background in which intelligence constitutes a sort of guarantee. All the representation is designed to do here is to explain and domesticate the unfamiliar, or to adapt to the requirements imposed by the child's education; it also operates as a sort of defence of the self-image when the social identity – in this case a parental one – is capable of threatening its positivity.

So a parental identity certainly exists, and has its own socio-cognitive operations. But to be quite sure of it, as it is a new notion, we carried out a further, more sophisticated and more difficult test: if this socio-psychological identity is real, ought it not to be more marked, and thus make the socio-psychological operations we have just seen more salient, in cases where the parents have more children?

The intensity of parental experience

The reason why parental experience constitutes a basic determinant of the representation of intelligence we have just been looking at is to do with the novelty, the unpredictability, the unfamiliarity of which that experience is made up. However, this interpretation deserves to be taken further. To do that, we have assumed that this unfamiliarity would become more marked at the birth of at least a second child. We know that all children are different (apart from monozygotic twins), whether they are brothers or sisters. This renewal of inter-individual differences ought therefore to accentuate further the representation of intelligence typical of parental experience.

To test this hypothesis, we looked only at the sample composed of the 279 parents, which we divided into sub-groups on the basis of the declared number of children. The first group consisted of the 99 parents who had only one child at the time of the questionnaire (indicated by PAR1), and the second of the 180 who had at least two (PAR2). The great majority of these subjects had two children, which prevented us from carrying out any more detailed analyses than those advanced here. The data are to be found in table 5.2.

Information

There is no significant difference between the two groups of subjects in the information they take from their parental experience (slightly higher for PAR2, but not significantly so). Two differences do appear, however. The PAR2 make less use of specialists than the PAR1 (Q7F1, PAR1 = +.39, PAR2 = +.12, $F = 5.664$ $p = .018$; the degree of freedom given here for all the instances is 1/277), which we believe shows that the interviews and consultations that parents have with doctors and paediatricians (see the previous section) actually provide very little information about intelligence

Table 5.2 *Mean factorial scores of non-student parents with an only child (PAR1; n = 99) or two or more children (PAR2; n = 180), and analyses of variance (F and p values are only given where p < .20). The sign '+' indicates agreement with the ideas summarised by the label attached to the factors.*

Q1	Intelligence	PAR1	PAR2	F(1/277)	p
F1	The theory of giftedness	+.11	+.39	6.610	.011
F2	Conformity	+.05	+.09	—	—
F3	Relativism	.00	−.08	—	—
F4	The cybernetic model	+.28	+.13	2.170	.142
F5	Adaptation	+.09	+.04	—	—
F6	Family heritage	+.02	−.07	—	—
F7	The differentiating school	−.04	−.10	—	—
F8	Personality	+.03	−.10	—	—
F10	Teachers and failure	+.02	.00	—	—
Q2	Development of intelligence	PAR1	PAR2	F(1/277)	p
F1	Learning social rules	+.22	+.12	—	—
F2	Socio-cognitive conflict	−.15	−.02	—	—
F3	Relational equilibrium	−.06	+.16	4.796	.029
F4	The effect of mass media	+.19	+.05	—	—
F5	Revelatory error	+.14	+.01	1.851	.175
F6	Heteronomy	+.20	−.11	9.938	.002
F7	Negation of the idea of development	+.10	+.24	1.872	.172
F8	Competence of teachers	+.03	+.10	—	—
F9	Autonomy	−.07	+.12	4.180	.042
F10	Strict assessment	+.09	+.15	—	—
Q3	Teaching methods	PAR1	PAR2	F(1/277)	p
F1	Pressures on the child	+.25	+.28	—	—
F2	Reformulating problems	−.08	+.09	2.736	.099
F3	Improving the 'psychological atmosphere'	−.05	+.14	3.099	.084
F4	Motivational diagnosis	+.13	+.24	—	—
F5	Severity	+.01	+.03	—	—
F6	Wait-and-see and *laissez-faire*	+.06	+.16	—	—
F7	Medical and psychological expertise	+.22	+.03	3.427	.065
F8	Tutoring	−.14	−.12	—	—
F9	Repetition	−.07	+.14	3.787	.053
F10	Modifying the curriculum	+.03	−.03	—	—
Q4	Models of the child	PAR1	PAR2	F(1/267)	p
F1	The gifted child	−.18	−.08	3.520	.062
F2	The sociable child	−.04	+.02	—	—
F3	The well-behaved child	+.05	+.02	—	—
F4	The child with no problems	+.21	.00	3.039	.082
F5	The communicative child	−.14	+.05	5.950	.015
F6	'Agnan'	+.05	−.02	—	—
F7	The 'inheritors'	−.05	+.04	—	—

Table 5.2 (*cont.*)

Q5	School subjects	PAR1	PAR2	F(1/277)	p
F1	Subjects with a high educational valency	+.20	+.17	—	—
F2	Subjects with a weak educational valency	−.06	−.10	—	—
F3	Language activities	+.09	+.28	3.380	.067
Q6	Scientific disciplines	PAR1	PAR2	F(1/277)	p
F1	Social sciences	−.02	−.07	—	—
F2	Clinical disciplines	+.08	−.17	5.969	.015
F3	Teaching and teaching methods	+.03	+.17	2.092	.149
F4	Humanism	+.28	+.05	5.373	.021
F5	Language and biology	+.11	+.27	3.478	.063
Q7	Sources of information	PAR1	PAR2	F(1/277)	p
F1	Specialists	+.39	+.12	5.664	.018
F2	Parental experience	+.49	+.63	—	—
F3	The mass media	+.14	−.11	5.858	.016
F4	Education	.00	−.05	—	—
F5	Informal social communication	.00	+.03	—	—

and its development. Such consultations are more likely to concern the physical and physiological care of the child, as the experience of the first child removes initial worries and makes the parents more independent from that point of view, something which can be seen from the lesser importance attributed to medical and clinical science (Q6F2, PAR1 = +.08, PAR2 = −.17, F = 5.969 p = .015) and to the recourse to medical and psychological expertise (Q3F7, PAR1 = +.22, PAR2 = +.03, F = 3.427 p = .065).

We also find that the informative value of the mass media and of reading declines as the number of children increases (Q7F3, PAR1 = +.14, PAR2 = −.11, F = 5.858 p = .016) and takes up even more of the parents' time than a single child. An important element to note, therefore, is that an increase in the number of children results in a diminution of information from outside their parental experience. Since parents in general seem to demonstrate an adequacy of information relative to non-parents, it seems legitimate to conclude that the intensity of parental experience accentuates this (relative) shortage of information.

The giftedness model

As predicted, the giftedness model is even more in evidence among the PAR2 than the PAR1. The theory of natural inequality is also more marked (Q1F1, PAR1 = +.11, PAR2 = +.39, F = 6.610 p = .011), as the negation of the whole idea of development would also be, if the effect were not at far too low a threshold (cf Q2F7). Reference to the biological aspect of maturation is also strengthened because of the importance attributed to linguistic activities (Q5F3, PAR1 = +.09, PAR2 +.28, $F = 3.380$ $p = .067$).

School is the criterion

There does not seem to be any difference when dealing with increased numbers of children at this level. The process of socialisation the first child goes through is enough to make a sort of dependence on the criteria of the educational institution salient once and for all.

Heteronomy

A sort of pattern emerges, linked to the socio-affective atmosphere. Good development is more regarded by PAR2 as presupposing a relational equilibrium between parents and/or peers (Q2F3, PAR1 = −.06, PAR2 = +.16, $F = 4.796$ $p = .029$) which they try to promote by improving the psychological atmosphere (Q3F3, PAR1 = −.05, PAR2 = +.14, $F = 3.099$ $p = .084$). Thus to this enduring heteronomy is added the management of the multiple relationships which flow from the new, triangular parent–child–child relationship, a context which also valorises the child's search for greater autonomy in his relationship with the adult (Q2F9, PAR1 = −.07, PAR2 = +.12, $F = 4.180$ $p = .042$), a further explanation for which can be found in the gradual achievement of real independence by the first-born.

Summary

The comparison between parents with several children and those who at the time of the questionnaire had only one thus makes clear the cognitive functions of the representation we saw parents develop, in the course of a real process of socialisation in which the new or renewed parental experience leads them to construct a specific model of intelligence and its development.

The fundamental point is that, as we anticipated, the intensity of parental experience, as defined by an increase in the number of offspring, gives new strength to the theory of natural inequality and the ideology of giftedness, coupled with a maturationist and biological view of development. Unfamiliarity, in this case the strangeness of the real differences between individuals, actually increases, and accentuates the search for a plausible explanation which we attribute (though without formal proof) to what we see as the current tendency of parents to believe 'they do as much for the one as for the other', which in cognitive terms means the exclusion of the family. Although we might 'regret' that the PAR2 do not go further in rejecting the role of the family background, we can nonetheless note that it is not accented, which would have constituted a plausible environmentalist explanation.

The second point of interest is the discovery that information sources outside parental experience gradually decline in importance as the number of children increases, and that this decline fundamentally affects the potential contribution of specialists such as doctors or paediatricians, as well as applying to books and the mass media. The popular theory of natural inequality would thus be based on a shortage of information, joined to the parental experience of inter-individual differences.

A third aspect concerns the family nucleus. The arrival at least of a second child obviously upsets the structure, the family nucleus. Relationships which have hitherto been almost entirely 'vertical' (parent–child) are now coupled with 'horizontal' relationships between peers, thus adding a relational complexity to the redefinition of vertical relationships which happens anyway as the first child grows older. These changes require a socio-cognitive adaptation to the new configuration of the family complex, one consequence of which is the importance the PAR2 attribute to relational equilibrium, psychological atmosphere, and the child's independence from the adult. These modifications in the parental representation stem from its adjustment to the new family scenario.

Finally, it becomes clear that the arrival of new children into the family has no effect at all on heteronomy, nor on reference to the school as the criterion of good development. From the birth of their first child, therefore, parents seem to develop two complementary attitudes which immediately crystallise. On the one hand they see development in terms of socialisation into social norms and rules, as a result of various kinds of pressure being exerted on the child. On the other hand, and also from the birth of the first child, there is a dependence on the ambient educational model for their definition of intelligence. Educational success thus tends from the outset to be seen more by parents than non-parents as the symbol of intelligence, and failure at school the symbol of its absence.

Parental experience and cultural background

To what extent are the systematic effects discovered so far, to wit the emergence of the ideology of giftedness as a function of parental experience and its intensity, generalisable, bearing in mind different social and cultural backgrounds? The most obvious question here is that of intercultural differences, which have been seen to affect representations of intelligence, as our study was conducted in and around Bologna in Italy, and Geneva in Switzerland. The very facts of each region's situation and history mean that some differences must emerge. However, we shall not be focussing on that problem; setting the differences aside, we shall be looking at the similarities of socio-cognitive function implied by parental experience, in order to demonstrate its general nature.

To do this, we shall again be comparing the ideas of parents and non-parents – but this time drawn from very different cultural backgrounds – on two counts, either of nationality or of professional training. Thus, in the Italian sample, we shall be looking at teachers, who are strongly represented there. In the Swiss sample, on the other hand, we disregard teachers and only look at those parents and non-parents whose jobs have nothing to do with education (also, of course, excluding students). The reasoning behind this is that parental experience, if it indeed has the socio-cognitive consequences we have attributed to it, ought to introduce the same sort of displacements of meaning, and adjustments to the representation of intelligence, into both contrasting sub-samples, thus transcending any specific discourses which might derive from cultural differences. We shall see that this is indeed the case.

Swiss non-teachers

Of the Genevan subjects who were neither students nor teachers, 42 had no children (NPAR), and 102 were parents (PAR). The data (see table 5.3) confirm that parents develop a representation of intelligence which is largely organised around the theory of giftedness (Q1F1, NPAR = +.36, PAR = +.94, F = 20.934 p = .000; the degree of freedom is 1/142), which is reinforced by the negation of the whole idea of development (Q2F7, NPAR = −.22, PAR = +.19, F = 8.821 p = .003), less recognition of the cultural relativism of the notion of intelligence (Q1F3, NPAR = +.15, PAR = −.10, F = 3.173 p = .077), and a reliance on a biologistic conception of language (Q6F5, NPAR = +.07, PAR = +.32, F = 4.699 p = .032). The Swiss parents consistently took a more favourable view of a motivational diagnosis where the child fails (Q3F4, NPAR = −.33, PAR = +.13, F = 11.307 p = .001), and of recourse to medical and psychological expertise (Q3F7, NPAR = −.18, PAR = +.21, F = 7.848 p = .006). Does the emphasis on pressure on the child (Q3F1, NPAR = +.26, PAR = +.65, F = 8.027 p = .005) reflect a special effort, faced with the reality of an absence of giftedness in children who fail? As for their model of intelligence, it tends to be cybernetic (Q1F4, NPAR = −.28, PAR = −.04, F = 2.928 p = .089), and to take its cue from the most important school subjects (Q5F1, NPAR = −.24, PAR = +.12, F = 5.587 p = .019).

The final point to note is that the emergence of the ideology of giftedness

Table 5.3 *Mean factorial scores of Swiss subjects without children (NPAR = 42) and parents (PAR = 102), and analyses of variance (F and p values are only given where p < .20). The sign '+' indicates agreement with the ideas summarised by the label attached to the factors.*

Q1	Intelligence	NPAR	PAR	F(1/142)	p
F1	The theory of giftedness	+.36	+.94	20.934	.000
F2	Conformity	+.09	−.04	—	—
F3	Relativism	+.15	−.10	3.173	.077
F4	The cybernetic model	−.28	−.04	2.928	.089
F5	Adaptation	+.46	+.27	1.856	.175
F6	Family heritage	+.40	+.18	2.056	.154
F7	The differentiating school	+.07	−.02	—	—
F8	Personality	+.25	−.18	7.282	.008
F10	Teachers and failure	.00	+.17	—	—
Q2	**Development of intelligence**	**NPAR**	**PAR**	**F(1/142)**	**p**
F1	Learning social rules	−.02	+.05	—	—
F2	Socio-cognitive conflict	−.34	−.19	—	—
F3	Relational equilibrium	+.15	+.18	—	—
F4	The effect of mass media	+.19	+.36	—	—
F5	Revelatory error	−.06	+.07	—	—
F6	Heteronomy	−.47	−.38	—	—
F7	Negation of the idea of development	−.22	+.19	8.821	.003
F8	Competence of teachers	−.02	+.22	3.094	.081
F9	Autonomy	+.43	+.30	—	—
F10	Strict assessment	−.08	+.10	1.674	.198
Q3	**Teaching methods**	**NPAR**	**PAR**	**F(1/142)**	**p**
F1	Pressures on the child	+.26	+.65	8.027	.005
F2	Reformulating problems	−.14	−.10	2.334	.129
F3	Improving the 'psychological atmosphere'	−.13	+.03	—	—
F4	Motivational diagnosis	−.33	+.13	11.307	.001
F5	Severity	−.04	−.07	—	—
F6	Wait-and-see and *laissez-faire*	+.06	+.13	—	—
F7	Medical and psychological expertise	−.18	+.21	7.848	.006
F8	Tutoring	+.24	+.09	—	—
F9	Repetition	+.43	+.62	1.740	.189
F10	Modifying the curriculum	+.08	−.06	—	—
Q4	**Models of the child**	**NPAR**	**PAR**	**F(1/142)**	**p**
F1	The gifted child	+.06	+.20	—	—
F2	The sociable child	+.12	+.08	—	—
F3	The well-behaved child	−.01	+.20	1.766	.186
F4	The child with no problems	−.11	.00	—	—
F5	The communicative child	−.16	−.16	—	—
F6	'Agnan'	−.08	−.16	—	—
F7	The 'inheritors'	−.01	−.14	—	—

Table 5.3 (*cont.*)

Q5	School subjects	NPAR	PAR	F(1/142)	p
F1	Subjects with a high educational valency	−.24	+.12	5.587	.019
F2	Subjects with a weak educational valency	−.21	−.37	—	—
F3	Language activities	+.32	+.53	2.471	.118
Q6	Scientific disciplines	NPAR	PAR	F(1/142)	p
F1	Social sciences	+.06	+.12	—	—
F2	Clinical disciplines	−.11	−.55	9.820	.002
F3	Teaching and teaching methods	+.15	+.33	2.244	.136
F4	Humanism	+.20	+.18	—	—
F5	Language and biology	+.07	+.32	4.699	.032
Q7	Sources of information	NPAR	PAR	F(1/142)	p
F1	Specialists	+.33	+.01	4.283	.040
F2	Parental experience	−.31	+.55	33.314	.000
F3	The mass media	−.13	−.50	5.751	.018
F4	Education	+.13	−.14	4.428	.037
F5	Informal social communication	−.20	+.02	2.695	.103

in this sub-sample is a concomitant of a specific focus on parental experience as a source of information (Q7F2, NPAR = −.31, PAR = +.55, F = 33.314 p = .000), which contrasts with the shortage of information already noted above. In fact, the specialists are seen as less important than by non-parents (Q7F1, NPAR = +.33, PAR = +.01, F = 4.283 p = .040), something which is confirmed by the lack of heuristic importance attributed to the clinical disciplines (Q6F2, NPAR = −.11. PAR = −.55, F = 9.820 p = .002), the fact that less use is made of the different media (Q7F3, NPAR = −.13, PAR = −.50, F = 5.751 p = .018), and that there is less input from parents' training (Q7F4, NPAR = +.13, PAR = −.14, F = 4.428 p = .037). On the positive side, there is nothing but a rather weak tendency for parents to make more use of informal social communication, probably with other parents (Q7F5, NPAR = −.20, PAR = +.02, F = 2.695 p = .103).

To sum up then, the ideology of giftedness – which is more marked in our sub-sample of non-teachers from Geneva – is produced by the conjunction of a particular focus on the differences between individuals stemming from parental experience and a relative shortage of information.

Teachers from Bologna

So what about the sample of teachers from the Bologna region, where we are dealing with a culture which is both geographically and occupationally different? If we compare the 93 childless teachers (NPAR) with the 75 teachers with at least one child (see table 5.4), we see that systematic

Table 5.4 *Mean factorial scores of Bologna teachers' subjects without children (NPAR = 93) and parents (PAR = 75), and analyses of variance (F and p are only given where p < .20). The sign '+' indicates agreement with the ideas summarised by the label attached to the factors.*

Q1	Intelligence	NPAR	PAR	F(1/166)	p
F1	The theory of giftedness	−.54	−.27	7.698	.006
F2	Conformity	−.14	+.07	4.076	.045
F3	Relativism	+.06	+.11	—	—
F4	The cybernetic model	+.13	+.26	—	—
F5	Adaptation	−.09	−.01	—	—
F6	Family heritage	+.04	−.13	2.362	.126
F7	The differentiating school	+.11	−.26	9.064	.003
F8	Personality	−.14	+.02	2.229	.137
F10	Teachers and failure	+.01	−.43	12.435	.001
Q2	Development of intelligence	NPAR	PAR	F(1/166)	p
F1	Learning social rules	−.07	+.05	—	—
F2	Socio-cognitive conflict	−.07	+.04	—	—
F3	Relational equilibrium	−.12	−.07	—	—
F4	The effect of mass media	−.13	−.13	—	—
F5	Revelatory error	−.13	.00	—	—
F6	Heteronomy	+.31	+.26	—	—
F7	Negation of the idea of development	−.13	+.16	6.755	.010
F8	Competence of teachers	−.17	−.09	—	—
F9	Autonomy	−.29	−.11	3.163	.077
F10	Strict assessment	−.20	+.03	4.980	.027
Q3	Teaching methods	NPAR	PAR	F(1/166)	p
F1	Pressures on the child	−.38	−.20	2.079	.151
F2	Reformulating problems	−.04	+.06	—	—
F3	Improving the 'psychological atmosphere'	+.01	−.02	—	—
F4	Motivational diagnosis	+.08	+.21	—	—
F5	Severity	+.02	+.05	—	—
F6	Wait-and-see and *laissez-faire*	−.05	+.01	—	—
F7	Medical and psychological expertise	+.02	+.05	—	—
F8	Tutoring	+.05	−.28	7.889	.006
F9	Repetition	−.49	−.56	—	—
F10	Modifying the curriculum	+.18	+.15	—	—
Q4	Models of the child	NPAR	PAR	F(1/156)	p
F1	The gifted child	+.06	+.12	—	—
F2	The sociable child	+.05	.06	—	—
F3	The well-behaved child	−.08	−.36	4.215	.042
F4	The child with no problems	−.16	−.16	—	—
F5	The communicative child	−.04	+.12	1.844	.176
F6	'Agnan'	−.06	+.10	1.737	.189
F7	The 'inheritors'	+.03	+.04	—	—

Table 5.4 (*cont.*)

Q5	School subjects	NPAR	PAR	F(1/166)	p
F1	Subjects with a high educational valency	+.12	+.32	3.527	.062
F2	Subjects with a weak educational valency	+.18	+.28	—	—
F3	Language activities	−.32	−.01	4.415	.037
Q6	Scientific disciplines	NPAR	PAR	F(1/166)	p
F1	Social sciences	+.19	−.09	6.346	.013
F2	Clinical disciplines	+.29	+.37	—	—
F3	Teaching and teaching methods	−.03	+.07	—	—
F4	Humanism	−.26	+.02	5.148	.025
F5	Language and biology	−.02	+.22	5.190	.024
Q7	Sources of information	NPAR	PAR	F(1/166)	p
F1	Specialists	−.10	+.44	13.522	.000
F2	Parental experience	−.30	+.60	63.000	.000
F3	The mass media	+.35	+.46	—	—
F4	Education	+.31	+.44	1.847	.176
F5	Informal social communication	+.04	+.01	—	—

differences emerge here too, and that they too are organised around the theory of natural inequalities (Q1F1, NPAR = −.54, PAR = −.27, F = 7.698 p = .006). The idea of development is similarly rejected in favour of hereditary programming (Q2F7, NPAR = −.13, PAR = +.16, F = 6.755 p = .010), which is consistent with the more marked reference to a biological conception of language (Q6F5, NPAR = −.02, PAR = +.22, F = 5.190 p = .024), which in turn is corollary to the importance attributed to linguistic activity (Q5F3, NPAR = −.32, PAR = −.01, F = 4.415 p = .037).

Turning to information, there is no differentiation between parents and non-parents as far as the cultural references – mass media and education – are concerned, which is understandable in view of the fact that they are all in the same profession. However, parents report more use of specialists (Q7F1, NPAR = −.10, PAR = +.44, F = 13.522 p = .000) and of their own parental experience (Q7F2, NPAR = −.30, PAR = +.60, F = 63.000 p = .000). The shortage of information is expressed here in different terms, at the level of scientific disciplines which are a potential rival to the ideology of giftedness. Basically, the ideology of giftedness that these teacher-parents develop is paralleled by a distrust of social science (Q6F1, NPAR = +.19, PAR = −.09, F = 6.346 p = .013), which contrasts with the reliance we have seen placed on a biologistic approach to language. Furthermore, the rival value (for the theory of giftedness) of the humanist disciplines most valorised by the parents seems extremely questionable (Q6F4, NPAR = −.26, PAR = +.02, F = 5.148 p = .025).

Finally, this time as a consequence of professional experience, some adjustments to the representation of intelligence can be perceived. Thus intelligence is more defined by parents in terms of conformity to social norms (Q1F2, NPAR = −.14, PAR = +.07, F = 4.076 p = .045), principally the ones defined by subjects with a high educational valency (Q5F1, NPAR = +.12, PAR = +.32, F = 3.527 p = .062). This is probably the reason for the Bologna teacher-parents' tendency towards strictness (Q2F10, NPAR = −.20, PAR = +.03, F = 4.980 p = .027) and a degree of distrust of 'tutoring' (Q3F8, NPAR = +.05, PAR = −.28, F = 7.889 p = .006), which in this context would be incompatible with learning respect for social rules.

In conclusion, we may note that the Bologna teacher-parents reject the idea of the school's differentiating function more forcefully than the non-parents (Q1F7, NPAR = +.11, PAR = −.26, F = 9.064 p = .003), which is also consistent with the ideology of giftedness. Similarly, they are strongly opposed to assigning responsibility for failure at school to the teachers (Q1F10, NPSAR = +.01, PAR = −.43, F = 12.435 p = .001). We shall come across the way social representations of intelligence can take on this function of defending identity again, in the chapter devoted to teachers.

Conclusion

Altogether, these results confirm the emergence of a social representation specific to the experience of being a parent. The fact that, at least in part, this representation is in some ways intensified by the birth of another child, and adjusted to the new relationships that entails, is confirmation that we must recognise the existence of parental identity as a specifically socio-psychological identity. It makes further adaptations to adjust to particular conditions (we saw, for example, the effect of the number of children). Further on, we shall have an opportunity to mention other adjustments, particularly in relation to sexual differences.

Yet over and above these partial adjustments it must be remembered that parental identity produces a representation which is built up around the problem of differences between individuals, and which tends towards an ideology of giftedness. Since those last comparisons showed that similar shifts take place as a result of parental experience, regardless of cultural barriers and occupation, it must be acknowledged that parental identity has general socio-cognitive consequences of its own.

6 Sexual differentiation and representations of intelligence

Does the fact that they belong to different sexes mean that men and women have divergent representations, or not? In this chapter, we shall try to show that, while there is no radical difference in their representations of intelligence (and this despite the fact that they clearly take diametrically opposite positions on other social topics), they do nevertheless diverge sometimes, because of the psychological significance of their different integrations, and they are modified, particularly in relation to family and occupational position. We shall begin by examining the youngest of our subjects, the students.

Sexual differentiation among students

Of the students in our sample, 193 were women (FEM) and 99 were men (MAL). Their responses are set out in table 5.1. We did find differences, which seem to be organised around three areas of opinion.

First of all, the male students present the outline of an ideology of giftedness. They were less inclined than the female students to reject the theory of natural inequality (Q1F1, FEM = −.29, MAL = −.04, F = 7.070 p = .008: the degree of freedom is 1/290), and more inclined to reject the whole idea of development (Q2F7, FEM = −.22, MAL = = +.08, F = 10.662 p = .001); they also tended (though the effect is very weak) to reject more often the idea of definitional relativism (Q1F3, FEM = +.06, MAL = −.10, F = 2.470 p = .117), one of the component items of which challenges male claims of intellectual superiority. Yet it is no more than an outline, as the differences on the other factors, which we have seen to be characteristic of this representation, are lacking, particularly the references to language and its biological nature.

The second point that emerged was a differentiation between male and female students in respect of one particular characteristic of the male stereotype: 'male autonomy'. This is the case for those students for whom intelligence, even incidentally, also involves an individual's personality (in the sense of having personality? see Q1F8, FEM = −.01, MAL = +.22, F = 5.527 p = .019), who regard intelligence as a product of interpersonal

Table 6.1 *Mean factorial scores of female students (FEM; n = 193) and male students (MAL; n = 99), and analyses of variance (F and p values are only given where p < .20). The sign ' + ' indicates agreement with the ideas summarised by the label attached to the factors.*

Q1	Intelligence	FEM	MAL	F(1/290)	p
F1	The theory of giftedness	−.29	−.04	7.070	.008
F2	Conformity	−.06	+.06	—	—
F3	Relativism	+.06	−.10	2.470	.117
F4	The cybernetic model	−.16	−.19	—	—
F5	Adaptation	−.10	−.14	—	—
F6	Family heritage	−.07	.00	—	—
F7	The differentiating school	+.06	−.06	—	—
F8	Personality	−.01	+.22	5.527	.019
F10	Teachers and failure	−.03	+.07	—	—
Q2	Development of intelligence	FEM	MAL	F(1/290)	p
F1	Learning social rules	−.09	−.15	—	—
F2	Socio-cognitive conflict	+.09	+.27	3.793	.052
F3	Relational equilibrium	−.02	−.11	—	—
F4	The effect of mass media	−.09	−.12	—	—
F5	Revelatory error	−.01	+.05	—	—
F6	Heteronomy	+.07	−.12	4.192	.042
F7	Negation of the idea of development	−.22	+.08	10.662	.001
F8	Competence of teachers	−.04	+.12	3.395	.066
F9	Autonomy	−.08	−.01	—	—
F10	Strict assessment	−.08	+.03	1.748	.187
Q3	Teaching methods	FEM	MAL	F(1/290)	p
F1	Pressures on the child	−.25	+.08	9.330	.002
F2	Reformulating problems	+.07	−.12	3.499	.062
F3	Improving the 'psychological atmosphere'	+.02	−.16	2.884	.091
F4	Motivational diagnosis	−.10	−.31	4.367	.038
F5	Severity	−.09	+.13	5.767	.017
F6	Wait-and-see and *laissez-faire*	−.11	−.13	—	—
F7	Medical and psychological expertise	−.02	−.17	1.904	.169
F8	Tutoring	−.05	+.26	9.570	.002
F9	Repetition	−.06	+.03	—	—
F10	Modifying the curriculum	−.03	−.16	1.939	.165
Q4	Models of the child	FEM	MAL	F(1/280)	p
F1	The gifted child	+.17	+.07	—	—
F2	The sociable child	−.04	+.14	1.829	.177
F3	The well-behaved child	−.04	−.11	—	—
F4	The child with no problems	−.12	−.22	—	—
F5	The communicative child	−.03	−.04	—	—
F6	'Agnan'	−.06	+.02	—	—
F7	The 'inheritors'	+.03	−.06	—	—

Table 6.1 (*cont.*)

Q5	School subjects	FEM	MAL	F(1/290)	p
F1	Subjects with a high educational valency	−.11	−.30	2.505	.115
F2	Subjects with a weak educational valency	+.06	+.12	—	—
F3	Language activities	−.15	−.22	—	—
Q6	Scientific disciplines	FEM	MAL	F(1/290)	p
F1	Social sciences	+.12	−.28	13.236	.000
F2	Clinical disciplines	+.05	+.02	—	—
F3	Teaching and teaching methods	−.06	−.26	4.745	.030
F4	Humanism	−.15	+.16	8.438	.004
F5	Language and biology	−.20	−.30	—	—
Q7	Sources of information	FEM	MAL	F(1/290)	p
F1	Specialists	−.19	−.26	—	—
F2	Parental experience	−.39	−.37	—	—
F3	The mass media	+.03	−.25	8.073	,005
F4	Education	−.02	−.41	16.668	.000
F5	Informal social communication	+.01	−.02	—	—

conflict (another male stereotype? Q2F2, FEM = +.09, MAL = +.27, F = 3.793 p = .052), particularly of 'tutoring' (Q3F8, FEM = −.05, MAL = +.26, F = 9.570 p = .002), teaching methods which may also derive from the competence of the teacher (Q2F8, FEM = −.04, MAL = +.12, F = 3.395 p = .066). This kind of developmental autonomy in a conflictual socio-cognitive relationship with another person could also explain why the male students do not regard reformulating problems as very effective (Q3F2, FEM = +.07, MAL = −.12, F = 3.499 p = .062), nor motivational diagnosis (Q3F4, FEM = −.10, MAL = −.31, F = 4.367 p = .038), results which are actually not inconsistent with the outline theory of giftedness.

From the point of view of the female students, the lesser degree of developmental autonomy might be taken to mean a more comprehensive approach (verification, motivation, reformulation), implying a sort of avoidance or minimisation of the conflictuality of interpersonal relationships. All of which in the end corresponds to a certain stereotyped view of men and women.

In addition to autonomy, the male students demonstrate an inclination towards strictness, something which was foreshadowed in connection with strict assessment (see Q2F10, but the effect is not statistically reliable), and advanced as an effective teaching method, except by the female students (Q3F5, FEM = −.09, MAL = +.13, F = 5.767 p = .017). Again, male students are more willing than female students to recognise the effectiveness of pressure exerted on the child (Q3F1, FEM = −.25, MAL = +.08, F = 9.330 p = .002) and recourse by the adult to restrictive relational regulation (Q2F6, FEM = +.07, MAL = −.12, F = 4.192 p = .042). Complementary to this, the male students do not regard improving the psychological atmosphere as very useful (Q3F3, FEM = +.02, MAL = −.16, F = 2.884 p = .091).

Finally, none of the definitions of intelligence – in terms of cybernetics, or education, or social intelligence – differentiates between male and female students.

The men and women in the student sample thus seem to differentiate themselves mainly by a certain stereotyped attitude to their sexual identity, the female students being less strict and more understanding or enthusiastic, and the males more autonomous and conflictual. All very stereotyped, in fact, and seemingly not related to any real differential in the actual structuring of the representations of intelligence, especially as there is no differentiation in its definition.

Why then, however, do the male students demonstrate the main elements of the ideology of giftedness? Our view is that the reasons for this are not to do with sexual differentiation in itself. To back this up, we shall look first of all at the sources of information. Male students seem to make less use of their reading and information from other mass media (Q7F3, FEM = +.03, MAL = −.25, F = 8.073 p = .005), which indicates a difference that is at least as much 'cultural' as sexual, and supports our hypothesis about the role of information. What is more, the male students refer much less to their education than do female students (Q7F4, FEM = −.02, MAL = −.41, F = 16.668 p = .000). This cultural difference, superimposed on sexual identity, also fits well with the courses taken by our student sample. The female students (in our sample, that is) tend to look towards careers in teaching or psychology, whereas many of the male students are preparing for prestigious careers in medicine or physics.

If this is indeed the case, there ought to be some difference in the theoretical reference of the two groups, which would also provide an explanation for the divergence of opinions, especially over giftedness. Male students, in fact, are less prepared than female students to accept the information value of the social sciences (which would constitute a sort of antidote to giftedness) (Q6F1, FEM = +.12, MAL = −.28, F = 13.236 p = .000) and of the teaching disciplines (Q6F3, FEM = −.06, MAL = −.26. F = 4.745 p = .030). The only positive reference of the male students is thus to the humanist subjects, which include the history of science (Q6F4, FEM = −.15, MAL = +.16, F = 8.438 p = .004). So, rather than sexual identity, it is cultural reference, in this case the university career (on which see Francès, 1980), which determines the differences.

But though this may be true for the outline theory of giftedness, how far does it also apply to those more 'masculine' attitudes and values of autonomy and severity? To discover this, we need to compare non-students who share the same sources of information and theoretical references. This is the only way in which we shall be able to find out whether, all other things being equal, men and women differ in their representations of intelligence. We could not do this with teachers, as most of our subjects came from the female-dominated primary sector, so we shall only look at non-students who are also not teachers.

Sexual differentiation among non-teachers

The first thing we discovered was that there was no differentiation between the 132 women (FEM) and the 87 men (MAL) as regards their sources of information (see table 6.2), the dominant aspects of which are parental experience and the absence of reference to the mass media and education, nor as regards their reference to scientific theories. But the two sub-samples differed very little in general in their responses to the questionnaire, as if when cultural references are constant sexual differences diminish, at least as far as the representation of intelligence is concerned.

The few differences which do appear, like the previous comparison, show autonomy and severity to be more marked among men than women. The autonomy tends, though feebly, to be explained as such (Q2F9, FEM +.04, MAL = +.20, F = 2.332 p = .128), but it lies mainly in the appeal to the socio-cognitive constructivism (Q2F2, FEM = −.21, MAL = +.06, F = 5.331 p = .022) which also underlies the acknowledged effectiveness of 'tutoring' (Q3F8, FEM = −.10, MAL = +.14, F = 4.799 p = .030). Men are also keener on severity than women (Q3F5, FEM = −.09, MAL = +.20, F = 5.466 p = .020).

Finally, although there are other tendencies, nothing clear or organised emerges from them. Except that, as in the familiar stereotype, women accord more importance than men to language (Q5F3, FEM = +.40, MAL = +.14, F = 5.788 p = .017).

Several general comments can be made on these results. First of all, it appears that differences in the sex of the subjects (at least in connection with intelligence, which is all we are talking about here) do not determine the way the representation is organised. The only systematic differences we found concern the two attitudes of autonomy and severity, which were more marked among the men than among the women, who tended to be milder and more relaxed. Apart from these stereotyped attitudes, there were no noteworthy differences.

Secondly, the most organised differences between male and female

Table 6.2 *Mean factorial scores of women (FEM; n = 132) and men (MAL; n = 87), excluding students, and analyses of variance (F and p values are only given where p < .20). The sign '+' indicates agreement with the ideas summarised by the label attached to the factors.*

Q1	Intelligence	FEM	MAL	F(1/217)	p
F1	The theory of giftedness	+.40	+.49	—	—
F2	Conformity	+.06	+.17		
F3	Relativism	+.01	−.15	2.001	.159
F4	The cybernetic model	+.12	+.03	—	—
F5	Adaptation	+.10	+.15	—	—
F6	Family heritage	−.05	+.14	2.797	.096
F7	The differentiating school	.00	−.11	—	—
F8	Personality	−.06	+.06	—	—
F10	Teachers and failure	+.16	+.31	1.859	.174
Q2	Development of intelligence	FEM	MAL	F(1/217)	p
F1	Learning social rules	+.25	+.07	2.048	.154
F2	Socio-cognitive conflict	−.21	+.06	5.331	.022
F3	Relational equilibrium	+.10	+.10	—	—
F4	The effect of mass media	+22.	+.11	—	—
F5	Revelatory error	+.01	+.17	1.934	.166
F6	Heteronomy	−.12	−.19	—	—
F7	Negation of the idea of development	+.12	+.06	—	—
F8	Competence of teachers	+.13	+.13	—	—
F9	Autonomy	+.04	+.20	2.332	.128
F10	Strict assessment	+.18	+.07	—	—
Q3	Teaching methods	FEM	MAL	F(1/217)	p
F1	Pressures on the child	+.48	+.49	—	—
F2	Reformulating problems	+.04	−.02	—	—
F3	Improving the 'psychological atmosphere'	+.08	+.04	—	—
F4	Motivational diagnosis	+.07	+.01	—	—
F5	Severity	−.09	+.20	5.466	.020
F6	Wait-and-see and *laissez-faire*	+.15	+.05	—	—
F7	Medical and psychological expertise	−.01	+.09	—	—
F8	Tutoring	−.10	+.14	4.799	.030
F9	Repetition	+.36	+.22	2.250	.135
F10	Modifying the curriculum	−.08	−.08	—	—
Q4	Models of the child	FEM	MAL	F(1/207)	p
F1	The gifted child	−.04	−.17	2.211	.139
F2	The sociable child	+.09	−.13	3.245	.073
F3	The well-behaved child	−.05	−.12	—	—
F4	The child with no problems	+.11	+.06	—	—
F5	The communicative child	+.09	−.01	—	—
F6	'Agnan'	+.08	+.10	—	—
F7	The 'inheritors'	+.06	+.03	—	—

Table 6.2 (*cont.*)

Q5	School subjects	FEM	MAL	F(1/217)	p
F1	Subjects with a high educational valency	+.09	.00	—	—
F2	Subjects with a weak educational valency	−.29	−.09	2.400	.123
F3	Language activities	+.40	+.14	5.788	.017
Q6	Scientific disciplines	FEM	MAL	F(1/217)	p
F1	Social sciences	+.02	−.12	—	—
F2	Clinical disciplines	−.16	−.30	—	—
F3	Teaching and teaching methods	+.10	+.22	1.861	.174
F4	Humanism	+.19	+.28	—	—
F5	Language and biology	+.15	+.16	—	—
Q7	Sources of information	FEM	MAL	F(1/217)	p
F1	Specialists	+.15	+.13	—	—
F2	Parental experience	+.43	+.38	—	—
F3	The mass media	−.19	−.26	—	—
F4	Education	−.20	−.23	—	—
F5	Informal social communication	−.03	−.05	—	—

students is related more to specific cultural integrations than to sexual differences, as the students commit themselves to university careers with divergent theoretical reference, in accordance with their sexual identity. When these references remain constant, as also with the sources of information, the only differences which show up in the analysis are the stereotypes of autonomy and severity which we have already seen.

The cultural context is therefore fundamental. Not that this means, of course, that there is no sexual differentiation in the representation of intelligence: we shall see later on that there is often a difference between fathers and mothers over some elements of the representation, as a result of their family or occupational integration. Yet here again we shall try to show that this is not the product of some basic 'natural' difference, to do with a *sui generis* sexual differentiation, but a differentiation linked to divergent cultural conditions stemming from the social integrations of the men and women concerned.

Parental identity and sexual differentiation

Whether one likes it or not, and whether one approves or not, it has to be recognised that, as a general rule, mothers play a special role in the education of children, particularly perhaps in early childhood. Not that the father does not also have a role to play (and a role which is increasingly

Table 6.3 *Mean factorial scores of parents who are women (FEM; n = 183) and those who are men (MAL; n = 95), and analyses of variance (F and p values are only given where p < .20). The sign ' + ' indicates agreement with the ideas summarised by the label attached to the factors.*

Q1	Intelligence	FEM	MAL	F(1/276)	p
F1	The theory of giftedness	+.18	+.48	7.279	.007
F2	Conformity	+.11	+.01	—	—
F3	Relativism	+.02	−.18	3.342	.069
F4	The cybernetic model	+.24	+.07	2.755	.098
F5	Adaptation	+.05	+.06	—	—
F6	Family heritage	−.08	+.05	1.833	.177
F7	The differentiating school	−.09	−.05	—	—
F8	Personality	−.07	−.02	—	—
F10	Teachers and failure	−.06	+.14	3.157	.077
Q2	The development of intelligence	FEM	MAL	F(1/276)	p
F1	Learning social rules	+.23	+.03	3.052	.082
F2	Socio-cognitive conflict	−.10	−.02	—	—
F3	Relational equilibrium	+.07	+.09	—	—
F4	The effect of mass media	+.12	+.05	—	—
F5	Revelatory error	+.02	+.12	—	—
F6	Heteronomy	+.06	−.12	3.018	.083
F7	Negation of the idea of development	+.20	+.15	—	—
F8	Competence of teachers	+.09	+.05	—	—
F9	Autonomy	−.01	+.17	3.895	.049
F10	Strict assessment	+.17	+.04	1.712	.192
Q3	Teaching methods	FEM	MAL	F(1/276)	p
F1	Pressures on the child	+.28	+.23	—	—
F2	Reformulating problems	+.10	−.11	3.487	.063
F3	Improving the 'psychological atmosphere'	+.12	−.01	—	—
F4	Motivational diagnosis	+.27	+.06	4.335	.038
F5	Severity	.00	+.07	—	—
F6	Wait-and-see and *laissez-faire*	+.13	+.11	—	—
F7	Medical and psychological expertise	+.07	+.14	—	—
F8	Tutoring	−.20	+.02	4.932	.027
F9	Repetition	+.02	+.14	—	—
F10	Modifying the curriculum	+.04	−.10	1.691	.195
Q4	Models of the child	FEM	MAL	F(1/266)	p
F1	The gifted child	−.10	−.17	—	—
F2	The sociable child	+.05	−.10	1.822	.178
F3	The well-behaved child	+.09	−.07	2.073	.151
F4	The child with no problems	+.08	+.06	—	—
F5	The communicative child	−.01	−.03	—	—
F6	'Agnan'	−.04	+.10	1.903	.169
F7	The 'inheritors'	−.02	+.07	—	—

Table 6.3 (*cont.*)

Q5	School subjects	FEM	MAL	F(1/276)	p
F1	Subjects with a high educational valency	+.25	+.03	5.008	.026
F2	Subjects with a weak educational valency	−.07	−.09	—	—
F3	Language activities	+.26	+.13	—	—
Q6	Scientific disciplines	FEM	MAL	F(1/276)	p
F1	Social sciences	−.01	−.15	1.762	.186
F2	Clinical disciplines	+.04	−.32	11.903	.001
F3	Teaching and teaching methods	+.12	+.13	—	—
F4	Humanism	+.08	+.24	2.505	.115
F5	Language and biology	+.24	+.16	—	—
Q7	Sources of information	FEM	MAL	F(1/276)	p
F1	Specialists	+.26	+.13	—	—
F2	Parental experience	+.62	+.51	—	—
F3	The mass media	+.07	−.19	5.798	.017
F4	Education	+.01	−.12	1.657	.199
F5	Informal social communication	+.07	−.09	2.595	.108

being acknowledged: see Lamb, 1975, 1981), but this discussion need not concern us here. It is enough for use to assume that there is a difference between the parental experience of mothers and fathers, and to attempt to identify the way this modifies parents' social representations. In order to look at this problem, we examined the responses of the 183 mothers (FEM) and 95 fathers (MAL) who composed our parent sample (note that one of the 279 parents was omitted, as there was no indication of his or her sex).

As our approach puts particular emphasis on the part played by information, we shall begin by looking at the importance of the different sources of information, stressing at the outset the marked importance given to parental experience by both sexes (see table 6.3). But there is a significant difference in relation to the information drawn from the various mass media, where it seems that mothers are better informed than fathers (Q7F3, FEM = +.07, MAL = −.19, F = 5.798 p = .017). It also appears that mothers derive more information from informal social communication, presumably with other parents (Q7F5, FEM = +.07, MAL = −.09, F = 2.595 p =.108).

A further aspect of the fathers' information shortage is that they are less convinced of the explanatory value of the scientific models which, as we have seen, offer rivals to social representations, especially in the area of giftedness. Fathers thus attribute less importance to the clinical and medical disciplines (Q6F2, FEM = +.04, MAL = −.32, F = 11.903 p = .001), and to the social sciences, though in the latter case the statistical threshold is definitely too weak (Q6F1, FEM = −.01, MAL = −.15, F = 1.762 p = .186). The only sign of an opposite tendency is in the greater reference to humanist subjects (Q6F4, FEM = +.08, MAL = +.24, F = 2.505 p = .115).

Given this (relative) shortage of information, the fathers draw on naturalising explanations in terms of giftedness, more than mothers (the difference between fathers and mothers needs to be emphasised here, because as parents they both tend to draw on it). So the theory of natural inequality is more widely accepted by fathers (Q1F1, FEM = +.18, MAL = +.48, F = 7.279 p = .007), who are also more opposed to the notion of the definitional relativism of intelligence (Q1F3, FEM = +.02, MAL = −.18, F = 3.342 p = .069). They also tend towards greater acceptance of the ideal of family heritage (but unfortunately the effect is not significant: Q1F6, FEM = −.08, MAL = +.05, F = 1.833 p = .177), and the direct, personal responsibility of the teacher (Q1F10, FEM = −.06, MAL = +.14, F = 3.157 p = .077), an idea which, as we have seen, often co-exists with the naturalising explanation of the differences in intelligence between one individual and another.

Finally, and presumably this time as a function of being male, the fathers valorise autonomy (Q2F9, FEM = −.01, MAL = +.17, F = 3.895 p = .049), which confirms our earlier findings.

But let us go back to the fathers' clear naturalisation of the explanation of the origin of intellectual processes, expressed in an attitude of non-intervention in the classroom, which also serves to confirm it. Fathers are also less willing than mothers to consider reformulating problems (Q3F2, FEM = +.10, MAL = −.11, F = 3.487 p = .063) or a motivational diagnosis (Q3F4, FEM = +.27, MAL = +.06, F = 4.335 p = .038). The only intervention they are more positive about is 'tutoring' (Q3F8, FEM = −.20, MAL = +.02, F = 4.932 p = .027). On the other hand, this provides confirmation for the lower level of interventionism on the part of fathers, who leave the business of development to the mutual interactions of peers, and on the other it fits in with the way fathers, as we have seen, valorise autonomy in children's development.

Among mothers, on the other hand, the naturalising explanation, although there by virtue of parental identity, is present to a lesser extent, or at any rate is less salient. Instead another organising element of the representation occupies a more central position: the child's socialisation into the rules of society, in which the mother would seem to be a kind of 'interface' between the school and the family.

In fact mothers do see development more in terms of learning social rules (Q2F1, FEM = +.23, MAL = +.03, F = 3.052 p = .082). These undoubtedly relate to schooling, as mothers are more likely than fathers to regard success in subjects with a high educational valency as a better criterion for assessing intelligence (Q5F1, FEM = +.25, MAL = +.03, F = 5.008 p = .026), and to agree with the logical and mathematical prototype in their definition of intelligence (Q1F4, FEM = +.24, MAL = +.07, F = 2.755 p = .098).

Mothers are more alert than fathers to the fact that a restrictive interpersonal relationship with a child carries the risk of limiting the child's cognitive development (Q2F6, FEM = +.06, MAL = −.12, F = 3.018 p = .083), and so they are more in favour of the teaching methods (motivational diagnosis, reformulation of problems) which mobilise the child's cognitive activity, as we saw earlier.

To sum up, then, parental position in the family is not without its effect on parental identity. The sex of the parent particularly can affect or modify the different components of parental identity (for a review of the literature, which shows that the differentiating effects of gender are often less than might have been expected, see Goodnow *et al.*, 1985).

In the case of the fathers, a sort of information shortage, perhaps linked with the fact that they are less directly concerned with the child (at least in quantitative and probabilistic terms: see particularly Belsky, Gilstrap and Rovine, 1984), accentuates two aspects. The first is a naturalising explanation, organised around the problem of the natural inequality of intelligence. And the second is that fathers, probably for the reasons we have just seen (less direct interaction with the child), seem to develop a less interventionist attitude to teaching and a preference for a developmental autonomy based partly on mutual teaching.

For mothers, the predominant function is concerned with socialisation, as the child has to adapt to the demands of his schooling, which implies a greater interest in teaching practices that involve motivating the child's cognitive activity. And as they have both more information (formal and informal) and the firm base provided by the model of social intelligence as learning social rules – and perhaps also simply because they are women – they are more aware of a relativist perspective in the definition of intelligence, and thus do not develop the naturalising explanation, based on natural inequality, to such a great extent.

Working women and full-time mothers

Although, as we have just seen, parental experience in the general sense plays a major role in the organisation of social representations of intelligence, it seems that sexual differentiations do orient, or modify, the representation associated with parental identity, while not actually

Table 6.4 *Mean factorial scores of mothers with no other declared occupation (MOT; n = 31) and mothers with another occupation (NMOT; n = 70), and analyses of variance (F and p values are only given where p < .20). The sign '+' indicates agreement with the ideas summarised by the label attached to the factors.*

Q1	Intelligence	NMOT	MOT	F(1/99)	p
F1	The theory of giftedness	+.22	+.77	8.535	.004
F2	Conformity	+.10	+.13	—	—
F3	Relativism	−.08	+.06	—	—
F4	The cybernetic model	+.37	−.06	4.695	.033
F5	Adaptation	−.08	+.18	2.703	.103
F6	Family heritage	−.16	−.04	—	—
F7	The differentiating school	−.05	.00	—	—
F8	Personality	−.14	−.01	—	—
F10	Teachers and failure	+.34	+.01	3.333	.071
Q2	Development of intelligence	NMOT	MOT	F(1/99)	p
F1	Learning social rules	+.35	+.35	—	—
F2	Socio-cognitive conflict	−.12	−.10	—	—
F3	Relational equilibrium	−.04	+.35	5.138	.026
F4	The effect of mass media	+.19	+.35	—	—
F5	Revelatory error	−.02	+.26	2.722	.102
F6	Heteronomy	+.08	−.34	5.204	.025
F7	Negation of the idea of development	+.36	−.15	8.451	.005
F8	Competence of teachers	+.11	+.50	4.227	.042
F9	Autonomy	.00	−.09	—	—
F10	Strict assessment	+.21	+.41	—	—
Q3	Teaching methods	NMOT	MOT	F(1/99)	p
F1	Pressures on the child	+.57	+.68	—	—
F2	Reformulating problems	+.09	+.18	—	—
F3	Improving the 'psychological atmosphere'	+.11	+.31	—	—
F4	Motivational diagnosis	+.17	+.26	—	—
F5	Severity	+.04	−.20	1.733	.191
F6	Wait-and-see and *laissez-faire*	+.17	+.12	—	—
F7	Medical and psychological expertise	+.05	+.11	—	—
F8	Tutoring	−.16	−.17	—	—
F9	Repetition	+.29	+.44	—	—
F10	Modifying the curriculum	−.19	+.08	2.011	.159
Q4	Models of the child	NMOT	MOT	F(1/89)	p
F1	The gifted child	−.14	+.25	2.592	.111
F2	The sociable child	+.12	+.22	—	—
F3	The well-behaved child	−.02	−.26	1.762	.188
F4	The child with no problems	+.14	−.02	—	—
F5	The communicative child	+.05	+.03	—	—
F6	'Agnan'	+.05	+.22	—	—
F7	The 'inheritors'	+.11	−.02	—	—

Table 6.4 (*cont.*)

Q5	School subjects	NMOT	MOT	F(1/99)	p
F1	Subjects with a high educational valency	+.15	+.36	—	—
F2	Subjects with a weak educational valency	−.27	−.25	—	—
F3	Language activities	+.24	+.82	12.025	.001
Q5	Scientific disciplines	NMOT	MOT	F(1/99)	p
F1	Social sciences	−.10	+.29	4.285	.041
F2	Clinical disciplines	−.09	−.34	1.745	.190
F3	Teaching and teaching methods	+.03	+.25	2.169	.144
F4	Humanism	+.25	.00	1.873	.174
F5	Language and biology	+.10	+.40	5.251	.024
Q7	Sources of information	NMOT	MOT	F(1/99)	p
F1	Specialists	+.13	+.01	—	—
F2	Parental experience	+.72	+.52	—	—
F3	The mass media	−.14	−.28	—	—
F4	Education	−.26	−.44	—	—
F5	Informal social communication	+.01	+.11	—	—

challenging the way it works; fathers seem to accentuate the maturationist aspect, mothers the 'functional', the socialisation, aspect.

The next question is whether there are any differences between mothers who have no occupation apart from motherhood, and those who also have a job outside the family, given that the increase in women's employment is one of the best-known changes in the contemporary family (see Lamb, Chase-Lansdale and Owen, 1979). To answer it, we compared the 31 full-time mothers with the 70 mothers who also had other jobs; we excluded teachers, as the model they developed in the course of their training and their work as educators might perhaps be too emphatic and would not enable us to grasp the true effects of working on the mothers, although of course effects associated with the kind of job they did were not excluded. So let us look at the results (table 6.4).

First of all, with one exception, the significance of which will become clear later, the full-time mothers (MOT: e.g. with no other declared occupation) tend to align themselves more on the side of the maturationist model of intelligence. They are more willing than working mothers (NMOT) to accept the theory of natural inequality (Q1F1, NMOT = +.22, MOT = +.77, F = 8.535 p = .004; the degree of freedom here is 1/99), and have a greater tendency to limit the function of error simply to indicating the cognitive level of the child (Q2F5, NMOT = −.02, MOT = +.26, F = 2.722 p = .102). They also give more importance to linguistic activity as a criterion of intelligence (Q5F3, NMOT = +.24, MOT = +.82, F = 12.025 p = .001), and as a corollary of that expect a great deal from the maturationist approach to language for an understanding of intelligence (Q6F5, NMOT = +.10, MOT = +.40, $F = 5.251$ $p = .024$).

Thus it seems that women who are 'just' full-time mothers, who in theory are defined solely (or at least very largely) by their parental identity, accentuate the maturationist aspect, which is one of the organisers of the parental representation of intelligence. This certainly provides another validation of the whole notion of parental identity.

One might therefore have expected to find an accentuation of the reference to parental experience, but this is not the case; indeed, it could even (see Q7F2) be the reverse, except that this result is not significant. Could the (somewhat simplified) reason for this be that working mothers have to defend themselves against the prejudices of a society which, despite all the progress in this area, still (today: social representations are historically dated!) regards women as mothers, and denigrates mothers who work outside the home (even if only implicitly) as being 'bad mothers'?

It is this self-justification which seems to provide an explanation for the responses of working mothers on the 'negation of the idea of development' factor (Q2F7, NMOT = +.36, MOT = −.15, $F = 8.451$ $p = .005$). Hitherto this clearly maturationist idea has been coupled with an acceptance of the theory of natural inequality. In this comparison, however, that is no longer the case. It is working mothers who are most convinced that the child spontaneously develops his innate capacity for intelligence (which may of course be a *post facto* justification, but may also fulfil an anticipatory function, making it easier to decide to take up, or return to, a job). We shall assume that by doing this they are defending themselves from the feeling, or the accusation, that they are not sharing sufficiently in the child's development (see Lamb, Chase-Lansdale and Owen, 1979). This is a specific attitude of self-defence of a personal identity that can be seen as deviating from a dominant model of what a mother should be. There is also the complementary explanation that ideas about educating children often have less to do with educational principles than with concrete situations, particularly demands and restrictions on time (Whiting, 1974).

This identity-defending attitude may be expressed in the attribution of failure, or difficulty at school, to factors outside the child, as we shall see when we look at teachers, and as we can sometimes glimpse with parents, who often put the responsibility for this on to each other, to a greater or lesser extent. The same attitude seems to be present among working mothers, tending thus to confirm our interpretation, since they are more likely to think that failure could be avoided if the teacher had a better attitude (Q1F10, NMOT = +.34, MOT = +.01, $F = 3.333$ $p = .071$), while at the same time manifesting a lack of confidence about teachers' abilities (Q2F8, NMOT = +.11, MOT = +.50, F = 4.227 p = .042).

This mechanism by which responsibility is projected on to the individual teacher is all the more noteworthy, as the same mothers put a higher value than the full-time mothers on the – educationally dominant – cybernetic model of intelligence (Q1F4, NMOT = +.37, MOT = –.06, F = 4.695 p = .033), and see little to be gained in modifying the curriculum (even though the result is not significant: Q3F10, NMOT = –.19, MOT = +.08, F = 2.011 p = .159). It is as if the working mothers place more reliance on the school as institution, give it the responsibility of developing the child's intelligence, and make the teachers more personally answerable for any educational difficulties that may arise.

Although we have sometimes extrapolated from some of these results, and although the results themselves clearly reflect the current situation of working women, it does seem to be the case that the attitudes developed, while not fundamentally altering the parental model of intelligence, operate to preserve an identity which is difficult because it happens to be marginal or ambivalent.

We return now to the women who are 'just' full-time mothers, and who as we have seen tend to accentuate the maturationist aspect of the parental representation. The adaptive function of intelligence is also slightly more marked for them (Q1F5, NMOT = –.08, MOT = +.18, F = 2.703 p =.103). But the accent there seems to be on a particularly relational kind of adaptation. They put greater emphasis on the importance of relational equilibrium with the adult and between peers (with the parents – the mother herself – and, where appropriate, between brothers and sisters?) for good development of intelligence (Q2F3, NMOT = –.04, MOT = +.35, F = 5.138 p = .026). They are also more inclined to reject the idea that relational regulations (like the restrictions and compliance which stem from them) may be harmful to this good development (Q2F6, NMOT = +.08, MOT = –.34, F = 5.204 p = .025). In short, they are valorising their interventionism with their own children.

This argument can also be seen from the point of view of mothers working outside the home: having less time for interaction with their children (from a quantitative viewpoint, which is in no way a prejudgement of their quality), they regard the relational equilibrium of these interactions as less important, and even take the view that certain forms of adult intervention may be detrimental to the child's cognitive development.

The method of analysis we have chosen does not make it possible to say who is responsible for these shifts in the representation of intelligence; and, in reality, it is not very important. On the other hand, it is very clear that these modifications to the parental representation seem to be ways of adjusting to the realities of daily life. They are justifications of specific situations, which both make it coherent and legitimate, and give it a positive socio-psychological identity.

To sum up, then. We may, admittedly, have gone a bit far occasionally, as one section of the effects discussed is not statistically very conclusive. But the psychological significance of the results is nonetheless quite coherent, and casts light particularly on the identity function of some of the attitudes which influence the parental model of intelligence, and which are found in both groups of mothers. What they basically demonstrate is that there are socio-psychological dynamics specific to a mother's identity, and that these vary depending on her occupational situation.

We have seen that mothers who are solely concerned with their children accentuate a maturationist view of intelligence which cannot be explained at the level of sources of information. However, this confirms one of our earlier demonstrations, namely that the intensification of parental experience (defined this time by non-reference to an identity outside the family, which here would mean working) accentuates this interpretation of intelligence.

On the other hand they also accentuate aspects of their experience centred on relations with children: they valorise certain constructive aspects of their intervention in children's lives, and particularly valorise the cognitive image of the child (Q4F1, NMOT $= -.14$, MOT $= +.25$, $F = 2.592$ $p = .111$). Both these modifications of the parental representation benefit the maternal identity.

Working mothers are, to some extent, more defensive, perhaps as a defence against some probably socially inspired 'bad conscience' about not being sufficiently involved with their children. They therefore see the child's development as something which happens spontaneously, and partially reject the effectiveness or utility of adult intervention, sometimes even regarding it as a potential obstacle to the development of intelligence. Alongside this, by a sort of projective mechanism, these mothers tend to make teachers personally responsible for any difficulties their children may encounter.

These results do not constitute a challenge to the parental model of intelligence. They merely reflect partial adjustments to it in the light of particular family or occupational situations. However one looks at them, from the point of view of full-time mothers as much as from that of mothers who also have other jobs, these modifications are designed to create an image of the world and of themselves which is both coherent and satisfying from the point of view of their socio-psychological identity.

7 Effects of occupation

The effect of social and occupational categories

Does membership of a social and occupational category have an organising effect on social representations of intelligence? To investigate this problem, we used only non-teachers, whom we differentiated largely on the basis of information from the Service de la Recherche Sociologique de Genève, with some modifications. It was not difficult to classify the subjects into class A (workers and junior employees), class B (middle class) and class C (managerial and professional class). The first analysis we carried out involved 116 A subjects, 67 B and 37 C, but it turned out to be misleading, as well as skewed by the small number of subjects from Bologna in classes B and C. We therefore only used the Swiss subjects, 58 A, 58 B and 28 C, who provided us with an adequate basis for comparison (bearing in mind that teachers are not included in this sample, for obvious reasons). It is important to note at this point that we do not accept the current notion of a complete homogenisation of class in Switzerland. As proof of this we can take the case of Geneva itself: Perrenoud (1982) shows that children of twelve to thirteen years are unevenly distributed between the classical and scientific streams and the general and practical ones, according to their social origin. The (1980) statistics thus reveal that only 53.2% of children from class A are in the more prestigious classical and scientific streams, as against 72.9% from class B, and 89.9% from class C. Our sample is therefore part of a social system in which, as in those elsewhere (even if to a lesser degree), academic level broadly coincides with social origin. Let us look now at the data given in detail in table 7.1 (for the univariate analyses for the comparisons between pairs of classes).

Only three factors show a progressive difference (to at least $p = < .10$) between the three classes. The most marked result is the importance attributed to language activity (Q5F3), which is greatest where the occupational level is lowest.

The second result concerns the recognition of the differentiating and, in fact, discriminatory effect of the school (Q1F7), where the higher the occupational level, the more the subjects deny discrimination. As we know,

Table 7.1 *Mean factorial scores for Swiss subjects in 'lower' (A; n = 58), 'middle' (B; n = 58) and 'higher' (C; n = 28) social and occupational categories, and analyses of variance (F and p values are only given where p < .20; comparisons are made between groups A and B, A and C, and B and C, respectively). The sign '+' indicates agreement with the ideas summarised by the label attached to the factors.*

					A–B		A–C		B–C	
Q1	Intelligence	A	B	C	F(1/114)	p	F(1/84)	p	F(1/84)	p
F1	Theory of giftedness	+.92	+.68	+.68	2.900	.091	1.989	.162	—	—
F2	Conformity	−.01	−.02	+.07	—	—	—	—	—	—
F3	Relativism	+.03	−.03	−.15	—	—	—	—	—	—
F4	The cybernetic model	−.03	−.22	−.06	1.785	.184	—	—	—	—
F5	Adaptation	+.24	+.36	+.44	—	—	—	—	—	—
F6	Family heritage	+.27	+.18	+.32	—	—	—	—	—	—
F7	The differentiation school	+.16	.00	−.27	—	—	6.090	.016	2.697	.104
F8	Personality	−.16	+.09	−.12	2.217	.139	—	—	—	—
F10	Teachers and failure	+.06	+.09	+.30	—	—	2.114	.150	—	—
Q2	Development of intelligence									
F1	Learning social rules	+.18	−.04	−.14	2.076	.152	2.732	.102	—	—
F2	Socio-cognitive conflict	−.24	−.27	−.17	—	—	—	—	—	—
F3	Relational equilibrium	+.28	+.11	+.08	—	—	—	—	—	—
F4	The effect of mass media	+.32	+.21	+.49	—	—	—	—	1.851	.177
F5	Revelatory error	+.16	−.07	−.01	2.295	.133	—	—	—	—
F6	Heteronomy	−.30	−.40	−.65	—	—	4.515	.037	2.224	.140
F7	Negation of the idea of development	+.13	+.06	−.03	—	—	—	—	—	—
F8	Competence of teachers	+.32	−.02	+.14	6.581	.012	—	—	—	—
F9	Autonomy	+.22	+.32	+.59	—	—	5.418	.022	2.919	.091
F10	Strict assessment	+.20	−.11	+.07	5.108	.026	—	—	—	—
Q3	Teaching methods									
F1	Pressures on the child	+.71	+.38	+.51	5.796	.018	—	—	—	—
F2	Reformulating problems	−.03	−.03	+.27	—	—	2.391	.126	2.225	.140

F3	Improving the 'psychological atmosphere'	+.12	−.14	−.03	2.896	.092	—	—	—	—
F4	Motivational diagnosis	+.01	−.08	+.12	—	—	—	—	—	—
F5	Severity	−.14	−.01	+.01	—	—	—	—	—	—
F6	Wait-and see-and *laissez-faire*	+.11	+.09	+.14	—	—	—	—	—	—
F7	Medical and psychological expertise	+.15	+.03	+.12	—	—	—	—	—	—
F8	Tutoring	+.12	+.10	+.21	—	—	—	—	—	—
F9	Repetition	+.71	+.44	+.51	3.471	.065	—	—	—	—
F10	Modifying the curriculum	.00	+.04	−.19	—	—	—	—	1.732	.192
Q4	Models of the child									
F1	The gifted child	−.06	−.17	−.35	—	—	—	—	—	—
F2	The sociable child	+.08	−.22	−.16	3.974	.049	2.661	.107	—	—
F3	The well-behaved child	−.29	+.08	−.26	5.840	.017	—	—	3.501	.065
F4	The child with no problems	+.10	−.01	−.03	—	—	—	—	—	—
F5	The communicative child	+.16	+.30	−.16	—	—	2.737	.102	9.125	.003
F6	'Agnan'	+.09	+.20	+.07	—	—	—	—	—	—
F7	The 'inheritors'	+.10	+.14	+.03	—	—	—	—	—	—
Q5	School subjects									
F1	Subjects with a high educational valency	+.14	−.14	+.07	3.168	.078	—	—	—	—
F2	Subjects with a weak educational valency	−.33	−.43	−.08	—	—	—	—	2.522	.116
F3	Language activities	+.70	+.37	+.18	6.597	.012	9.611	.003	—	—
Q6	Scientific disciplines									
F1	Social sciences	+.14	+.05	+.13	—	—	—	—	—	—
F2	Clinical disciplines	−.44	−.52	−.19	—	—	2.024	.159	—	—
F3	Teaching and teaching methods	+.34	+.25	+.18	—	—	—	—	—	—
F4	Humanism	+.12	+.25	+.20	—	—	—	—	—	—
F5	Language and biology	+.34	+.15	+.27	2.630	.108	—	—	—	—
Q7	Sources of information									
F1	Specialists	−.05	+.29	+.05	4.622	.034	—	—	—	—
F2	Parental experience	+.36	+.33	+.13	—	—	—	—	—	—
F3	The mass media	−.55	−.27	−.34	3.230	.075	—	—	—	—
F4	Education	−.41	+.21	+.09	25.901	.000	10.691	.002	—	—
F5	Informal social communication	−.08	+.01	−.11	—	—	—	—	—	—

superior or dominant groups do often tend to deny their social advantages (see Hewstone, Jaspers and Lalljee, 1982).

Last, the higher the occupational level, the more importance is granted to autonomy in development (Q2F9). This is especially true for the C environment, which we know (see Deschamps, Lorenzi-Cioldi and Meyer, 1982) develops an ideology which is largely based on autonomy-related values. Moreover, Kohn (1963) had already pointed out that attitudes towards autonomy (particularly on the part of the father) account for much of the connection between social class and parental values.

Interesting though these differences are, though, they are clearly not sufficient to organise the really fundamental and specific differences of social representations of intelligence. So let us turn to the characteristics which clearly differentiate one of the three classes from the other two.

There is not very much to be said about the middle class (B), except that they least accept the usefulness of the teacher's competence (Q2F8), and tend to be somewhat less severe (Q2F10). And, for reasons we are not aware of, they make more reference to consulting experts (Q7F1).

If we slightly exaggerate the statistics, the A subjects (the 'disadvantaged' classes) provide a rather more organised picture. They tend to uphold the theory of natural inequality more (Q1F1) and to see development in terms of learning social rules (Q2F1), which results in a pedagogy based on pressure to adapt to the correct model answer (Q3F1). A further important result is that A subjects are the ones who make least use of information derived from their professional training (Q7F4) or the mass media (Q7F3). These results, however, are obviously too weak at the statistical level.

In conclusion, there only seems to be even a relative coherence in the case of the lower social class (measured by occupation). A representation of intelligence seems, in fact, to be defined on the basis of an absence or a lack of information relative to occupation. This lack leads to the attribution of major importance to linguistic and communicational activity (does not everyone desire what they most lack?). The theory of natural inequality tends (only tends, because the result is a weak one) to provide an explanation, and fits in with the idea that one of the functions of the school is to reinforce the initial differentiations between individuals. These subjects see development as based on the learning of social rules, which also fits in with their approval of pedagogic norms of pressure to conform to correct answers.

As for the class B and C subjects, although there are some significant results, they cannot be regarded as constituting a representation of intelligence differentially organised around a principle, a 'hard nucleus'.

What conclusions are we to draw from this? Social class has no specific organisational effect on the representations of intelligence and its development (at least in Switzerland; but note, nonetheless, that when we analysed the Swiss and Italian subjects together there was no improvement in the picture, which resulted in a similar degree of incoherence. The same is true if the subjects' highest educational level is taken as the criterion.) The variable of socio-economic status has a similar (relative) lack of effect, as has been noted by other writers (Hess *et al.*, 1980; Goodnow *et al.*, 1984). Social and occupational category does of course give rise to different opinions or expressions of attitude (such as the lesser degree of severity among B subjects, or the refusal by C subjects, who of course are best served by them, to see schools as instruments of social reproduction). These, however, are only isolated opinions, non-systematic effects.

Only class A, the least-advantaged class, provides some, admittedly weak, elements of coherence, which we regard as mediated by the relative lack of information for them to latch on to, especially at the level of education, but also in the mass media.

If social class is not the organising element – or one of the organising elements – of social representations of intelligence (at least at this stage of the research), we shall have to look elsewhere.

The teaching profession: teachers and future teachers

However it is defined, the subject of intelligence is necessarily relevant to those who have made, or want to make, teaching their profession. Thus it is important to two sub-samples in this study: the 216 teachers (the majority of them, although not all, working in the primary sector) and the 123 student teachers, either as students of education or at an 'école normale' training for a teaching career. Study of these groups should be particularly interesting, because for them the representation of intelligence and related problems has to play both a directly practical or functional part in the way they organise their current or future teaching activity and a dynamic role in professional identification. The dynamics, moreover, should become salient as teachers move from the period of training to the actual practice of their profession.

Seen from our socio-psychological perspective, this encounter with the reality of teaching ought to present two kinds of change in the representations. The first would be an accentuation of institutional constraints (see particularly Morrison and McIntyre, 1976), in some cases accompanied by loss of certain 'noble' or 'idealistic' educational principles which cannot be sustained in the face of the often difficult objective teaching conditions (such as the number of pupils, for example). The second kind of problem we regard as linked with the identity of being a teacher; it becomes all the more salient as the practice of teaching, especially the failures, makes it an issue, and even calls it into question. We may therefore expect some modifications of a self-defensive sort.

We shall also be asking one other question in this connection: to what extent are education students – the teachers of the future – already teachers in their outlook? We shall see that this is not obvious.

A preliminary analysis of the differences between the 123 student teachers and the 216 teachers in fact revealed a huge difference between the two samples. Quite obviously, the student teachers are not already teachers in their outlook, as far as their representations are concerned. The entry into the profession introduces a kind of socialisation which consists of socio-cognitive adaptations to the new conditions of the realities of teaching.

However, we shall not spend any time on this comparison. When we pursued the analysis further, we saw that there was a real gulf which separated the teachers into two sub-categories: teachers with and without children. The fact of being a parent, as we shall see, introduces its own particular dynamics into the representation, which are much more powerful than we had anticipated. We shall see this difference later.

For a stricter assessment of the effect of 'professionalisation', we therefore compared the 115 teachers without children (TEAC) with the 122 students (also without children: STUD). The results (see table 7.2; the means on each item for the two sub-samples are given in appendices 1–7) seem to be organised around three axes.

Before we look at those, however, it should be noted that in a way the teachers base their ideas more on their education, logically enough, as they have completed it (Q7F4, STUD = .00, TEAC = +.42, $F = 23.448$ $p = .000$: the degree of freedom is 1/235), with the implication of slightly more reading (Q7F3, STUD = +.12, TEAC = +.26, $F = 2.109$ $p = .148$), as well as on their more direct experience of contact with children (Q7F2, STUD = −.49, TEAC = −.32, $F = 3.854$ $p = .051$). We shall see the consequences of this obvious professionalisation for the representations of intelligence.

The first axis relates to the explanation of intelligence in terms of giftedness. It turns out that although teachers are by and large clearly opposed to the theory of natural inequality, they are less convinced opponents than students or future teachers (Q1F1, STUD = −.48, TEAC = −.31, $F = 2.869$ $p = .092$), and tend more to reject the whole idea of development (Q2F7, STUD = −.23, TEAC = −.08, $F = 2.691$ $p = .102$). These tendencies are confirmed by the teachers' regarding intelligence as more revelatory of inherited traits (Q1F6, STUD = −.12, TEAC = +.06, $F = 3.317$ $p = -.070$). Related to these is the fact that teachers also tend to attribute informative importance to the biological, maturationist approach

Table 7.2 *Mean factorial scores of teachers (TEAC; n = 115) and student teachers (STUD; n = 122), all without children, and analyses of variance (F and p values are only given where p < .20). The sign '+' indicates agreement with the ideas summarised by the label attached to the factors.*

Q1	Intelligence	STUD	TEAC	F(1/235)	p
F1	The theory of giftedness	−.48	−.31	2.869	.092
F2	Conformity	−.14	−.16	—	—
F3	Relativism	−.04	+.05	—	—
F4	The cybernetic model	−.17	+.09	7.341	.007
F5	Adaptation	−.16	−.01	2.657	.104
F6	Family heritage	−.12	+.06	3.317	.070
F7	The differentiating school	+.24	+.12	—	—
F8	Personality	−.01	−.12	—	—
F10	Teachers and failure	+.01	−.03	—	—
Q2	Development of intelligence	STUD	TEAC	F(1/235)	p
F1	Learning social rules	−.14	−.10	—	—
F2	Socio-cognitive conflict	+.11	−.09	3.916	.049
F3	Relational equilibrium	−.12	−.12	—	—
F4	The effect of mass media	−.10	−.06	—	—
F5	Revelatory error	−.07	−.14	—	—
F6	Heteronomy	−.05	+.16	4.746	.030
F7	Negation of the idea of development	−.23	−.08	2.691	.102
F8	Competence of teachers	−.09	−.20	—	—
F9	Autonomy	−.22	−.14	—	—
F10	Strict assessment	−.18	−.16	—	—
Q3	Teaching methods	STUD	TEAC	F(1/235)	p
F1	Pressures on the child	−.28	−.39	—	—
F2	Reformulating problems	+.16	−.04	3.142	.078
F3	Improving the 'psychological atmosphere'	−.07	−.02	—	—
F4	Motivational diagnosis	−.13	+.08	3.991	.047
F5	Severity	−.09	+.01	—	—
F6	Wait-and-see and *laissez-faire*	−.23	−.03	4.068	.045
F7	Medical and psychological expertise	+.01	+.01	—	—
F8	Tutoring	+.03	+.07	—	—
F9	Repetition	−.25	−.24	—	—
F10	Modifying the curriculum	+.14	+.19	—	—
Q4	Models of the child	STUD	TEAC	F(1/225)	p
F1	The gifted child	+.15	−.03	4.068	.045
F2	The sociable child	+.07	.00	—	—
F3	The well-behaved child	−.08	+.07	2.376	.125
F4	The child with no problems	−.13	+.16	7.855	.006
F5	The communicative child	−.08	+.08	2.949	.087
F6	'Agnan'	−.08	+.04	—	—
F7	The 'inheritors'	+.01	−.03	—	—

Table 7.2 (*cont.*)

Q5	School subjects	STUD	TEAC	F(1/235)	p
F1	Subjects with a high educational valency	−.09	+.09	2.550	.112
F2	Subjects with a weak educational valency	+.32	+.08	5.502	.020
F3	Language activities	−.16	−.20	—	—
Q6	Scientific disciplines	STUD	TEAC	F(1/235)	p
F1	Social sciences	+.17	+.15	—	—
F2	Clinical disciplines	+.19	+.14	—	—
F3	Teaching and teaching methods	−.01	−.03	—	—
F4	Humanism	−.18	−.29	—	—
F5	Language and biology	−.12	+.05	3.011	.084
Q7	Sources of information	STUD	TEAC	F(1/235)	p
F1	Specialists	−.15	−.10	—	—
F2	Parental experience	−.49	−.32	3.854	.051
F3	The mass media	+.12	+.26	2.109	.148
F4	Education	.00	+.42	23.448	.000
F5	Informal social communication	−.08	+.04	—	—

to language development (Q6F5, STUD = −.12, TEAC = +.05, F = 3.011 p = .084).

This tendency to naturalise intelligence can be interpreted as a way of shifting intelligence and the random factors associated with it on to the outside world (Nature, the immeasurable), which may have a self-defensive function, a function, that is, of defending the teachers' socio-psychological identity, especially in relation to educational failure.

What is thus a socio-cognitive tendency at the level of explanations of intelligence is expressed very directly at the level of attitudes towards teaching, which is marked by a propensity (which might be regarded as paradoxical, given the profession in question) for a minimum of intervention, as Perret's (1981) study has already pointed out. This is how we understand the fact that teachers are more likely than student teachers to advocate a policy of wait-and-see and a degree of *laissez-faire* (Q3F6, STUD = −.23, TEAC = −.03, F = 4.068 p = .045), calling into question particularly the usefulness of reformulating problems (Q3F2, STUD = +.16, TEAC = −.04, F = 3.142 p = .078). Further concomitants of this wait-and-see policy are the ideas that socio-cognitive conflict – including that initiated by the adult – is not a source of development (Q2F2, STUD = +.11, TEAC = −.09, F = 3.916 p = .049), and that relational regulations entailing an 'authoritarian' or forceful intervention by an adult can be an obstacle to cognitive development (Q2F6, STUD = −.05, TEAC = +.16, F = 4.746 p = .030).

Finally, recourse to testing children's knowledge (Q3F4, STUD = −.13, TEAC = +.08, F = 3.991 p = .047) may well also be related to the diagnostic search for the child's gifts (which may or may not be present), rather than a simple search for motivation.

Thus far things seem quite clear: teachers develop a more innatist explanation (or, if you like, less anti-innatist than the student teachers, to be faithful to the explicit rejection of this theory by the teachers: see the itemised results in the appendix), which is a corollary of a wait-and-see policy which might be thought paradoxical in the light of the children's capacity for 'spontaneous' development.

Then there is a second axis which organises the differences between teachers and future teachers in terms of the educational norms that define intelligence. What we are seeing here is in fact a kind of normalisation, because, with professionalisation, the 'real' criteria of the educational institution come to prominence. Thus, for example, expressive activities are more highly regarded by the student teachers (Q5F2, STUD = +.32, TEAC = +.08, F = 5.502 p = .020), which contrasts with the teachers' tendency to inflate the normative value of subjects with a high educational valency (Q5F1, STUD = −.09, TEAC = +.09, F = 2.550 p = .112). Attitudes to the cybernetic prototype of intelligence confirm this, as it is more widely accepted by practising teachers (Q1F4, STUD = −.17, TEAC = +.09, F = 7.341 p = .007). We may assume that it is against the background of these educational demands that intelligence has an adaptive function (Q1F5, STUD = −.16, TEAC = −.01, F = 2.657 p = .104). In short, the teachers demonstrate an institutionalisation of the whole definition of intelligence, so that it comes to be seen in terms of success in the most institutionally valorised school subjects.

Finally there is a third set of differences between teachers and student teachers, to examine which we need, for once, to look at the models of the child. What we find is a sort of de-idealisation of the image of the child. Future teachers see the child as a model child (Q4F1, STUD = +.15, TEAC = −.03, F = 4.068 p = .045). After encountering actual groups of children presenting obvious differences of aptitude, the model of the cognitively model child retreats somewhat, and shifts towards the mean. Practising teachers, on the other hand, usually see the child as calmer and more relaxed (Q4F4, STUD = −.13, TEAC = +.16, F = 7.855 p = .006) and communicative (Q4F5, STUD = −.08, TEAC = +.08, F = 2.949 p = .087). There is also a slight, though not significant, tendency to regard the child as fairly well-behaved (Q4F3, STUD = −.08, TEAC = +.07, F = 2.376 p = .125). So altogether the teachers seem to develop a more positive image of the child in terms of interpersonal relations and the atmosphere in the classroom, although they are prepared more bluntly to recognise the differences between individuals in their 'cognitive aptitudes', and to carry out a sort of regression towards the mean.

The image of the child changes with the professionalisation of the teacher, becoming one which, although relaxed about relations with the child, is more pessimistic about intelligence itself. It is this, we believe, which is responsible for the tendency to naturalisation which appears in teachers' explanations of intelligence. In fact, it seems that the surplus of information they derive from their training is not sufficient to make up for the 'discovery' or 'revelation' of differences in intelligence that they encounter in their teaching. This discovery and this explanation (it does not matter whether the explanation is rational and scientifically well founded, or not: all we are concerned with here is the representation) gives teachers their wait-and-see, slightly defeatist, certainly not interventionist conception of the attitude to teaching which best encourages the development of intelligence.

Once again, therefore, Moscovici's hypothesis seems to be confirmed: it is the experience of the unfamiliar, of something inexplicable despite the models that have been developed during education, especially during professional training, which seems to underlie the transformation of social representations, in this case of intelligence.

We shall now see how the experience of parenthood constitutes another 'shock' with a structuring effect on social representations.

The parental experience of teachers

The fact of having children therefore seems to be one of the organising elements of teachers' social representations of intelligence, in addition to the experience of transition from being a student to being a responsible teacher, which will already have restructured them.

So let us look at what effect the advent of children has on the 101 teachers (PAR), in comparison with the 115 who, at the time of the questionnaire, had no children. The data are given in table 7.3; the means for each item are given for both sub-samples in appendices 1–7.

At the outset it is worth noting that, in connection with sources of information, PAR do make more reference to their experience as parents (Q7F2, NPAR $= -.32$, PAR $= +.58$, $F = 79.946$ $p = .000$) and to consulting experts (Q7F1, NPAR $= -.10$, PAR $= +.41$, $F = 16.828$ $p = .000$).

Now let us look at the effects on the representations themselves, taking them in order of the questionnaires.

Table 7.3 *Mean factorial scores of teachers who are parents (PAR; n = 101) and teachers without children (NPAR; n = 115), and analyses of variance (F and p values are only given where p < .20). The sign '+' indicates agreement with the idea summarised by the label attached to the factors.*

Q1	Intelligence	NPAR	PAR	F(1/214)	p
F1	The theory of giftedness	−.31	−.02	7.474	.007
F2	Conformity	−.16	+.04	4.782	.030
F3	Relativism	+.05	+.05	—	—
F4	The cybernetic model	+.09	+.21	—	—
F5	Adaptation	−.01	+.08	—	—
F6	Family heritage	+.06	.00	—	—
F7	The differentiating school	+.12	−.08	3.109	.079
F8	Personality	−.12	−.01	—	—
F10	Teachers and failure	−.03	−.45	15.363	.000
Q2	**Development of intelligence**	**NPAR**	**PAR**	**F(1/214)**	**p**
F1	Learning social rules	−.10	+.04	1.955	.163
F2	Socio-cognitive conflict	−.09	−.12	—	—
F3	Relational equilibrium	−.12	+.07	3.610	.059
F4	The effect of mass media	−.06	−.03	—	—
F5	Revelatory error	−.14	−.04	—	—
F6	Heteronomy	+.16	+.13	—	—
F7	Negation of the idea of development	−.08	+.20	7.564	.006
F8	Competence of teachers	−.20	−.09	—	—
F9	Autonomy	−.14	+.09	5.506	.020
F10	Strict assessment	−.16	+.03	4.171	.042
Q3	**Teaching methods**	**NPAR**	**PAR**	**F(1/214)**	**p**
F1	Pressures on the child	−.39	−.20	2.936	.088
F2	Reformulating problems	−.04	−.01	—	—
F3	Improving the 'psychological atmosphere'	−.02	+.01	—	—
F4	Motivational diagnosis	+.08	+.32	4.533	.034
F5	Severity	+.01	+.01	—	—
F6	Wait-and-see and *laissez-faire*	−.03	+.13	1.982	.161
F7	Medical and psychological expertise	+.01	+.12	—	—
F8	Tutoring	+.07	−.24	8.441	.004
F9	Repetition	−.24	−.30	—	—
F10	Modifying the curriculum	+.19	+.17	—	—
Q4	**Models of the child**	**NPAR**	**PAR**	**F(1/204)**	**p**
F1	The gifted child	−.03	−.17	—	—
F2	The sociable child	.00	−.06	—	—
F3	The well-behaved child	+.07	+.26	2.294	.131
F4	The child with no problems	+.16	+.07	—	—
F5	The communicative child	+.08	−.08	2.688	.103
F6	'Agnan'	+.04	−.14	3.033	.083
F7	The 'inheritors'	−.03	−.07	—	—

Table 7.3 (*cont.*)

Q5	School subjects	NPAR	PAR	F(1/214)	p
F1	Subjects with a high educational valency	+.09	+.27	3.059	.082
F2	Subjects with a weak educational valency	+.08	+.15	—	—
F3	Language activities	−.20	+.08	4.934	.027
Q6	Scientific disciplines	NPAR	PAR	F(1/214)	p
F1	Social sciences	+.15	−.06	3.886	.050
F2	Clinical disciplines	+.14	+.20	—	—
F3	Teaching and teaching methods	−.03	+.09	—	—
F4	Humanism	−.29	−.05	4.400	.037
F5	Language and biology	+.05	+.29	6.411	.012
Q7	Sources of information	NPAR	PAR	F(1/214)	p
F1	Specialists	−.10	+.41	16.828	.000
F2	Parental experience	−.32	+.58	79.946	.000
F3	The mass media	+.26	+.35	—	—
F4	Education	+.42	+.42	—	—
F5	Informal social communication	+.04	+.04	—	—

On intelligence in general

Statistically, the strongest result is the parent-teachers' rejection of the idea that teachers have a direct responsibility for a child's failure (Q1F10, NPAR = −.03, PAR = −.45, F = 15.363 p = .000). This marked refusal to take the responsibility on themselves is a product of their combined identities as parents and teachers. There is no such rejection on the part of the non-teacher parents, who put the blame very clearly on the teacher, nor is the issue so clear for future teachers (non-teacher parents: +.27, future teachers: +.01, parent-teachers: −.45). Parent-teachers find themselves with a conflict of identity, the attitude which stems from being parents to some extent contradicting that derived from their identity as teachers. The solution these subjects opt for is de-individuation: responsibility is, so to speak, doubly rejected, both as a teacher and as a parent.

A second result is an increase in agreement with the theory of natural inequalities (Q1F1, NPAR = −.31, PAR = −.02, F = 7.474 p = .007), which is to some extent a corollary of a less widely held belief in the differentiating or 'selective' function of the school (Q1F7, NPAR = +.12, PAR = −.08, F = 3.109 p = .079). We can see a process at work here, taking away responsibility from the school environment, accompanied at the same time by a more marked naturalisation of intelligence. This tendency is not unrelated to the result we saw above, where the teacher's direct and therefore personal responsibility was rejected. What happens here is that an identification with the institution may entail the defence of that institution against the children, including their own.

Finally, parent-teachers are more inclined to define intelligence as conformity to social rules (Q1F2, NPAR = −.16, PAR = +.04, F = 4.782 p = .030).

The development of intelligence

The most prominent result concerns the negation of the idea of development in favour of a biological innatism, which is stressed more by the parent-teachers (Q2F7, NPAR −.08, PAR = +.20, F = 7.564 p = .006), which confirms what we have just seen in connection with the theory of natural inequalities.

Parent-teachers are also more often confronted with relational questions, and thus valorise socio-affective equilibrium in relations between individuals more highly (Q2F3, NPAR = −.12, PAR = +.07, F = 3.621 p = .059), and autonomy from the adult model (Q2F9, NPAR = −.14, PAR = +.09, F = 5.506 p = .020), while paradoxically looking for stricter assessment (Q2F10, NPAR = −.16, PAR = +.03, F = 4.171 p = .042). This seems to reveal a kind of ambivalence in the parent-teachers, who are both more severe (from the educational point of view?) and more 'empathetic' (from the familial point of view?).

Teaching methods

'Tutoring' is most strongly rejected here (Q3F8, NPAR = −.07, PAR = −.24, F = 8.441 p = .004). Curiously, the fact of having children reduces teachers' confidence in children's capacity to manage their own cognitive development collectively. Is this because they see intelligence as a gift?

Paradoxically, though, the teachers tend to consider a more interventionist activity, in the forms of motivational diagnosis (Q3F4, NPAR = +.08, PAR = +.32, F = 4.533 p = .034), and pressure to conform to the correct model (Q3F1, NPAR = −.39, PAR = −.20, F = 2.936 p = .088).

The ambivalence we have seen so far in relation to teachers with children finds expression in attitudes to teaching as well: if intelligence is seen as a gift bestowed naturally on the child, and thus immutable, it leads to both a wait-and-see policy, and to a (slightly desperate?) attempt to intervene. A Sisyphean task indeed! Yet the fact that most stress is laid on motivational diagnosis might also imply that they are in fact only assessing the child's maximum capacities.

School subjects

The parental experience of teachers accentuates the use of the school subjects with the highest valency to determine the child's intelligence. The need to succeed in subjects with a very high valency thus tends to be more pronounced (Q5F1, NPAR = +.09, PAR = +.27, $F = 3.059$ $p = .082$), as well as language activities (Q5F3, NPAR = −.20, PAR = +.08, $F = 4.934$ $p = .027$). Their parental experience, in short, further accentuates the normalisation of the definition of intelligence as success at school.

Scientific disciplines

In this connection, teachers' parental experience has a dual consequence: on one hand the social sciences do not seem to be so competitive as for teachers without children (Q6F1, NPAR = +.15, PAR = −.06, $F = 3.886$ $p = .050$), while on the other the biological maturation of linguistic functions becomes salient (Q6F5, NPAR = +.05, PAR = +.29, $F = 6.411$ $p = .012$). Note, too, the slightly esoteric appeal to philosophy and the history of science (Q6F4, NPAR = −.29, PAR = −.05, $F = 4.400$ $p = .037$)!

Summary

In our view, these varied results are organised on the basis of two fundamental principles. First, the representations developed by parent-teachers seem to be a response to a difficult conflict of identity, between their identity as parents and their identity as teachers. This identity conflict is expressed in a set of attitudes designed to remove the burden of responsibility from the teacher, both as an individual and as part of the educational institution.

This tension is also expressed at the level of attitudes to educational types of relationship, which will be more tense than those within the family, which are likely to be more empathetic. 'Other people's children are not our children' is a statement that is likely to be especially true for parent-teachers.

A consequence of this (relative) rejection of teachers' responsibility is the systematic appearance of a naturalisation of intelligence, in the form of a psychology of giftedness, a conservative, *laissez-faire* approach, and an appeal to biological maturationism. In this context, we can also regard these representations as playing a part in preserving the social identity which is most likely to be threatened by the vexed question of failure at school.

In conclusion, then, it is also one of the functions of social representations to forge the social identity of social actors, and to adjust the self-image to fit in with difficult social identities. This function would, in fact, be more visible where there is a threat to the identity, as when two contradictory identities intersect each other.

8 Models of the child: experimental approach

We now come to the experimental part of our study of the social representations of intelligence. The question we shall be looking at is this: are bright children perceived differently from mediocre or dull children; over what dimensions; and does this happen in the same way for mathematics, language and drawing, i.e. whether the subject is of high or low educational valency?

The measurements we shall be dealing with are derived from the seven factors identified in the factor analysis and detailed, for models of the child, on pages 73–5. First of all, we shall look at the results of the experimental manipulations for the whole sample, with no reference to any of the sociological or socio-psychological variables, as is justified by the fact that the different experimental conditions are distributed entirely at random in the various sub-populations.

Then we shall look for experimental validation of some of our earlier assertions about the effects of identity, whether it be that of teachers or parents.

The bright child and the child who is not bright

It will be remembered that the first operation consisted of asking the subjects to describe the characteristics of bright or dull children. The second induction related to the valency or importance of the subject in which the child described demonstrates brightness or mediocrity: mathematics, language or drawing. Table 8.1 indicates the number of subjects in each experimental group, with the degree of freedom corresponding to the simple results of first-degree interaction, the F value and probability of which (when the latter is at least .10) will be given for each factor analysed subsequently. Note that the factorial scores will be presented in such a way that a plus sign always relates to the enhanced perception of the characteristic of the label designating one of the factors.

Table 8.1. *Frequency of subjects and degrees of freedom*

	Maths (b1)	Language (b2)	Drawing (b3)
Bright (a1)	117	130	118
Mediocre (a2)	122	128	113

A: df = 1/722; B: df = 2/722; A × B: df = 2/722

The gifted child

The most striking of the results shown in table 8.2 is the overwhelming difference between the bright child and the mediocre one, regardless of subject. The bright child has important capacities for motivation and creativity as well as cognitive functioning, qualities of the gifted, model child which the mediocre child is deprived of. At the very least, there is a fundamental division in the image of educational success and failure which emphasises very well the differences between individuals which we have seen lie at the root of representations of intelligence.

Table 8.2. *The 'gifted' child*

	Maths	Language	Drawing
Bright	+.87	+.64	+.46
Mediocre	−.76	−.72	−.48

A: F = 656.825 p = .000; A × B: F = 14.871 p = .000

The second important result takes the form of an interaction between the two experimental manipulations, and consists of an accentuation of the differences between bright and mediocre children where the importance of the subject for the school career is increased. Thus the difference is least marked in the case of drawing, though it is, nonetheless, still very important (which is a serious argument for putting forward the salience of the question of differences between individuals); it is moderately important in the case of language, and most important in the case of mathematics, where there is the most discrimination in the assessment of the child's intelligence. This is also another indirect indication that the cybernetic or the logical and mathematical model is indeed the main criterion of intelligence.

To sum up, the first result shows that educational success determines a very positive general impression of the child and his cognitive capacities, and failure (or at least difficulties) a very negative image, while the second

Table 8.3. *The 'sociable' child*

	Maths	Language	Drawing
Bright	−.36	.00	+.09
Mediocre	+.28	+.05	−.08

A: $F = 7.486$ $p = .006$; A × B: $F = 13.927$ $p = .000$

makes salient the institutional definition of intelligence seen in cybernetic terms.

The sociable child

Two significant effects appear in the results set out in table 8.3. First, the mediocre child is judged more favourably than the bright child on this 'sociability' dimension. Although, as we have already seen, his cognitive capacities are week, he is nevertheless regarded as pleasant, amusing, talkative, and generally nice. Sociability is thus regarded as a contrast to the seriousness of the gifted, that is the intelligent, child. However, this representation also gives rise to an interaction that limits the application of this to the sphere of mathematics, as that is where the contrast between the bright (−.36) and mediocre (+.28) child is most striking. Children who are very good at mathematics are thus not very sociable, while most sociable children are not very good at mathematics. This seems to provide a further demonstration of the centrality of the cybernetic model in the definition of intelligence, since there is very little opposition between the two in language work, and the situation in drawing is reversed.

The well-behaved, disciplined child

It is only the interaction here which is significant, as can be seen from the data in table 8.4. Let us try to analyse the significance of this, beginning with the bright child, who is most disciplined in mathematics ($m = +.31$). But then that is a subject which in fact demands the rigour and respect for rules implicit in the idea of discipline. The child who is good at language work is around zero, this dimension being to some extent irrelevant to him, while the child who excels in drawing is very undisciplined ($m = -.26$). Which makes enough sense if we consider that creativity does not in the end have much to do with rigour and respect for rigid norms.

The mediocre child on the other hand is seen as undisciplined in mathematics ($m = -.12$) and in language work ($m = -.13$). both of which are subjects which carry a high educational valency, and both of which

Table 8.4. *The 'disciplined' child*

	Maths	Language	Drawing
Bright	+.31	+.04	−.26
Mediocre	−.12	−.13	+.18

$A \times B$: $F = 15.313$ $p = .000$

Table 8.5. *The calm child*

	Maths	Language	Drawing
Bright	−.04	−.01	+.42
Mediocre	−.16	+.01	−.22

A: $F = 13.586$ $p = .000$; B: $F = 3.358$ $p = .035$; $A \times B$: $F = 9.523$ $p = .000$

entail the interiorisation of rules (in mathematical proofs and demonstrations, and in linguistic, grammar and spelling rules). It might seem strange that a child who is mediocre at drawing should be described as disciplined ($m = +.18$), but in our view this indicates a profound contrast between intelligence in the strict sense, which requires a disciplined approach, and creativity, of which intelligence is in a sense a negation (on the social representation of creativity, see Le Disert, 1983).

The child with no problems

Should bright children be calmer, as a result of their visible educational success? The results on this factor, set out in table 8.5, show that this is not really the case.

Although the two simple effects seem to indicate that on the one hand bright children are in fact likely to be calmer, and on the other that their calmness should increase in inverse ratio to the educational valency of the subject, the interaction between the two effects means that our interpretation needs to be qualified somewhat. We can see, first of all, that this dimension does not have a great deal of relevance to language work, and also that children who are mediocre at mathematics tend to be less relaxed than those who do well at it, which can probably be explained by the fact that having difficulty or failing in that subject does actually put the child in a position of disequilibrium, at least in regard to the demands of school. It is therefore quite normal for him to be a bit 'preoccupied'.

Finally, this dimension seems to be the one most relevant to drawing. As

Table 8.6. *The 'communicative' child*

	Maths	Language	Drawing
Bright	−.47	+1.07	−.23
Mediocre	+.19	−.60	−.03

A: $F = 37.775$ $p = .000$; B: $F = 25.080$ $p = .000$; A × B: $F = 201.237$ $p = .000$

an expressive subject it reveals the equilibrium of those who are good at it and the relative disequilibrium of those who experience difficulty in expressing themselves.

The communicative child

The fifth factor is concerned, it will be remembered, with the child who has a rich vocabulary and an extensive communicative capacity. The results are set out in table 8.6. The different conditions are clearly very strongly contrasted on this factor. Given the complexity of the effects, let us start by looking at the significance of the interaction between the two variables. First, the strongest opposition is naturally the one between children who are good at language work and those who are not. This is natural and obvious.

More interesting, perhaps, is the inversion of the effect for mathematics, where the bright child appears to be a poor speaker, unlike the mediocre child who has the best faculty of communication out of the three mediocrities, which fits in with his greater sociability. The idea here is that mathematics demands such abstract cognitive capacities that not only do they not require any great communicative abilities, they imply their complete absence. And finally, drawing, which provokes the least description of the child in communication terms – less, in fact, the better the child is at it – the implication being that the dominant function of drawing is exclusively individual expression.

'Agnan'

This factor, the results for which are shown in table 8.7, describes the child who is smug, and who tells tales. The first result, to do with the simple effect of the subjects, can be interpreted as a reflection of the pointlessness of being smug when judgements are based on subjects with a low educational valency, such as drawing. The child who is good at drawing thus has the fewest pretensions. What the interaction shows up most clearly is that the smuggest child is the one who does well in maths. Although there is

Table 8.7. *The 'smug' child*

	Maths	Language	Drawing
Bright	+.24	+.05	−.20
Mediocre	−.08	+.07	−.09

B: $F = 5.504$ $p = .004$; $A \times B$: $F = 4.336$ $p = .013$

Table 8.8. *The 'inheritor'*

	Maths	Language	Drawing
Bright	+.12	+.12	−.09
Mediocre	−.06	−.23	+.16

A: $F = 2.985$ $p = .084$; $A \times B$: $F = 8.968$ $p = .000$

admittedly a critical tone to this, it surely also reflects a recognition that vanity of this sort has a degree of legitimacy?

The inheritors

The last factor is concerned with the image of the child as the heir of a good (but also less good) family, the child of intellectual or rich parents, which in fact constitutes a sort of sociological explanation of educational success and failure. The results are set out in table 8.8. Overall, the bright child tends to be a worthy representative of a family from a culturally and/or economically advantaged background. Moreover, this is particularly true, as the strong interaction between the two variables implies, of the child who is good at mathematics or language, the most highly valorised subjects. This is not, however, the case with the child who is good at drawing, either because drawing is not, in the end, deemed to be a criterion of intelligence, or perhaps because popular thought allows the socially and culturally disadvantaged the benefit of a certain amount of (individual) creativity. This leads us to examine the fact that the children who are mediocre at drawing also come from 'good' families. So failure in drawing seems in some sense to be the luxury of the well-off, whereas failure in other subjects, especially in language (either Bernstein, 1971, did not invent anything, or else his ideas have had considerable social resonance), is evidence of disadvantaged socio-economic and cultural origins. The results of this factor indicate that our subjects have a clear awareness of the social determinants of educational success and failure, or in other words of intelligence (and contrast therefore with the frequently expressed rejection of social determinism: this is clearly one of the advantages of experimentation which, by comparing conditions, enables us to reveal the complex aspects which are likely to affect the social desirability of the response).

Intelligence profiles

Having conducted that analysis, let us try to establish a sort of identikit picture of the child as perceived by our subjects through the prism of the experimental position they were assigned.

The child who is good at maths, first of all, is highly gifted from the cognitive point of view (he is motivated, creative, synthetically minded, etc.). Although he seems to have little aptitude for communication, this is not very important, as he is not very sociable either. A bit like the popular prototype of the scientist, in fact. On the other hand, he is highly disciplined, and respects rules, which should counterbalance his smugness and tale-telling. Predictably, this bright child comes from a 'good' family.

The child who is good at language would be a more rounded character, from the point of view of the image people have of him. After his linguistic and communicational aptitudes have received special recognition, there are still the considerable cognitive abilities he inherits from his privileged social and cultural background. His image is an entirely positive one, perhaps because he does seem more rounded and less specialised or limited than the child who is only good at mathematics and who is prototypical of what may be assumed to be a rarer type of intelligence.

The child who is good at drawing does not necessarily come from a well-off social background. He is 'not stupid' (his cognitive abilities are good), although he is somewhat lacking in linguistic skills; primarily, though, he is well balanced and fairly sociable. He is not smug, but he is very undisciplined.

The mediocre child, on the other hand, lacks adequate cognitive tools in all these cases, and thus does not have the qualities required for doing well. The short reason is that he is not gifted. Depending on the subject in question, however, he manifests particular differentiating characteristics.

Thus *the child who is mediocre at mathematics* is somewhat of a mirror-image of the bright child. So he is particularly sociable, does not have much discipline, and has no Agnan-like traits. He is also relatively uncalm, perhaps precisely because of the difficulties he is having in this area.

The image of *the child who is mediocre at language* is also the opposite of the well-rounded child, who is very good at it. In fact, his image is especially negative. He quite clearly does not come from a privileged social background, and as well as lacking linguistic skills he is undisciplined, and even tends towards smugness and telling tales.

The case of *the child who is mediocre at drawing*, on the other hand, is singular. He is fairly well-behaved (perhaps too well-behaved to be creative), but he is not well-balanced from the socio-affective point of view; he is relatively unsociable and has few pretensions. Primarily, though, he comes from a privileged social and cultural background. So what does this add up to? Is this a 'difficult' child, such as one finds even in the 'best' families? Or is drawing the only acceptable subject to fail in, the luxury which children from this background can allow themselves?

Whatever the answer, popular thought seems to be highly structured at this level, as it reacts in a very systematic way with our experimental inductions. While they have revealed the supremacy of the logical and mathematical model of intelligence, they have also brought to light the existence of different social and psychological typologies of children, which constitute additional proof that there are genuine popular 'psychologies', which are no less coherent and strongly structured for being 'implicit' (on implicit psychologies, see Beauvois, 1984, and Leyens, 1983).

But for these to make a more significant contribution to our socio-psychological approach to the social representations of intelligence, we need to demonstrate the ways in which they modify and are modified by the different identities whose operation we described earlier, particularly parental and teacher identity. This is what we shall do next.

Models of the child and parental experience

In the preceding chapters we were able to establish that parental identity tends to organise a representation of intelligence around the theory of natural inequalities, and we tried to show that this was a response to their experience of intellectual differences between one person and another. If our interpretation is correct, it should be possible to detect traces of this focus on inter-individual differences, by looking at the divergent experimental conditions according to whether the subjects had had any parental experience, because in fact the manipulation relating to bright or mediocre children is, implicitly at least, concerned with the question of these differences. Our reasoning is straightforward: if parental experience does in fact make recognition of these differences salient, then those who have it should show a more marked divergence between their judgements of gifted and ungifted children. Moreover, this divergence ought to be valid essentially for the first factor of the image, which is concerned with gifted and ungifted children. So, to test our hypothesis we examined the factorial scores of parents and non-parents (all of them non-students) on the first factor, for bright and mediocre children in the different subjects.

First, this naturally reiterates the effects we saw above for all the experimental subjects: a huge bias of favour of the bright children, who are seen as gifted, and an accentuation of the differences between bright and

Table 8.9. *The 'gifted' child, as seen by parents and non-parents (n in brackets)*

		Maths	Language	Drawing
Non-parents	Bright	+.60 (25)	+.79 (31)	+.35 (26)
	Mediocre	−.76 (27)	−.92 (26)	−.47 (22)
Parents	Bright	+.93 (43)	+.56 (48)	+.53 (39)
	Mediocre	−1.07 (49)	−.82 (52)	−.55 (48)

mediocre in relation to educational valency of the subject in question. What concerns us here, however, is the second-degree significant interaction, because that implies that these judgements vary in practice depending on whether or not the subjects have children ($F\ 2/424 = 4.468\ p = .012$).

In order to simplify the interpretation of this interaction, we shall point out that the fundamental aspect for parents is the reference to mathematics (the cybernetic prototype which we have seen is more dominant among parents), which creates the most marked differentiation between the bright child who is gifted ($m = +.93$) and the mediocre child who is not ($m = -1.07$). This differentiation is more marked than that made by non-parents. So reference to the educational institution and its dominant definition of intelligence blurs even the differentiation the parents apply in the case of language work (bright, $m = +.56$; mediocre, $m = -.82$) which, however, we have also seen to be linked to the theory of giftedness by its reference to biology. The explanation for this should be simple. We can assume that language, at least in its basics, is acquired before going to 'big school', and that it is in fact a prerequisite (implicit, because obvious). Since the experimental manipulation is explicitly concerned with educational success and failure, it will be the dominant model of the school (in this case, the logical and mathematical model most of all) that becomes salient to the point where it gives rise to a more marked accentuation of the differences between gifted and ungifted children. It is an accentuation, as we need to remember that similar differentiations also exist in relation to language and even to drawing, as is the case for non-parents too.

To conclude, it seems that the judgements passed on the child (who may be more or less gifted) share some of the characteristics of the socio-cognitive functions which underlie the social representations of intelligence, and that it is possible to act experimentally on them in order to create some kind of reaction, as it is actually from the experimental conditions that responses stemming from the social logic we have uncovered derive.

We could, of course, have tried the exercise with other factors identified in our analysis of the image of the child, but to have done that would obviously have been to risk extending and complicating the analysis needlessly. So we have limited it to the first factor, which nonetheless does not prevent us from pointing out one particularly illuminating effect. A significant interaction appears in connection with the seventh factor (the 'inheritor'), which relates to parental experience and whether the judgements have to do with bright children or not ($F\ 1/424 = 4.550\ p = .033$). If we look at non-parents, we find that they regard bright children, obviously enough in some ways, as fortunate inheritors ($m = +.14$), and mediocre children as underprivileged inheritors ($m = -.18$). However, when we turn to the parents, this difference is less visible, the factorial scores being almost equal at zero for the bright child ($m = .00$) and the mediocre child ($m = +.01$). Again, the refusal to blame the family, which we have imputed to a defence of personal identity against the threat of a parental identity which does not necessarily have a positive connotation as a result of the subjects' occupational category, confirms and thus validates by other means an important result which we identified before any experimental manipulation.

But let us go back to the principal factor (the gifted child), and look at it in connection with teaching identity.

Models of the child and teaching identity

Just as we did in the case of the parents, we shall compare the judgements organised around the image of the gifted child, this time by contrasting education students preparing for the teaching profession with teachers who are already in the job (making no distinction this time between those with and those without children: it is only the process of professionalisation that interests us here). The results are set out in table 8.10.

There are two relevant effects. The first is the greater 'severity' of practising teachers, who generally regard children as less gifted ($m = -.10$; student teachers: $m = +.15$; $F\ 1/327 = 6.614\ p = .014$). Is this part of a less positive overall view of the child, or is it a consequence of the painful experience of educational failure? The latter is the explanation implied by the first-degree interaction between type of subject and type of child to be assessed ($F\ 1/327 = 2.6855\ p = .102$). If we compare students and teachers in relation to the bright child, in fact, we do not find any important differences in situations where educational success is assured, and so the images are not differentiated on the basis of teaching experience. Differences do appear, though, when the child is judged to be mediocre, and implicitly relate to the question of failure at school: teachers in fact regard the mediocre child as less gifted than the student teachers do.

As we have said several times already, it is the experience of differences of intelligence between individual pupils, especially when they take the form

Table 8.10. *The 'gifted' child, as seen by student teachers and teachers (n in brackets)*

		Maths	Language	Drawing
Student teachers	Bright	+.86 (24)	+.80 (19)	+.63 (22)
	Mediocre	−.44 (19)	−.65 (22)	−.51 (17)
Teachers	Bright	+.86 (33)	+.74 (42)	+.45 (33)
	Mediocre	−1.02 (39)	−1.03 (37)	−.55 (32)

of failure (as is also suggested by the recent study by Thommen, 1984), which constitutes one of the organising nuclei of the representation of intelligence (or perhaps unintelligence) among teachers. It will be recalled, indeed, that teachers, although they were overtly opposed to the ideology of giftedness (to go by the average responses to the relevant questionnaires), tend to modify their representations towards greater acceptance of the theory of inequalities and its implications. And it is precisely this kind of inequalities that we are concerned with in the model of the gifted child we are examining here.

We should note, finally, one more aspect of the results which is consistent with the representation of intelligence we have assigned to teachers (in relation to non-teachers): these differences between gifted and ungifted children seem to be more marked for subjects with a high educational valency (mathematics and language) than for drawing, at least as far as teachers are concerned, as there is no such difference among education students. This result fits in well with the increased importance the teachers attribute to institutional definitions of intelligence, and confirms the findings of Gilly (1980) on the values governing the teacher's representation of his pupils.

As in the case of the parents, then, our experimental manipulations introduced kinds of agitation which aroused dynamics concerned with the actual nature of the social representations of intelligence we discerned in the responses to the earlier questionnaires. And because it is capable of arousing dynamics of this sort, the more experimental part of our study has shown itself to be useful as a way of validating certain aspects of our modelling of the social representations, which is perhaps the main purpose of experimentation (Grisez, 1975).

9 Conclusions

'It is quite wrong to regard social thought as a site of incoherence and disorder', writes Rouquette (1973, p. 327) and, as the evidence we have seen demonstrates very clearly, the same thing is true of intelligence. Rouquette continues:

> Everything in fact seems to point to the opposite conclusion, that it is constructed on the basis of rigorous patterns and in conformity with precise rules. In other words, the whole of its discourse obeys its own particular syntax, which can in theory be explained in its entirety. Far from dissolving into an arbitrary sequence of errors and an absence of traditional logic, 'natural' thought has a coherence of its own, and is indeed a type of rationality.

It is a rationality, though, which assumes what Moscovici calls 'cognitive polyphasia', in that it is based on a multiplicity of different orders of reasoning and a diversity of socio-cognitive functions which accounts for the heterogeneity of the way different groups and individuals talk about intelligence, as well as their variation in response to particular social experiences or significant moments in people's lives.

Yet having acknowledged that there is this multiplicity of discourses, we still have to reconstruct the socio-psychological pattern, or rather patterns, which generate them, modify them or otherwise affect them. In order to prevent this work from becoming unwieldy and incoherent, we have consciously left a number of questions unanswered, but the data we have employed suggest that there are several organising principles behind the representations of intelligence which can be illustrated by effects that recur frequently enough for us to be confident that they have a general application. We will conclude by looking briefly at them, in turn.

The multiple meanings of the concept of intelligence

Intelligence only exists as a mental construct, and like all mental constructs it is social or collective in nature. So we would expect its meanings to vary, depending on the individual or the group who transmit these social representations, and even for one individual or one group to use the term to mean different things.

Anthropologists seem to adopt a relativist attitude as a matter of course: all definitions of intelligence, or attempts to measure it are dependent on cultural values specific to each society, as a result of which certain kinds of behaviour, attitudes or particular mental processes are valorised. This multiple significance can often also be seen in the impossibility of finding a literal translation of the word 'intelligence' in its dominant western sense, different cultures using a variety of terms to provide what they judge to be an appropriate equivalent (see particularly Dasen, 1984; Goodnow, 1976; Serpell, 1977; Wober, 1974).

This multiplicity of meanings is not just a consequence of intercultural disparities. As Sternberg *et al.* (1981) suggest, an analysis of the representations of intelligence in western society reveals a plurality of definitions rather than a single concept of intelligence. So although intelligence certainly relates to the logical and mathematical model operating in the scientific process, the psychogenetic development of which the Piagetian school undertook to describe and explain (from a structural standpoint), intelligence cannot simply be defined in terms of the formal logic that characterises it. People do not only think of it in terms of abstract logical operations, it is also seen in terms of elaborating and interiorising norms of social conduct and values, the nature of which may be specific to different social groups. In those situations, intelligence is what defines an individual's language and communication skills, his discipline and social attitudes, as well as the other personal or sociological characteristics which we have seen to be associated with models of the intelligent child. Finally, we also have to recognise that some groups, although they may deny it, see intelligence primarily as a matter of succeeding in fulfilling the institutionally defined aims of the school, which obviously covers the acquisition of a heterogeneous group of skills and social values. This definition may also be the meeting point for the frequently co-occurent conceptions of 'logical' intelligence and 'social' intelligence.

The polysemous nature of the popular concept of intelligence contrasts with the more monolithic scientific approaches which, like Piaget's in particular, argue for a single unambiguous meaning of the word, with the inevitable implication of abstraction from the specific content the mental operations are dealing with, and from the social relations which govern the elaboration of logical systems just as much as other, socio-psychological, systems of norms and values. The importance of these other definitions of intelligence (which for the sake of simplicity we will call 'social') ought to encourage intelligence specialists to take more account of them in their analyses (especially psychogenic ones), if they do not want to run the risk of studying mental processes in terms which have no relation to the actual social practices which create them and organise them. Recent work in the field of genetic social psychology seems to be opening up promising perspectives in this area.

So, paradoxically, these popular views of intelligence seem to be closer to the psychometric approach, in which intelligence tests enable an intellectual quotient to be assessed, given that such an approach is only capable of reflecting the cultural values dominant in a particular historical or cultural context and translating them into tests (Valsiner, 1984). This would also explain why the practice of using these intelligence tests still continues, in spite of the virulent criticisms which have been levelled against them. The reason for this is that the logic of these popular conceptions may well be homologous with the factorial structure of the tests, which assumes that the variety of dimensions which go to make up intelligence are complementary (even though they are organised hierarchically), especially given the movement towards the theory of giftedness which, as we have said, is closely connected with the ideology underlying testing. This is the only explanation for such a close similarity between the conceptions of the man in the street and the models developed by experts (Sternberg *et al.*, 1981). Taking this at its face value (Sternberg, 1980), we even end up by thinking of all popular conceptions of intelligence as ultimately correct.

This multiplicity of meanings, then, is the reason why social representations appear to be assemblages made up of apparently contradictory discourses, not only among the different groups we looked at but also within groups and even within one individual. As part of social thought, intelligence is not monolithic or unambiguous; its model is multi-factorial, with each factor covering a particular definition and conception of intelligence. This is the only way of grasping the coherence of a discourse (that of parents, especially) which veers between asserting a genetic and maturationist conception of abstract intelligence (the 'bump of mathematics') and arguing for an environmentalist conception of social intelligence, or taking success at school as the best indication of it. This is not a question of logical contradiction, or inadequate cognitive organisation: it is a matter of complexity and richness, with a variety of discourses complementing each other in order to take account of the totality of discourses covered by the single concept of intelligence.

The socio-cognitive roots of the ideology of giftedness

The ideology of giftedness is a well-known social phenomenon which resurfaces regularly, even in discourses where it is least expected. It is a conception which has hitherto been regarded negatively, because of the reactionary ideology spread by social groups who take advantage of it to hide or naturalise (both of which come to the same thing in the end) sociological differentiations, especially of race, class and sex. It is not our intention to deny this explanation, despite its overtones of conspiracy theory and machiavellianism, but to provide a further, complementary, socio-psychological explanation, which both derives from and supports Moscovici's theory of social representations (1984a). It consists of looking at the theory of natural inequalities as the result of socio-cognitive operations designed to overcome an unfamiliarity when accompanied by a shortage of information.

The question is really one of accounting for recurrent, systematic modifications of the representations of intelligence, beyond their diversity. There are several characteristic aspects of these shifts in meaning, which often happen without the knowledge of the groups or individuals who transmit the representations. The first has to do with what has been called the dissemination of information. In other words, the groups who are bearers of representations in which the theory of natural inequalities is dominant, or at least accentuated, seem to have insufficient 'rational' information to explain the unfamiliarity constituted by the evidence of the disparity of intelligence between individuals, which no competing explanation, such as social heritage or the differentiating effects of school, seems to them to account for. Having no explanatory model, the man in the street (and sometimes the expert, too) tends to naturalise these differences, to attribute them to the gifts which nature bestows on some and withholds from others, in accordance with the mysterious operations of chance which some branch of biology, probably genetic biology, will one day finally be able to uncover. Within this conception is also a contrast between the confidence in biology and a growing distrust of social science. The experts may perhaps like to draw their own conclusions about the implications this has for their activity (especially as regards popularisation).

Of course we have to recognise that this ideology of giftedness, which adds elitism and discriminatory tendencies to the theory of natural inequalities, is not overtly advertised. Going by the 'raw' responses to our questionnaire, in fact, it is usually denied. A particular analytic methodology, in this case factor analysis, is required for it to be brought into the open. Social discourse, though, is riddled with prohibitions and subject to censorship and self-censorship. And elitist and discriminatory discourse is not socially desirable, it is not part of the 'Zeitgeist', the spirit of our time, apart from among a few groups generally convinced of their legitimate superiority and desirous of preserving it. Yet other groups are also particularly liable to become involved in these ideas, for reasons which are socio-psychological as well as political. These reasons are clearly based on the personal experience of unfamiliarity provided by perceived differences of intelligence, which gives rise to a selective focus on them. As we have seen, this applies to parents first and foremost, but teachers are also involved in it. The differences, which for them are basically ones between children, are all the more salient because they introduce additional complications into running a family or a classroom. But there is no alternative model, not even a scientific one, which offers even a remotely complete explanation of these differences or any advice on ways to come to terms with them. Confronted with them, broad educational principles often turn out to be so generalised as to be powerless, which adds a further tension to the cognitive unfamiliarity.

The result of this is that the extremes become prototypes, against which the whole range of other individuals is assessed. It is the brilliant ones, in extreme cases the ones with genius, who become the parameters for assessing the mass of individuals, or, at the opposite end of the scale, the 'mediocre' children, the ones who are failures at school. Both groups being extreme cases, they call for special explanations which take fundamental account of their unusual nature, of the sort offered by the theory of natural inequality of giftedness. In a socially quite logical way the same reasoning is then applied by analogy to people in general.

Obviously this theory, or ideology, satisfies a psychological economy principle, by reducing everything to a single unifying explanatory principle, which naturalises and thus objectivises what cannot otherwise be rationally explained, using a phenomenal causality which transforms effect into cause.

The identity function of representations

There is therefore one central principle orienting the social representations, which in turn mentally structure particular and unusual experiences. But what governs the way this reconstruction is carried out? This is the point at which a second principle, the principle of identity, directs the socio-cognitive management of unfamiliarity: the solution involves psychologically salient social identities, as well as the need to protect the individual identity when multiple social identities intersect.

The main consequence of this identity principle is that specially organised representations are presented by the social groups for whom intelligence is part of everyday experience and for whom it constitutes a significant component of their identity. We have seen how it is primarily parents and teachers who construct their own highly complex representation of intelligence, and that they are the very people who are confronted daily with the question of intelligence by their children and their pupils. Their representations contain a number of principles which generate opinions which they constantly deploy. Student identity, on the other hand, if there is such a thing, is by the same title not likely to organise its own specific social representation of intelligence.

Recent work in Australia, the United States and Japan, in particular (see Goodnow, 1985; Sigel, 1985) has revealed differences, decisive from a number of viewpoints, between various methods of education and parental attitudes. In a complementary way our study has revealed the generic specificity of identity which is entailed in the new experience of socialisation which becoming a parent involves. It is essential to take account of this identity which of course is obviously liable to variation, because it is a modality of social integration which creates radical changes in the representational systems which have hitherto been largely underestimated, or completely unconsidered. Indeed, it appears that the parental condition plays at least as important a part in people's social identity as the weightier sociological variables like nationality, social class or even sexual identity. However, we ought to be cautious here, where we are dealing with variables which have not appeared to play a determining part in the shaping of the representations of intelligence: the absence or weakness of the differentiating effects of these variables can hide other differentiations, particularly in practical situations and in social interactions with children, which we have not dealt with in this study.

Returning to the effects of parental identity, they seem to be sufficiently general to enable us to observe what happens when they are joined with the teaching identity. In both instances we can see an evolution, a genuine socialisation, from non-parents into parents, from apprentice-teachers to practising professionals, even from teachers without children to parent-teachers. Moreover, this evolution happens in broadly similar directions (even if by slightly different degrees) and according to three general axes.

The first turning point, as we know, is linked to a sense of the unfamiliarity of differences of intelligence, and finds expression in an increased appeal to the theory of giftedness or even to its ideology. This sort of explanation also provides a ready protection of personal identity, as the naturalisation takes away most of the responsibility from both teachers and parents.

The second is a gradually increasing emphasis on a definition of intelligence as conformity to social norms, and on the call for various sorts of pressure to be put on the child to ensure that he learns these normative systems and social rules. In other words, the multi-factorial conception of intelligence develops to the extent–or so we can assume–that the educational aims become diversified, and this concerns social as much as intellectual development in its more cognitive sense, i.e. the totality of the socialisation process of the developing individual.

Finally, and perhaps as a consequence of the foregoing, there is the simultaneous emergence of a particular focus on school and educational success as the criterion of intelligence, with the emphasis falling more and more on the subjects most valorised by the educational institution (especially in selection processes), by a sort of increased symbiosis with it. Some people would say, in a sort of coalition against the child. This is, however, too serious a question to be answered hastily; it is better left to our conscience as adults, parents or teachers.

Briefly, then, parents–or the family in general–and teachers appear to be mediating in their day-to-day activity between the child and the educational institution in the socialisation process from one to the other. This mediating function, with its assumption of differentiated educational aims, and different levels of aims, thus takes account of the multiplicity of their discourses and their multifactorial definition of intelligence. It is a process which involves a number of mental constructions which simultaneously serve to overcome the unfamiliarity of inter-individual differences of intelligence and 'personality' (since intelligence is also related to social attitudes), and to provide a vision which is consistent with the achievement of the educational aims which stem from the constraints of the educational institution. We believe they also complement the arguments advanced by Gilly (1980, 1981) about the social representations of teachers.

As well as these generic effects of parental or teaching identity on the functions and the socio-cognitive organisation of representations of intelligence, there are a number of modifications of them, perhaps more partial but no less important from a psychological point of view, which in a dynamic way help to preserve the identity of the individuals and groups who are the bearers of these representations. It will be remembered, too, that the theory of giftedness also helps to shift responsibility for the cognitive difficulties of their children or their pupils away from parents and teachers. The situation is equally clear in cases of conflicts of identification where divergent opinions and attitudes clash as a result of different identities. We have seen several typical instances of this: it happens when there is a conflict between parental and teaching identity, so that parents attribute a large share of responsibility to individual teachers, while teachers reject this all the more strongly if they are themselves parents. We have also seen it in the case of mothers who also have a job outside the home, and who are more committed to the idea of the autonomous development of the child, no doubt to defend themselves against accusations, including self-accusations, of failing in their 'maternal duty' as it is defined by a dominant current in our society. Again, when members of an 'advantaged' social group deny the benefits of a social heritage which privileges their children, or when parents reject the idea of a family heritage which perhaps does not show them in a favourable light, these modifications, minor though they may seem, are primarily designed to preserve a personal identity likely to be threatened as a result of conflictual social identities and integrations, for whatever reason, at a given historical moment.

So, to summarise, social representations, particularly representations of intelligence, are structured, and evolve, in accordance with the 'chances' of everyday experience, by a dual socio-cognitive function which implies a number of specific socio-cognitive operations: on the one hand, the construction of a social universe which is mentally intelligible and coherent, and on the other, the elaboration of a satisfying social and personal identity, one that is which is compatible with socially and historically determined systems of norms and values.

Conclusion

Concluding the afterword to the second edition of his analysis of the social representations of psychoanalysis, Moscovici (1961; 1976, p.504) wrote: 'through all the uncertainties and all the perspectives we have outlined emerges the still unresolved question which we have been asking all the time: how does man create his reality? This is not a question we could have expected to answer straight away.' The same thing is true of the approach to intelligence which we have put forward.

The main point of uncertainty concerns the relations between representations of intelligence and what happens in practice, especially in education. Of course, we questioned the subjects about different educational principles or teaching methods to be considered for children in difficulty, and the responses were amply structured and very varied (and in fact confirmed several theoretical currents in the psychology of development and learning), and they also correlated with and thus confirmed more general assertions about intelligence and its development, in their various senses. Yet we did not observe the actual behaviour of adults in interaction with children, either in experimental situations or in their normal settings. Furthermore, the recent reviews of this question (see Goodnow, 1985; Sigel, 1985) have shown that although the connections between them are clear, they are not as close as one might hope. We have discussed one reason for this in the introduction, which is that representations are actualised in concrete situations, and are therefore 'translated' each time, in the form of particular social episodes worked out reciprocally in relation to the specific task and the reactions of the child himself (on episodes of this sort in nurseries, see Emiliani and Zani, 1984). The transition from representation to action is thus the product of a new cognitive elaboration which in some ways is more specific than the social representation (Von Cranach, 1982).

A further reason which emerges from our analysis lies in the nature of the actual system of communication governing the representation of intelligence, which Moscovici (1961) sees as related primarily to diffusion, and sometimes to propagation, but seldom to propaganda. In the latter, the aim of communication is precisely the transition into action, the adoption of a position, and so the gap between the two tends towards zero. This, however, is not the case with propagation, the aim of which is more concerned with developing a general attitude in which a connection between action and representation, while probable, is not necessary; nor *a fortiori* is it the case with diffusion which, like rumour, only involves individual elements of representation. These personal opinions, which we know from other sources are likely to be, or at least to appear to be, contradictory (Stoetzel, 1943), would therefore be heavily dependent on specific situations, and would lead to highly specific actions. Because systems of communication play a particularly important part in controlling representations of intelligence, it may be in their nature to be linked to action in a way that is more probabilist than determinist.

In other words, the question of these links is likely to turn out to be complex, in terms of systems of communication, in terms of the multiple meanings of the whole idea of intelligence and the widely separate conceptions it encompasses, and lastly in terms of the local reconstructions demanded by concrete situations (particularly the kinds of tasks, however they are interpreted) and the personal relationship established with the child, who himself needs to be seen as an individual. This sense of the random nature of the links between actions and representations thus derives from a complex combinatory of changes of which we can only catch a momentary and fragmentary glimpse. There is no doubt that the field of research this opens up is a particularly difficult and absorbing one for genetic social psychology. Any study of it should also take on the insufficiently explored question of education for parents (which would have to do more than simply list the basic information needed by parents; see Kohn, 1959; Cohen, 1981), for which this study has reminded us that there is an urgent need, at the same time as emphasising the part that representations of intelligence should play in it.

The reason why this is such a complex question is that, like any social phenomenon, intelligence as a collective and historical construct needs to be analysed at a variety of levels which have to be identified and isolated and then articulated (Doise, 1986). The lessons to be drawn from our study of the representations of intelligence agree with the approach adopted by recent work in genetic social psychology in emphasising the theoretical and cultural inadequacy of treating certain intra-psychological processes in isolation (particularly when the label of intelligence excludes other processes), since intelligence – or, to be more precise, intelligences – is concerned both with the inter-individual dynamics and with relations of position or situation within the social system, and thus with specific experiences and identities which modify, and involve differentially, a variety of cognitive processes, including those of the developing child himself. At the ideological level, we can no longer ignore the systems of norms and values which are dominant at any given point in history, and which claim to define as universal one dominant conception of intelligence out of the many competing definitions which surround us. If psychology, particularly genetic or developmental psychology, does not consider the totality of the dimensions which constitute intelligence, it will lack the socio-psychological articulation which the fundamentally social nature of intelligence demands.

To say this may well be to give the impression that we have merely extended the agenda instead of solving the problem. But this does not matter, as there is no point in providing easy solutions to complex problems, as the economy principle that still operates in positivist approaches would like us to do. The real need is to guard against simplifying problems through one of the forms of reductionism, and to ensure that the whole range of conceptually significant dimensions is taken into account in order to understand a social phenomenon of which they are all constitutive. And the social representations of intelligence are what constitutes intelligence.

This book claims to have contributed one important element to this project, by extending the concept of intelligence to include aspects which have hitherto been ignored by so many people, particularly by psychologists, who have been led by too great a focus on western society to regard them as mere curiosities, only useful for differentiating 'our' definition of intelligence (the true one) from the more esoteric definitions of 'primitive' peoples, who are not yet 'civilised' because not yet 'westernised'. Yet it is abundantly clear that these conceptual differences in relation to intelligence are not the province of Third World specialists: the divisions are present in western societies, if we are prepared to see them and to acknowledge the psychological attention they deserve, as we hope we have done. This will mean changing our habits and assumptions, because it is going to become increasingly difficult to carry on talking about intelligence in the singular when it is so undeniably a plural noun.

Appendix 1
Questionnaire 1 : Intelligence

Means on the scale from 1 (do not agree) to 7 (agree) for parents (PAR) and non-parents (NPAR), for trainee teachers (STUD) and teachers with (PAR) and without children (NPAR) and for non-teacher parents from Bologna (BOL) and Geneva (GEN). The full numbers are given in brackets, as are $p < .20$.

					Teachers				Non-teaching parents		
		NPAR (157)	PAR (279)	df 1/434 p	STUD (123)	NPAR (115)	PAR (101)	df 2/336 p	BOL (76)	GEN (102)	df 1/176 p
2	Success at school is not a sign of intelligence	5.11	4.63	.008	5.02	5.10	4.49	.018	4.47	4.89	.144
7	Logic and mathematics are the prototypes of intelligence	3.13	3.75	.000	2.79	3.06	3.72	.000	3.97	3.62	—
8	Intelligence tests enable the intellectual capacities of children to be measured with precision	2.67	2.96	.053	2.35	2.67	2.95	.008	2.84	3.05	—
10	Intelligence is an invention of our society for the purpose of adapting to new economic demands and current technological conditions	2.64	2.22	.005	2.29	2.40	2.43	—	1.88	2.26	.085
11	Intelligence is above all a question of character	2.44	2.41	—	2.40	2.25	2.35	—	2.59	2.32	—
12	The first-born in a family is usually the least intelligent	1.45	1.56	—	1.42	1.41	1.68	.066	1.55	1.44	—
13	It is his degree of intelligence which indicates what job a child may hope to have, not the child's personal preference	2.14	2.48	.019	1.83	2.13	2.71	.000	2.16	2.48	.149
14	It is the school which creates intellectual differences between children	3.45	3.15	.097	3.52	3.30	2.84	.012	3.49	3.22	—
17	The computer is the perfect model of what intelligence is	2.07	2.13	—	1.84	2.12	2.19	.094	2.58	1.75	.000
19	Intelligence is a rationalisation of affectivity	2.96	3.14	—	2.85	2.86	3.17	.191	3.08	3.15	—
20	Intelligence is gauged by the capacity for abstract thought	3.90	4.14	.168	3.50	3.84	4.15	.012	3.64	4.49	.002
23	Homework is important because it enables a relationship to be established between the parents and the school	3.14	3.99	.000	3.07	2.85	3.78	.001	3.45	4.59	.000

Appendix 1 (*cont.*)

					Teachers				Non-teaching parents		
		NPAR (157)	PAR (279)	df 1/434 p	STUD (123)	NPAR (115)	PAR (101)	df 2/336 p	BOL (76)	GEN (102)	df 1/176 p
27	Basing curricula on the child of average intelligence results in the impoverishment of the most intelligent	3.35	3.42	—	2.89	3.31	3.08	.168	2.87	4.18	.000
29	Being intelligent means agreeing to disagree with other people	4.36	4.17	—	3.61	4.23	3.93	.043	3.70	4.75	.001
32	Intelligence tests are misleading: all they do is measure the differences (particularly economic differences) that exist between different social categories	4.22	4.01	—	3.89	4.10	4.23	—	3.47	4.19	.010
35	The brain is the birthplace of intelligence	4.68	5.06	.017	4.04	4.64	4.51	.008	5.24	5.48	—
36	Intelligence is a problem of personality	3.24	3.21	—	3.19	3.09	3.24	—	3.20	3.19	—
41	The average man has a 'concrete' intelligence but is incapable of thinking abstractly	3.18	3.48	.056	3.18	3.35	3.47	—	3.51	3.48	—
46	A child who does not value intelligence will never be intelligent	2.66	2.90	.096	2.33	2.62	2.73	.058	2.76	3.17	.097
47	Intelligence is primarily a rigorous attitude in thinking and in action	3.36	3.95	.001	3.11	3.15	3.92	.000	3.68	4.19	.058
48	Failure is generally due to the teacher's lack of understanding of the child	3.83	3.74	—	4.06	3.92	3.01	.000	4.42	3.96	.073
50	The feeling of failure induces frustration and makes the child want to give up	4.95	4.90	—	5.17	5.14	5.09	—	5.14	4.53	.019
51	Careers advice mainly benefits the less gifted	2.73	2.99	.098	2.11	2.57	2.97	.000	2.92	3.07	—
52	Differences of intelligence between individuals exist before children start school	5.43	5.73	.037	5.15	5.39	5.86	.001	5.51	5.75	—
53	Being intelligent means knowing how to take advantage of an opportunity	3.43	3.49	—	2.89	3.01	3.25	—	2.92	4.17	.000
55	'Like father, like son': this is equally true for intelligence	2.01	1.96	—	1.61	1.91	2.11	.005	1.78	1.94	—
56	The existence of differences of intelligence between individuals is a mysterious problem which science has been unable to solve	3.67	4.57	.000	3.41	3.50	4.29	.000	4.57	4.85	—
57	Intelligence can be measured by the shape and size of a person's cranium	1.57	1.73	.196	1.36	1.58	1.74	.044	1.34	2.01	.000

58	Intelligence is simultaneously a question of biology, psychology and sociology	5.78	5.44	.013	5.89	5.83	5.66	—	5.26	5.36	—
59	Intelligence sanctions social injustice: when it comes to intelligence, it is the rich who get that, too	3.64	3.13	.010	2.85	3.44	3.11	.071	2.55	3.58	.001
60	Only science can define what intelligence is	3.05	3.34	.094	2.61	3.19	3.35	.001	3.70	3.06	.019
62	You have to be intelligent to do well at school	2.94	3.45	.003	2.66	2.99	3.50	.000	3.17	3.61	.101
64	Being intelligent means having good manners	1.85	1.95	—	1.78	1.86	1.99	—	2.33	1.63	.001
66	Failure could generally be avoided, given more patience on the part of the teacher	4.32	4.51	—	4.02	4.12	3.55	.032	5.00	5.09	—
69	Intelligence is the individual's capacity to adapt to the society in which he lives	4.17	4.20	—	3.56	3.89	4.06	.100	3.67	4.75	.000
73	Intelligent children come from families where the parents value intelligence	3.27	3.12	—	2.85	3.01	3.17	—	2.33	3.67	.000
74	There can be only one definition of what intelligence is	2.14	2.38	.163	1.71	2.02	2.24	.015	2.26	2.60	—
75	The school only reveals differences of intelligence which already exist by virtue of different social backgrounds	3.66	3.49	—	3.72	3.76	3.33	.183	3.63	3.55	—
78	An intelligent person is someone who can adapt to the dominant ideology	1.71	2.05	.006	1.76	1.52	2.01	.006	1.83	2.26	.037
79	We need to design school curricula in accordance with children's real capacities, not impose adult demands on them	6.01	5.82	.148	6.11	6.19	5.86	.128	5.84	5.75	—
82	Intelligence is the child's capacity to understand the meaning that the teacher gives to a question	3.59	4.39	.000	3.42	3.31	3.66	—	4.36	5.13	.002
87	Being intelligent means knowing how to look after yourself in life	3.89	4.00	—	3.37	3.67	4.02	.013	3.87	4.08	—
88	Being intelligent means conforming to the norms of a society which has become bureaucratic	2.03	2.20	.161	2.00	2.07	2.27	—	2.47	1.94	.008
89	Intelligence means managing to get on with other people despite initial differences of outlook	4.21	4.54	.068	4.09	4.14	4.37	—	4.95	4.40	.053
90	Parent's separation or divorce are frequently a source of intellectual deficiencies	3.94	4.14	—	3.85	3.83	4.17	—	4.37	3.94	.131
91	The rich invented the notion of intelligence to justify their wealth and power	3.10	3.00	—	3.05	3.12	3.16	—	3.57	2.41	.000
93	The different intellectual functions are clearly localised in the brain	4.31	4.70	.016	4.41	4.46	5.05	.004	4.42	4.55	—
94	Psychology should be regarded as a genuinely scientific discipline	4.37	4.41	—	4.48	4.43	4.45	—	4.34	4.43	—
95	'Tell me the parents' occupation and I will tell you the child's intelligence'	2.11	1.90	.092	1.85	2.02	1.99	—	1.72	1.94	—

Appendix 1 (*cont.*)

					Teachers				Non-teaching parents		
		NPAR (157)	PAR (279)	df 1/434 p	STUD (123)	NPAR (115)	PAR (101)	df 2/336 p	BOL (76)	GEN (102)	df 1/176 p
96	Being intelligent means knowing how to present yourself in the best light	2.38	2.43	—	2.05	2.18	2.32	—	2.28	2.67	.095
98	Everyone is intelligent in their own way	4.58	5.00	.012	4.83	4.43	4.71	.155	4.91	5.34	.089
99	Western culture is the prototype of intelligence	1.78	1.94	.177	1.85	1.84	2.00	—	2.12	1.75	.050
100	If men are seen as more intelligent than women this is because men define intelligence to their own advantage	4.78	4.86	—	4.60	4.90	5.04	—	4.66	4.84	—
102	Members of so-called ‘primitive’ cultures are also intelligent in their own way	6.04	6.18	—	6.18	6.06	6.17	—	6.18	6.19	—
103	If parents do not valorise a particular subject, efforts to teach it will be in vain	4.47	5.28	.000	3.83	4.48	5.18	.000	5.42	5.28	—
104	Being intelligent means adapting to school	2.46	2.65	.195	2.00	2.21	2.57	.003	2.58	2.78	—
106	People whose weight is ‘balanced’ are usually more intelligent than people who are very thin or overweight	1.87	1.81	—	1.39	1.76	1.92	.002	1.61	1.86	.161
109	Some people are born with more intelligence, others with less	4.17	4.97	.000	3.50	4.03	4.94	.000	4.63	5.25	.022
113	If certain social categories seem to be more intelligent, this is because they define what intelligence is themselves and impose their definition on others	4.42	3.93	.009	4.55	4.41	3.88	.022	4.08	3.87	—
115	Seeming intelligent is not the same as being intelligent	5.61	5.61	—	5.77	5.70	5.54	—	5.92	5.45	.041
118	Boys are more intelligent than girls: it is a question of nature	1.40	1.42	—	1.11	1.39	1.41	.012	1.39	1.46	—
119	Every culture has its own definition of intelligence	5.33	5.29	—	5.33	5.30	5.32	—	5.14	5.36	—
120	Intelligence defines the individual’s adaptation to his physical environment	4.24	4.20	—	3.68	4.02	4.31	.017	3.89	4.33	.086
121	School curricula try to do too much, they are too demanding	3.44	3.13	.059	3.33	3.33	3.42	—	2.88	3.02	—
122	There must be more advanced curricula for intelligent children than for less intelligent ones	3.03	3.18	—	2.23	2.71	2.78	.017	2.00	4.45	.000
123	School further accentuates the differences of intelligence that exist between individuals	4.41	4.07	.059	4.77	4.32	4.06	.012	3.55	4.47	.001

Appendix 2
Questionnaire 2: The development of intelligence

Means on the scale from 1 (do not agree) to 7 (agree) for parents (PAR) and non-parents (NPAR), for trainee teachers (STUD) and teachers with (PAR) and without children (NPAR) and for non-teacher parents from Bologna (BOL) and Geneva (GEN). The full numbers are given in brackets, as are $p < .20$.

					Teachers				Non-teaching parents		
		NPAR (157)	PAR (279)	df 1/434	STUD (123)	NPAR (115)	PAR (101)	df 2/336	BOL (76)	GEN (102)	df 1/176
1	If the child had to rely entirely on his own potentialities he would never develop his intelligence	4.30	3.94	.063	4.02	4.44	3.69	.012	4.04	4.12	—
3	It is by contradicting the child when he makes mistakes that you help him develop his intelligence	4.55	4.76	—	4.88	4.95	4.93	—	5.92	3.73	.000
4	To develop the child's intelligence, the teaching should be as individualised as possible	4.24	4.23	—	4.08	3.93	4.06	—	3.33	5.07	.000
5	The frequent repetition of exercises is indispensable to the development of intelligence	3.48	3.57	—	3.55	3.30	3.13	.149	3.37	4.17	.005
6	The child's errors reflect the inadequacy of his thinking	2.78	3.05	.108	2.69	2.74	2.90	—	3.20	3.08	—
9	The development of intelligence progresses according to a biological programme fixed at birth	2.71	3.22	.004	2.51	2.71	3.21	.006	3.32	3.16	—
15	For the child to make progress, all you have to do is show him the correct answer	2.05	2.26	.115	2.16	1.93	1.95	—	2.24	2.58	.146
16	The child needs negative assessment of his work in order to understand the necessity for improvement	3.70	4.19	.010	4.15	3.71	3.64	.058	4.74	4.33	.180
18	You can teach a child good manners, but not intelligence	4.12	4.63	.009	4.40	4.14	4.52	—	4.72	4.67	—

Appendix 2 (*cont.*)

					Teachers				Non-teaching parents		
		NPAR (157)	PAR (279)	df 1/434	STUD (123)	NPAR (115)	PAR (101)	df 2/336	BOL (76)	GEN (102)	df 1/176
21	The development of intelligence happens gradually, not in an all-or-nothing way	6.01	5.96	—	6.11	6.12	5.94	—	6.07	5.91	—
22	When a child makes a mistake in generalising a new rule to a situation where it is inadequate, it shows that he is making progress	3.90	4.06	—	3.92	3.68	3.92	—	3.84	4.37	.040
24	The use of audio-visual means (TV etc.) enables use to be made of a situation familiar to the child to stimulate his intellectual development	3.75	3.99	.167	3.67	3.46	3.64	—	3.62	4.61	.000
25	The child does not have to be shown the correct answer in order to make progress	3.98	4.14	—	3.92	3.89	4.32	.160	4.07	4.01	—
26	Punishment is a spur to progress	1.95	2.20	.062	2.13	1.90	1.92	—	2.18	2.49	.195
28	The child spontaneously develops his innate capacity for intelligence	3.20	3.86	.000	3.47	3.11	3.66	.044	3.72	4.17	.117
30	Within the family, the father plays the most important role in the development of the child's intelligence	1.68	1.75	—	1.52	1.57	1.59	—	1.59	2.03	.032
31	Intelligence does not develop; it is a hereditary gift	1.87	2.28	.003	1.67	1.91	2.43	.000	2.09	2.26	—
33	The development of intelligence occurs in stages, each of which results in the reorganisation of previous capacities	5.79	5.87	—	5.66	5.73	5.75	—	5.99	5.89	—
34	Television encourages the child's intellectual development	3.54	3.68	—	3.41	3.49	3.49	—	3.59	3.93	—
37	The development of language is dependent on the development of intelligence	4.15	4.13	—	4.02	4.18	4.19	—	3.82	4.31	0.79
38	Permissive education is all very well, but it is not effective when it comes to developing children's intelligence	3.78	4.10	0.60	3.66	3.83	4.23	.050	4.57	3.62	.000
39	The child only learns what his background teaches him	3.75	3.95	—	3.63	3.84	3.84	—	3.91	4.08	—
40	The child develops his intelligence by his own activity	4.73	4.82	—	4.99	4.82	5.30	.068	4.58	4.53	—
42	The child's errors are evidence of the level of his intelligence	3.01	3.23	.175	3.12	2.94	3.19	—	3.33	3.20	—
43	The child learns to respect the social rules of logical knowledge by learning respect for adult authority	2.21	2.76	.000	2.13	2.14	2.57	.013	3.16	2.66	0.60

44	Homework is important for the development of intelligence because it provides the child with practice at intellectual exercises	3.36	4.03	.001	3.87	3.12	3.47	.005	4.64	4.12	.079
45	Comics hinder the development of intelligence	2.46	2.74	.073	2.51	2.67	2.57	—	3.39	2.41	.000
49	The child only benefits from collective work if he does it with a more intelligent child	2.61	2.89	.061	2.41	2.46	2.87	.029	2.76	3.01	—
54	School curricula are the basic instruments for the development of children's intelligence	2.24	2.87	.000	2.46	2.03	2.27	.027	3.11	3.30	—
61	Coercion is never a source of intellectual development	4.82	5.02	—	4.76	5.21	5.23	.102	5.47	4.48	.000
63	Have a group of children working together; they will develop their intelligence better than if they each work for themselves	5.15	5.26	—	5.20	5.30	5.03	—	5.54	5.28	—
65	In order to develop his intelligence the child must be autonomous, and particularly be able to resist the suggestions of adults	3.78	3.75	—	3.10	3.50	3.76	.007	3.09	4.24	.000
67	Children who do not like school will not develop their intelligence	2.39	2.66	.054	2.16	2.39	2.72	.004	2.58	2.65	—
68	You have to use the child's mistakes to help him make progress	5.43	5.31	—	5.55	5.55	5.34	—	5.25	5.33	—
70	The development of intelligence requires a balanced affective development	5.37	5.57	.151	5.03	5.27	5.79	.000	5.45	5.44	—
71	The development of intelligence is the gradual learning of the rules of social life	3.62	3.62	—	3.37	3.52	3.51	—	3.82	3.59	—
72	A friendly relationship with the teacher is the best teaching technique for developing intelligence	4.35	4.84	.002	4.45	4.31	4.69	.180	4.86	4.96	—
76	The child has to be intelligent before he can be moral	2.55	2.81	.090	2.54	2.57	2.89	.162	2.93	2.64	—
77	A hierarchical relationship can never be the source of genuine intellectual progress	4.30	4.20	—	4.69	4.55	4.35	—	4.17	3.68	.000
80	The parents are the child's main model for the development of his own intelligence	4.55	4.57	—	4.60	4.38	4.45	—	4.57	4.71	—
81	It is reciprocity in relationships with other children which enables intelligence to develop	5.50	4.99	—	5.07	5.08	4.88	—	5.36	4.83	.005
83	For intelligence to develop, the child must first develop his language	3.74	3.93	—	3.57	3.71	3.79	—	3.70	4.24	.050
84	Mistakes are a source of progress for the child	4.90	5.10	.114	5.14	4.87	4.90	—	5.22	5.21	—
85	The child first of all learns logic from human relationships, and only later generalises this to natural phenomena	3.93	4.32	.009	3.71	3.91	4.22	.025	4.66	4.17	.033
86	Brothers and sisters are an essential element in the development of the child's intelligence	3.99	4.30	.069	4.34	3.70	3.89	.014	4.62	4.46	—
92	Going to a nursery from infancy onwards encourages the development of the child's intelligence	3.37	3.17	—	3.75	3.47	3.22	.062	3.58	2.81	.003

Appendix 2 (*cont.*)

				Teachers				Non-teaching parents		
	NPAR (157)	PAR (279)	df 1/434	STUD (123)	NPAR (115)	PAR (101)	df 2/336	BOL (76)	GEN (102)	df 1/176
97 The child develops his intelligence with his family as much as at school	5.66	6.06	.001	5.19	5.68	5.91	.000	6.08	6.21	—
101 The child is capable of understanding logic because he understands the rules of social life	3.37	3.55	—	3.28	3.44	3.39	—	3.95	3.42	.044
105 It is essential to the development of the child's intelligence that he should be able to establish good communication with his friends and with adults	4.99	5.28	.036	5.11	4.94	5.26	—	5.11	5.44	.132
107 For group work to be effective the children need to be at the same intellectual level	2.60	2.73	—	2.50	2.49	2.64	—	2.26	3.17	.000
108 Judgements of the child's work are more valuable than reports for the development of intelligence	5.14	5.08	—	5.16	5.15	4.93	—	5.00	5.28	—
110 The competence of teachers is the best guarantee of the development of children's intelligence	4.30	4.58	.104	4.29	4.22	4.40	—	4.67	4.69	—
111 The child develops his intelligence when he has to explain problems to a child less advanced than himself	4.57	4.88	.061	4.67	4.50	4.81	—	4.67	5.11	.087
112 The best stimulus to development is assessment, especially by means of reports	1.96	2.49	.000	1.73	1.83	2.03	.123	2.22	3.16	.000
114 To encourage the development of children's intelligence they should go to nursery school from the age of four	3.68	3.78	—	3.56	3.73	3.68	—	4.07	3.68	.165
116 The child's habitual compliance towards the adult does not allow him to develop his intelligence	4.18	3.90	.069	3.79	4.18	3.92	.149	4.36	3.53	.001
117 In order to understand the workings of society, the child must first have a grasp of logic and mathematics	3.00	3.22	.164	2.76	3.10	3.34	.017	3.54	2.87	.011

Appendix 3
Questionnaire 3: Teaching methods

Means on the scale from 1 (not effective) to 7 (effective) for parents (PAR) and non-parents (NPAR), for student teachers (STUD) and teachers with (PAR) or without children (NPAR) and for non-teaching parents from Bologna (BOL) and Geneva (GEN). The full numbers are given in brackets, as are $p < .20$.

					Teachers				Non-teaching parents		
				df				df			df
		NPAR (157)	PAR (279)	1/434 p	STUD (123)	NPAR (115)	PAR (101)	2/336 p	BOL (76)	GEN (102)	1/176 p
1	Make him collaborate with the child he is best friends with	5.13	5.15	—	5.04	5.11	4.99	—	5.28	5.22	—
2	Not to worry him, let him go at his own pace	3.63	3.66	—	3.24	3.65	3.77	.051	3.82	3.44	.164
3	Explain the task to him again	4.71	5.00	.042	4.72	4.76	4.70	—	5.11	5.22	—
4	Make him work with a child who is less advanced than himself	3.29	2.92	.026	3.07	3.24	2.77	.105	2.80	3.15	.188
5	Spur him on by making fun of him in front of his friends	1.33	1.30	—	1.20	1.29	1.39	.182	1.36	1.19	.098
6	Ground the examples in the child's everyday life	5.48	5.40	—	5.73	5.63	5.53	—	5.32	5.33	—
7	Talk to the parents about the child's difficulties	4.68	5.19	.000	5.00	4.69	4.62	.116	5.55	5.47	—
8	Refer the child to the inspector or the headteacher	1.90	2.15	.078	1.80	1.86	1.97	—	2.03	2.42	.088
9	Give him a punishment	1.34	1.47	.153	1.41	1.34	1.40	—	1.57	1.46	—
10	Show him a solution which is even less correct than his own	2.45	2.30	—	2.18	2.36	2.04	—	2.16	2.68	.030
11	Show him how the question often arises in relations with other people	4.47	4.62	—	4.87	4.46	4.57	.078	4.59	4.70	—
12	Check that he really understands the data of the problem	5.84	6.00	.133	5.85	5.85	5.92	—	5.92	6.13	.153
13	Modify the school curriculum so as to adapt it to the child's intelligence	4.76	4.43	.054	4.72	4.81	4.75	—	4.20	4.28	—

Appendix 3 (*cont.*)

					Teachers				Non-teaching parents		
		NPAR (157)	PAR (279)	df 1/434 p	STUD (123)	NPAR (115)	PAR (101)	df 2/336 p	BOL (76)	GEN (102)	df 1/176 p
14	Use more sitmulating methods, such as television	4.49	4.42	—	4.58	4.44	4.52	—	4.20	4.48	—
15	Tell him he is wrong without giving him the solution	3.17	2.72	.015	2.63	3.28	3.09	.025	2.86	2.25	.023
16	Suggest games which involve the problem to be solved	5.78	5.95	.107	6.05	5.84	5.89	—	5.99	5.97	—
17	Avoid concrete examples so that the child learns to reason abstractly	2.39	2.53	—	2.39	2.26	2.18	—	2.67	2.76	—
18	Help the child regain self-confidence	6.10	6.26	.095	6.09	6.12	6.27	—	6.34	6.20	—
19	Give the child responsibilities	5.64	5.85	.058	5.76	5.77	5.81	—	6.03	5.75	.075
20	Promise him a reward if he does better	3.41	3.83	.009	3.41	3.25	3.50	—	3.59	4.34	.001
21	Be more patient with him	5.50	5.84	.001	5.44	5.43	5.64	—	5.96	5.93	—
22	Make him do other problems of the same kind	5.19	5.52	.009	5.24	5.17	5.21	—	5.58	5.77	—
23	Give him a bad report	1.74	2.16	.001	1.59	1.63	1.62	—	2.55	2.40	—
24	Make him work with a child who makes the same mistakes as he does	2.76	2.31	.002	2.71	2.75	2.22	.011	1.95	2.68	.001
25	Advise the parents that the child should have extra tuition or stay down a year	2.09	2.62	.000	1.92	1.93	1.99	—	2.38	3.43	.000
26	Make him compete with other children	2.94	3.36	.017	2.72	2.62	2.27	.094	3.68	4.20	.044
27	Improve the classroom atmosphere	5.13	5.04	—	4.89	5.23	4.88	.106	5.16	5.12	—
28	Find out whether the child has family problems	5.39	5.51	—	5.46	5.50	5.61	—	5.46	5.43	—
29	Revise the formulation of the problem	5.59	5.66	—	5.59	5.64	5.70	—	5.43	5.79	.030
30	Ask for a consultation with a psychiatrist	2.48	2.81	.023	2.52	2.55	2.87	.143	2.51	2.96	.054
31	Present the question in a simpler form	5.52	5.65	—	5.16	5.52	5.55	.022	5.61	5.76	—
32	Tell the parents he should have private tuition	2.95	3.58	.000	2.93	2.47	2.65	.063	3.12	4.83	.000
33	Make him observe a friend who gives the right answer	3.30	3.75	.006	3.05	3.23	3.30	—	3.92	4.08	—
34	Give the child extra homework in the area where he has difficulty	2.46	2.89	.008	2.37	2.18	2.37	—	2.80	3.47	.009
35	Not to force him, things will come with time	4.08	4.13	—	3.54	4.06	4.09	.009	3.96	4.28	.155
36	Make him repeat the exercise several times	3.45	3.86	.009	3.23	3.10	3.14	—	3.68	4.70	.000
37	Show him that he is falling behind the others	1.93	2.14	.091	1.76	1.79	1.71	—	2.42	2.34	—

38	Make him explain his reasoning	5.51	5.84	.001	5.90	5.56	5.76	.034	5.84	5.91	—
39	Try to make him attentive	5.28	5.66	.000	5.41	5.24	5.65	.028	5.72	5.62	—
40	Check the vocabulary he knows	4.83	5.22	.011	4.46	4.92	5.19	.003	5.20	5.25	—
41	Help to dispel his psychological resistance to the subject in which he has failed	5.76	5.87	—	5.93	5.96	5.93	—	5.93	5.77	—
42	Teach him to be rigorous in his work	4.75	5.32	.000	4.50	4.80	5.30	.000	5.18	5.45	.168
43	Interest him in the problem posed	5.75	5.91	.090	5.91	5.78	5.97	—	5.87	5.88	—
44	Determine the level of his understanding before trying anything else	5.58	5.75	.136	5.40	5.70	5.87	.010	5.47	5.84	.031
45	Ignore him, if the majority of the class does the task correctly	1.47	1.53	—	1.37	1.38	1.42	—	1.46	1.69	.132
46	Show him the correct solution	3.63	3.92	.101	3.73	3.40	3.28	.122	4.05	4.46	.120
47	Warn him that you will tell his parents	1.88	2.32	.003	1.66	1.75	1.91	—	2.55	2.54	—
48	Do not tell him he is wrong	2.54	2.67	—	2.41	2.40	2.67	—	2.54	2.77	—
49	Ask for the child to be given a psychological examination	3.05	3.28	.141	2.85	3.05	3.14	—	2.99	3.65	.005
50	Ask him to respect the rules as he respects the teacher	2.49	3.31	.000	2.48	2.43	2.84	.076	3.46	3.67	—
51	Make him play the role of teacher to a younger child	4.34	4.74	.011	4.33	4.20	4.44	—	4.46	5.25	.000
52	Practise different problems which will help him find the right answer	5.63	5.75	—	5.76	5.68	5.67	—	5.70	5.85	—
53	Make the children work in small groups	5.61	5.67	—	5.77	5.68	5.77	—	5.70	5.56	—
54	Give a concrete example of the question	5.48	5.73	.037	5.67	5.44	5.54	—	5.70	5.95	.126
55	Make him repeat the correct answer several times	3.07	3.68	.000	3.22	2.92	3.35	.137	3.88	3.87	—
56	Do not intervene, as intelligence is a gift that cannot be altered	1.84	2.03	.111	1.72	1.77	1.97	—	2.11	2.03	—
57	Show him that the correct solution means everybody can be in agreement	3.60	4.07	.005	3.46	3.57	3.86	—	3.99	4.33	.164

Appendix 4
Questionnaire 4: Images of the child

Means on the scale from 1 to 7 (the left pole is given first, then the right) for parents (PAR) and non-parents (NPAR), for student teachers (STUD) and teachers with (PAR) and without children (NPAR) and for non-teaching parents from Bologna (BOL) and Geneva (GEN). The full numbers are given in brackets, as are $p < .20$.

					Teachers				Non-teaching parents		
		NPAR (157)	PAR (279)	df 1/434 p	STUD (123)	NPAR (115)	PAR (101)	df 2/336 p	BOL (76)	GEN (102)	df 1/176 p
1	Critical – conformist	3.78	3.80	—	3.26	3.72	4.10	.003	3.50	3.74	—
2	Likes to play with friends – does not like to play with friends	3.69	3.73	—	3.24	3.63	3.59	.032	3.50	4.03	.009
3	Educated – ignorant	3.63	3.78	—	3.35	3.65	3.77	.027	3.82	3.77	—
4	Smug – modest	3.93	4.20	.020	3.98	3.94	4.36	.016	4.04	4.17	—
5	Sensitive – insensitive	3.38	3.48	—	3.08	3.36	3.65	.017	3.22	3.50	—
6	Balanced – unbalanced	3.66	3.76	—	3.46	3.64	3.74	—	3.55	3.94	.043
7	Does not like studying – likes studying	4.10	4.02	—	4.28	4.10	4.08	—	3.86	4.09	—
8	Advantaged – disadvantaged	3.94	3.97	—	3.88	3.93	4.12	—	3.88	3.89	—
9	Chatty – silent	3.94	4.04	—	3.80	3.88	4.12	.159	3.91	4.07	—
10	Has a good vocabulary – has a poor vocabulary	3.75	3.89	—	3.85	3.70	4.00	—	3.87	3.78	—
11	Happy – unhappy	3.82	3.80	—	3.86	3.83	3.93	—	3.62	3.79	—
12	Does not imitate friends – imitates friends	3.80	3.59	.159	3.55	3.74	3.77	—	3.36	3.60	—
13	Curious – not curious	3.61	3.56	—	3.26	3.58	3.64	—	3.32	3.65	—
14	Tense – relaxed	4.17	4.13	—	3.98	4.15	4.08	—	4.18	4.13	—
15	Untiring – easily tired	4.04	4.14	—	4.18	4.02	4.20	—	3.80	4.33	.005
16	Jealous – not jealous	4.11	4.01	—	3.89	4.11	4.05	—	4.12	3.89	.167

17	Good at expressing himself – has difficulty in expressing himself	3.59	3.97	.020	3.96	3.60	4.09	.087	3.83	3.97	—
18	Has permissive parents – has demanding parents	4.13	4.22	—	4.14	4.15	4.29	—	4.22	4.15	—
19	Distracted – absorbed	4.40	4.21	—	4.34	4.36	4.23	—	4.28	4.14	—
20	Calm – excitable	3.92	4.09	—	4.26	3.89	4.12	.058	3.95	4.16	—
21	Uninterested – interested	4.38	4.40	—	4.53	4.37	4.30	—	4.80	4.20	.013
22	Has a good teacher – does not have a good teacher	3.89	4.08	.119	3.96	3.84	4.11	—	3.91	4.19	.194
23	Meticulous – disorganised	3.76	4.14	.004	4.04	3.77	3.97	—	4.17	4.29	—
24	Impulsive – self-controlled	4.15	3.94	.115	3.80	4.12	4.02	.154	3.96	3.85	—
25	Pleasant – unpleasant	3.59	3.71	—	3.72	3.65	3.72	—	3.68	3.71	—
26	Goes to bed early – goes to bed late	3.96	3.98	—	4.10	3.97	3.96	—	3.91	4.05	—
27	Impertinent – respectful	4.09	4.06	—	4.04	4.10	4.25	—	4.12	3.83	.063
28	Often ill – seldom ill	4.06	4.12	—	4.16	4.11	4.19	—	4.09	4.07	—
29	Helped by his parents – not helped	3.80	3.97	.147	3.77	3.81	3.86	—	3.93	4.12	—
30	Precocious – backward	3.69	3.78	—	3.53	3.71	3.80	.173	3.75	3.78	—
31	Solitary – has lots of friends	4.13	4.02	—	3.86	4.19	4.19	.027	3.95	3.90	—
32	Concrete – abstract	3.99	3.87	—	4.10	3.98	3.77	.196	3.89	3.94	—
33	Communicative – withdrawn	3.71	3.82	—	3.80	3.68	3.86	—	3.59	3.94	.102
34	Has a good memory – does not have a good memory	3.61	3.64	—	3.52	3.63	3.79	—	3.49	3.61	—
35	Child of rich parents – child of poor parents	3.99	4.01	—	3.89	3.98	4.05	—	4.11	3.91	.072
36	Superficial – profound	4.31	4.18	—	4.59	4.30	4.09	.037	4.38	4.12	.189
37	Creative – superficial	3.70	3.89	—	3.40	3.75	4.20	.002	3.75	3.68	—
38	Has no self-confidence – self-confident	4.10	3.92	—	4.08	4.07	3.84	—	4.12	3.84	—
39	Well-integrated – marginalised	3.81	3.89	—	3.89	3.77	3.91	—	3.80	3.93	—
40	Slow to understand – understands quickly	4.36	4.30	—	4.38	4.43	4.22	—	4.42	4.29	—
41	Mature – immature	3.75	3.68	—	3.58	3.66	3.74	—	3.50	3.75	—
42	Applies himself – couldn't care less	3.65	3.79	—	3.72	3.70	3.66	—	3.83	3.89	—
43	Reads a lot – does not read	3.70	3.80	—	3.79	3.70	3.97	—	3.82	3.62	—
44	Clumsy – adroit	4.31	4.23	—	4.23	4.32	4.30	—	4.38	4.04	.094
45	Likes playing – does not like playing	3.55	3.36	.117	3.33	3.46	3.47	—	2.92	3.59	.001
46	Anxious – calm	4.03	4.14	—	4.01	4.16	4.23	—	4.46	3.81	.000
47	Has brothers or sisters – has no brothers or sisters	4.01	3.90	—	3.90	4.00	3.87	—	3.92	3.90	—
48	Child of intellectuals – child of manual workers	4.10	4.10	—	4.05	4.16	4.23	—	4.12	3.96	.185
49	Does not watch TV – often watches TV	4.31	4.26	—	4.20	4.34	4.20	—	4.36	4.25	—
50	Disobedient – obedient	4.15	4.16	—	3.95	4.17	4.35	.005	4.13	3.99	—
51	Imitates adults – does not imitate adults	3.83	3.94	—	4.13	3.92	4.02	—	3.79	3.98	—

Appendix 4 (*cont.*)

					Teachers				Non-teaching parents		
		NPAR (157)	PAR (279)	df 1/434 p	STUD (123)	NPAR (115)	PAR (101)	df 2/336 p	BOL (76)	GEN (102)	df 1/176 p
52	Indifferent – motivated	4.39	4.23	—	4.60	4.42	4.28	—	4.45	4.01	.052
53	Surrounded by friends – left alone	3.81	3.96	.186	4.06	3.80	3.85	.171	4.07	3.98	—
54	Succeeds at school – does not succeed at school	3.68	3.72	—	3.72	3.68	3.63	—	3.72	3.79	—
55	Disciplined – undisciplined	3.82	3.91	—	3.80	3.82	3.73	—	3.72	4.22	.008
56	Asks questions – does not ask questions	3.70	3.70	—	3.54	3.70	3.63	—	3.53	3.90	.128
57	'Is always right' – recognises his mistakes	4.17	4.20	—	4.35	4.16	4.50	.109	4.11	3.98	—
58	Tell tale – loyal	4.35	4.35	—	4.55	4.43	4.35	—	4.61	4.18	.007
59	Capable of synthesis – incapable of synthesis	3.65	3.94	.074	3.42	3.73	4.08	.013	3.59	4.07	.062
60	Has a sense of humour – no sense of humour	3.65	3.82	.178	3.66	3.63	4.03	.035	3.63	3.75	—
61	Dominating – dependent	4.04	4.04	—	3.88	4.04	4.22	.083	3.96	3.93	—
62	Attentive – easily distracted	3.85	4.01	—	3.75	3.85	3.94	—	3.74	4.29	.026

Appendix 5
Questionnaire 5: School subjects

Means on the scale from 1 (not important) to 7 (important) for parents (PAR) and non-parents (NPAR), for student teachers (STUD) and teachers with (PAR) and without children (NPAR) and for non-teacher parents from Bologna (BOL) and Geneva (GEN). The full numbers are given in brackets, as are $p < .20$.

					Teachers				Non-teaching parents		
		NPAR (157)	PAR (279)	df 1/434 p	STUD (123)	NPAR (115)	PAR (101)	df 2/336 p	BOL (76)	GEN (102)	df 1/176 p
1	Geography	4.35	4.48	—	4.11	4.46	4.94	.001	4.16	4.27	—
2	Art	4.87	4.83	—	5.37	5.01	5.24	.184	4.93	4.35	.018
3	French/Italian	5.40	5.57	.183	5.59	5.61	5.65	—	5.53	5.51	—
4	Mathematics	5.76	6.02	.017	5.63	5.82	6.13	.003	5.95	5.96	—
5	Grammar	4.68	5.17	.001	4.64	4.56	4.97	.155	5.08	5.44	.088
6	Reading	5.01	5.44	.005	4.93	5.04	5.39	.120	5.45	5.49	—
7	Natural sciences	5.11	5.21	—	4.97	5.15	5.39	.082	5.08	5.14	—
8	Geometry	5.24	5.52	.028	5.15	5.36	5.78	.001	5.55	5.25	.123
9	Craft work	5.11	5.10	—	5.63	5.23	5.26	.035	5.38	4.75	.009
10	Handwriting	2.77	3.19	.021	3.14	2.76	3.54	.010	3.24	2.79	.090
11	Religious education	3.57	4.18	.001	3.46	3.38	3.90	.097	3.84	4.71	.001
12	History	4.97	4.90	—	5.20	5.13	5.30	—	4.58	4.75	—
13	Gymnastics	4.17	4.19	—	4.49	4.22	4.52	—	4.13	3.89	—
14	Music	4.58	4.69	—	5.04	4.57	4.78	.075	4.68	4.61	—
15	Poetry	3.38	3.74	.045	2.89	3.09	3.76	.001	2.97	4.29	.000
16	Composition	5.28	5.44	—	5.37	5.32	5.48	—	5.24	5.55	.097

Appendix 6
Questionnaire 6: Scientific disciplines

Means on the scale from 1 (not important) to 7 (important) for parents (PAR) and non-parents (NPAR), for student teachers (STUD) and teachers with (PAR) and without children (NPAR) and for non-teaching parents from Bologna (BOL) and Geneva (GEN). The full numbers are given in brackets, as are $p < .20$.

					Teachers				Non-teaching parents		
		NPAR (157)	PAR (279)	df 1/434 p	STUD (123)	NPAR (115)	PAR (101)	df 2/336 p	BOL (76)	GEN (102)	df 1/176 p
1	Theories of personality	5.31	5.23	—	5.36	5.30	5.30	—	4.87	5.44	.007
2	Comparisons between cultures	5.32	5.29	—	5.37	5.34	5.10	—	5.24	5.53	.131
3	Group dynamics	5.24	5.11	—	5.32	5.24	5.07	—	5.13	5.14	—
4	Social psychology	5.59	5.31	.021	5.53	5.59	5.36	—	5.21	5.33	—
5	Logic and mathematics	5.07	5.51	.001	4.81	5.08	5.61	.000	5.45	5.45	—
6	Paediatrics	4.38	4.58	—	4.26	4.26	4.50	—	4.67	4.60	—
7	Sociology of education	5.31	5.18	—	5.28	5.24	5.19	—	4.93	5.36	.032
8	Teaching techniques	4.75	5.29	.001	4.46	4.52	5.05	.032	4.47	6.15	.000
9	Biological maturation	4.92	5.03	—	4.70	4.84	5.28	.015	4.70	5.03	.119
10	Psychology of language	5.65	5.54	—	5.47	5.74	5.75	.100	5.18	5.60	.028
11	Psychoanalysis	4.43	4.39	—	4.96	4.51	4.58	.066	4.63	4.03	.018
12	Education	5.61	5.73	—	6.04	5.63	5.53	.007	5.29	6.25	.000
13	Psychology of reinforcement	4.84	4.66	.171	4.76	4.90	4.86	—	4.70	4.44	.177
14	Theories of motivation	5.35	5.30	—	5.08	5.35	5.34	—	4.70	5.72	.000
15	Body language	4.95	4.93	—	5.30	5.03	5.12	—	4.66	4.95	—
16	Ideologies of education	4.10	4.18	—	4.15	3.97	4.16	—	4.24	4.16	—
17	Programmed teaching	4.59	4.39	—	4.54	4.75	4.64	—	4.22	4.27	—
18	Clinical psychopathology	4.43	4.22	.135	4.41	4.47	4.53	—	4.34	3.82	.014
19	Sociometrics	4.16	4.22	—	4.07	4.11	4.50	.023	4.26	3.90	.011
20	Philosophy	4.03	4.31	.105	3.97	3.77	4.17	—	4.46	4.34	—
21	History of science	3.59	4.20	.000	3.54	3.39	3.91	.063	4.38	4.34	—

Appendix 7
Questionnaire 7: Sources of information

Means on the scale from 1 (not important) to 7 (important) for parents (PAR) and non-parents (NPAR), for student teachers (STUD) and teachers with (PAR) and without children (NPAR) and for non-teaching parents from Bologna (BOL) and Geneva (GEN). The full numbers are given in brackets, as are $p < .20$.

					Teachers				Non-teaching parents		
		NPAR (157)	PAR (279)	df 1/434 p	STUD (123)	NPAR (115)	PAR (101)	df 2/336 p	BOL (76)	GEN (102)	df 1/176 p
1	Books I have read	5.10	4.53	.008	4.72	5.40	5.61	.001	4.55	3.44	.002
2	Magazines or newspapers (even radio or TV programmes)	4.50	4.38	—	4.19	4.63	5.23	.000	4.79	3.25	.000
3	My education	5.06	4.13	.000	5.07	5.35	5.27	—	3.03	3.83	.018
4	Consultations with a psychologist	2.68	3.01	.134	2.47	2.58	3.88	.000	2.63	2.44	—
5	Consultation with work colleagues	4.83	4.51	.135	3.74	5.18	5.80	.000	4.20	3.45	.032
6	Talks with doctors	2.65	3.11	.039	1.97	2.42	3.56	.000	2.96	2.76	—
7	Discussions with friends	4.70	4.70	—	4.84	4.74	4.66	—	4.71	4.74	—
8	My professional training	4.18	3.79	.086	2.80	4.06	4.61	.000	2.86	3.67	.018
9	Discussions with other parents	3.82	4.70	.000	3.85	4.03	4.90	.001	4.61	4.56	—
10	Consultations with a paediatrician	2.19	3.08	.000	2.11	1.97	3.29	.000	3.37	2.66	.036
11	Contacts with welfare workers	2.86	2.72	—	2.37	2.83	3.47	.001	2.58	2.09	.085
12	(If you have children): discussions with your child or children's teacher(s)	3.41	4.75	.000	3.20	3.50	4.88	.000	4.93	4.49	.168
13	(If you have children): difficulties I have encountered with my child(ren)	3.61	4.76	.000	3.28	3.63	4.64	.000	4.95	4.74	—
14	(If you have children): discussions I have had with my child(ren)	3.71	5.51	.000	3.33	3.66	5.69	.000	5.45	5.37	—
15	My personal experience	5.62	5.51	—	4.67	5.77	5.93	.000	5.03	5.46	.141

References

Abelson, R. P. 1976. Script processing in attitude formation and decision making. In J. Carroll and J. Payne (eds.), *Cognition and social behaviour*. Hillsdale: Erlbaum

Abric, J. C. 1976. Jeux, conflits et représentations sociales. Unpublished thèse de doctorat d'état, Université de Provence

1984. A theoretical and experimental approach to the study of social representations in a situation of interaction. In R. Farr and S. Moscovici (eds.), *Social representations*. Cambridge: Cambridge University Press

Allen, V. L. and R. S. Feldman 1973. Learning through tutoring: low-achieving children as tutors. *The Journal of Experimental Education*, 42, 1–5

Anderson, N. H. 1968. Likableness ratings of 555 personality-trait words. *Journal of Personality and Social Psychology*, 9, 272–9

Ariès, P. 1973. *L'Enfant et la vie familiale sous l'Ancien Régime*. Paris: Seuil

Autrement. 1984. Intelligence, intelligences. *Autrement*, 57.

Balacheff, N. and C. Laborde 1985. Langage symbolique et preuves dans l'enseignement mathématique: une approche sociocognitive. In G. Mugny (ed.), *Psychologie sociale du développement cognitif*. Berne: Lang

Baldwin, J. M. 1913. *History of psychology*. London: Watts

Bandura, A. 1971. *Theories of modeling*. New York: Atherton Press

1977. *Social learning theory*. Englewood Cliffs, N.J.: Prentice-Hall

Beaudichon, J. 1982. *La Communication sociale chez l'enfant*. Paris: Presses Universitaires de France

Beauvois, J. L. 1984. *La Psychologie quotidienne*. Paris: Presses Universitaires de France

Bell, N. and A. N. Perret-Clermont 1985. The social-psychological impact of school selection and failure. *International Review of Applied Psychology*, 34, 149–60

Belsky, J., B. Gilstrap and M. Rovine 1984. The Pennsylvania infant and family development project, I: stability and change in mother–infant and father–infant interaction in a family setting at one, three, and nine months. *Child Development*, 55, 692–705

Bernstein, B. 1960. Language and social class. *British Journal of Sociology*, 2, 217–76

1971. *Class, codes and control*. London, Routledge, Kegan Paul

Berry, J. W. 1974. Radical cultural relativism and the concept of intelligence. In J. W. Berry and P. R. Dasen (eds.), *Culture and cognition*. London: Methuen

1984. Towards a universal psychology of cognitive competence. *International Journal of Psychology*, 19, 335–61

Berry, J. W. and P. R. Dasen (eds.). 1974. *Culture and cognition: readings in cross-cultural psychology*. London: Methuen

Bourdieu, P. and M. De Saint-Martin 1975. Les Catégories de l'entendement professoral. *Actes de la Recherche en Sciences Sociales*, 3, 68–93

Bourdieu, P. and J. C. Passeron 1964. *Les Héritiers*. Paris: Editions de Minuit

1970. *La Reproduction*. Paris: Editions de Minuit

Bruner, J. S., D. Shapiro and R. Tagiuri 1958. The meaning of traits in isolation and in combination. In R. Tagiuri and L. Petrullo (eds.), *Person perception and interpersonal behavior*. Stanford: Stanford University Press

Cantor, N. 1978. *Prototypicality and personality judgement*. Unpublished doctoral dissertation, Department of Psychology, Stanford University

Carugati, F. 1979. *Il Sé e l'identità: alla ricerca di una teoria*. Faenza: Fratelli Lega

Carugati, F., P. De Paolis and G. Mugny 1979. A paradigm for the study of social interactions in cognitive development. *Italian Journal of Psychology*, 6, 147–55

1980–1. Conflit de centrations et progrès cognitif III: régulations cognitives et relationnelles du conflit sociocognitif. *Bulletin de Psychologie*, 34, 845–52

Carugati, F. and G. Mugny 1985. La théorie du conflit sociocognitif. In G. Mugny (ed.), *Psychologie sociale du développement cognitif*. Berne: Lang

Cashmore, J. and J. Goodnow 1985. Agreement between generations: a two process approach. *Child Development*, 56, 493–501

Cattaneo, C. 1864. Dell' antitesi come metodo di psicologia sociale. *Il Politecnico*, 20, 262–70

Chance, M. & R. R. Larsen 1976. *The social structure of attention*. London: Wiley

Château, J. 1983. *L'Intelligence ou les intelligences*. Brussels: Mardaga

Chombart de Lauwe, M. J. 1979. *Un monde autre, l'enfance: de ses représentations à son mythe*. 2nd edn. Paris: Payot

Cohen, G. 1981. Culture and educational achievement. *Harvard Educational Review*, 51, 270–85

Cole, M. and J. S. Bruner 1971. Cultural differences and inferences about psychological processes. *American Psychologist*, 26, 867–76

Coll Salvador, C., C. Coll Ventura and M. Miras Mestres. 1974a. Génesis de la clasificacion y medio socioeconomico. *Anuario de Psicologia*, 10, 51–76

1974b. Génesis de la seriacion y medio socioeconomico. *Anuario de Psicologia*, 10, 77–99

Conroy, M., R. Hess, H. Azuma and K. Kashiwagi 1980. Maternal strategies for regulating children's behavior. Japanese and American families. *Journal of Cross-Cultural Psychology*, 11, 153–72

Dasen, P. R. 1984. The cross-cultural study of intelligence: Piaget and the Baoulé. *International Journal of Psychology*, 19, 301–6

Dasen, P. R., D. Bartélémy, E. Kan, K. Kouamé, K. Daounda, K. Kouakou Adéj and N. Assanolé 1985. N'glouélé, l'intelligence chez les Baoulé. *Archives de Psychologie*, 53, 293–324

De Paolis, P., W. Doise and G. Mugny 1981. Social marking in cognitive operations. In W. Doise and S. Moscovici (eds.), *Current issues in European psychology*, vol. 2 Cambridge: Cambridge University Press

De Paolis, P. and G. Mugny 1985. Régulations relationnelles sociocognitives du conflit cognitif et marquage social. In G. Mugny (ed.), *Psychologie sociale du développement cognitif*. Berne: Lang

Deconchy, J. P. 1971. *L'Orthodoxie religieuse. Essai de logique psycho-sociale.* Paris: Editions Ouvrières

1980. *Orthodoxie religieuse et sciences humaines.* La Haye: Mouton

Deschamps, J. C. 1977. *L'Attribution et la catégorisation sociale.* Berne: Lang

Deschamps, J. C., F. Lorenzi-Cioldi and G. Meyer 1982. *L'Echec scolaire: élève modèle ou modèles d'élèves?* Lausanne: Favre

Dickson, W. P., R. D. Hess, N. Miyake and H. Azuma 1979. Referential communication accuracy between mother and child as a predictor of cognitive development in the United States and Japan. *Child Development*, 50, 53–9

Doise, W. 1976. *L'Articulation psychosociologique et les relations entre groupes.* Brussels: De Boeck

1978a. L'elaborazione sociale degli strumenti cognitivi: dal postulato alla sperimentazione. In A. Palmonari and P. E. Ricci Bitti (eds.), *Aspetti cognitivi della socializzazione in eta evolutiva.* Bologna: Il Mulino

1978b. *Groups and individuals: explanations in social psychology.* Cambridge: Cambridge University Press

1981. La Construction sociale des instruments cognitifs: du postulat à l'expérimentation. *Psychologie Scolaire*, 36, 5–28

1985a. Le Développement social de l'intelligence: aperçu historique. In G. Mugny (ed.), *Psychologie sociale du développement cognitif.* Berne: Lang

1985b. Les représentations sociales: définition d'un concept. *Connexions*, 45, 243–53

1986. *Levels of explanation in social psychology.* Cambridge: Cambridge University Press

Doise, W., J. C. Deschamps and G. Mugny 1978. *Psychologie sociale expérimentale.* Paris: Armand Colin

Doise, W. and G. Mugny 1984. *The social development of the intellect.* Oxford: Pergamon Press

Doise, W. and A. Palmonari (eds.) 1984. *Social interaction in individual development.* Cambridge: Cambridge University Press

D'Unrug, M. C. 1974. *Analyse de contenu.* Paris: Editions Universitaires

Durkheim, E. 1983. (21st edn; 1st edn 1895.) *Les Règles de la méthode sociologique* Paris: Presses Universitaires de France

Durkheim, E. and M. Mauss 1969. (1st edn 1903) De quelques formes primitives de classifications; contribution à l'étude des représentations collectives. In M. Mauss (ed.), *Oeuvres*, vol. 2. Paris: Editions de Minuit

Emiliani, F. 1982. Azione concreta e rappresentazione sociale: uno studio su operatrici di asilo nido. *Giornale Italiano di Psicologia*, 1, 143–51

Emiliani, F. and F. Carugati 1985. *Il mondo sociale dei bambini.* Bologna: Il Mulino

Emiliani, F., B. Zani and F. Carugati 1982. Il bambino e l'asilo nido: immagini a confronto. *Giornale Italiano di Psicologia*, 3, 455–68

Emiliani, F. and B. Zani 1984. Behaviour and goals in adult-child interaction in the day-nurseries. In W. Doise and A. Palmonari (eds.), *Social interaction in individual development.* Cambridge: Cambridge University Press

Emler, N. and M. Glachan 1985. L'apprentissage social: perspectives récentes. In G. Mugny (ed.), *Psychologie sociale du développement cognitif.* Berne: Lang

Entwisle, D. and L. A. Hayduk 1978. *Too great expectations: the academic expectations of young children.* Baltimore: Johns Hopkins Press

Farr, R. M. and S. Moscovici 1984. *Social representations*. Cambridge: Cambridge University Press

Finn, G. P. T. 1985. L'intelligibilité sociale de la tâche. In G. Mugny (ed.), *Psychologie sociale du développement cognitif*. Berne: Lang

Flugel, J. C. 1947. An inquiry as to popular views on intelligence and related topics. *British Journal of Educational Psychology*, 17, 140–52

Forgas, J. P. 1981. Affective and emotional influences on episode representations. In J. P. Forgas (ed.), *Social cognition*. London: Academic Press

Francès, R. 1980. *L'Idéologie dans l'université*. Paris: Presses Universitaires de France

Fry, P. S. (ed.). 1984a. Changing conceptions of intelligence and intellectual functioning: current theory and research. *International Journal of Psychology*, 19 (special issue)

(ed.). 1984b. Introduction: changing conceptions of intelligence and intellectual functioning: current theory and research. *International Journal of Psychology*, 19, 301–6

Gartner, A., M. C. Kohler and F. Riessman 1971. *Children teach children: learning by teaching*. New York: Harper and Row

GFEN (Groupe Français d'Education Nouvelle). 1976. *L'Echec scolaire: doué ou non doué*. Paris: Editions Sociales

Ghiglione, R. and B. Matalon 1978. *Les Enquêtes sociologiques. Théories et pratique*. Paris: Armand Colin

Gilly, M. 1980. *Maître-élève: rôles institutionnels et représentations*. Paris: Presses Universitaires de France

1981. Rôles institutionnels facteurs idéologiques et représentation de l'élève par le maître. Colloque, 'Représentations sociales et champ éducatif', Aix-en-Provence

Girod, R. 1984. L'Inégalité des chances: quelques aspects de l'évolution des théories. *Pouvoirs*, 30, 7–13

Goodnow, J. 1976. The nature of intelligent behavior: questions raised by cross-cultural studies. In L. Resnik (ed.), *The nature of intelligence*. Hillsdale: Erlbaum

1984. On being judged 'intelligent'. *International Journal of Psychology*, 19, 391–406

1985. Change and variation in ideas about childhood and parenting. In I. Sigel (ed.), *Parental belief systems*. Hillsdale, N.J.: Lawrence Erlbaum

Goodnow, J., R. Knight and J. Cashmore 1985. Adult social cognition: implications of parents' ideas for approaches to development. In M. Perlmutter (ed.), *Social cognition*. Hillsdale, N.J.: Lawrence Erlbaum

Goodnow, J., J. Cashmore, S. Cotton and R. Knight 1984. Mother's developmental timetables in two cultural groups. *International Journal of Psychology*, 193–205

Gould, S. J. 1981. *The mismeasure of man*. New York: Norton

Grawitz, M. 1974. *Méthodes des sciences sociales*. Paris: Dalloz

Grisez, J. 1975. *Méthodes de la psychologie sociale*. Paris: Presses Universitaires de France

Gritti, J. 1978. *Elle court, elle court, la rumeur*. Ottawa: Stanké

Haroche, C. and M. Pêcheux 1971. Etude expérimentale de l'effet des représentations sociales sur la résolution d'une épreuve logique à présentation variable. *Bulletin du C.E.R.P.*, 20, 115–29.

Henderson, B. 1984. Social support and exploration. *Child Development*, 55, 1246–51

Herzlich, C. 1969. *Santé et maladie. Analyse d'une représentation sociale*. Paris: Mouton

1972. La Représentation sociale. In S. Moscovici (ed.), *Introduction à la psychologie sociale*, vol. 1. Paris: Larousse

Hess, R., K. Kashigawi, H. Azuma, G. G. Price and W. Dickson 1980. Maternal expectations for mastery of developmental tasks in Japan and the United States. *International Journal of Psychology*, 15, 259–71

Hewstone, M., J. M. F. Jaspers and M. Lalljee 1982. Social representations, social attribution and social identity: the intergroup images of 'public' and 'comprehensive' school-boys. *European Journal of Social Psychology*, 12, 241–69

Humphrey, N. K. 1976. The social function of intellect. In P. P. G. Bateson and R. A. Hinde (eds.), *Growing points in ethology*. Cambridge: Cambridge University Press

Inhelder, B., H. Sinclair and M. Bovet 1974. *Apprentissage et structures de la connaissance*. Paris: Presses Universitaires de France

Jodelet, D. 1983. Civils et bredins: représentations sociales de la maladie mentale et rapport à la folie en milieu rural. Paris, Unpublished thèse de doctorat d'état

1984. Représentation sociale: phénomènes, concept et théorie. In S. Moscovici (ed.), *Psychologie sociale*. Paris: Presses Universitaires de France

Kelley, H. H. 1967. Attribution theory in social psychology. In L. Levine (ed.), *Nebraska Symposium on Motivation*. Lincoln: University of Nebraska Press

Kohn, M. L. 1959. Social class and parental values. *The American Journal of Sociology*, 64, 337–51

1963. Social class and parent-child relationship. *American Sociological Review*, 68, 471–80

Kuhn, D. 1972. Mechanisms of change in the development of cognitive structures. *Child Development*, 43, 833–44

Labov, W. 1970. The logic of non-standard English. In F. Williams (ed.), *Language and poverty*. Chicago: Markham Press, 153–89

Lamb, M. E. 1975. Fathers: forgotten contributors to child development. *Human Development*, 18, 245–66

(ed.) 1981. *The role of the father in child development*. New York: Wiley

Lamb, M. E., L. Chase-Lansdale and M. T. Owen 1979. The changing American family and its implications for infant social development: the sample case of maternal employment. In M. Lewis and L. A. Rosenblum (eds.), *The child and its family*. New York: Plenum Press

Lautrey, J. 1980. *Classe sociale, milieu familial, intelligence*. Paris: Presses Universitaires de France

Le Disert, D. 1983. De la sociophobie au retour de l'individualisme: la représentation sociale de la créativité. Unpublished thèse de doctorat, Université de Paris VIII

Lefebvre-Pinard, M. and L. Reid 1980. A comparison of three methods of training communication skills: social conflict, modeling, and conflict-modeling. *Child Development*, 51, 179–87

Lemaine, G. and B. Matalon 1985. *Gens supérieurs, gens inférieurs. La controverse hérédité-environnement dans la psychologie différentielle de l'intelligence*. Paris: Armand Colin

Lévy, M. 1981. La Nécessité sociale de dépasser une situation conflictuelle générée par la présentation d'un modèle de solution de problème et par le questionnement d'un agent social. Unpublished thèse de doctorat, Université de Genève

Leyens, J. P. 1983. *Sommes-nous tous des psychologues?* Brussels, Mardaga

Luria, A. K. 1971. Towards the problem of the historical nature of psychological processes. *International Journal of Psychology*, 6, 259–72

McGillicuddy-De Lisi, A. V. 1982. Parental beliefs about developmental processes. *Human Development*, 25, 192–200

Mackenzie, B. 1984. Explaining race differences in IQ: the logic, the methodology, and the evidence. *American Psychologist*, 39, 1214–1233

Mead, G. H. 1934. *Mind, self and society*. Chicago: University of Chicago Press

Miller, S. A., N. White and M. Delgado 1980. Adults' conceptions of children's cognitive abilities. *Merill-Palmer Quarterly*, 26, 135–51

Monteil, J. M. 1985. *Dynamique sociale et systèmes de formation*. Paris: Editions Universitaires

Morrison, A. and D. McIntyre 1976. *The social psychology of teaching*. Harmondsworth: Penguin Books

Mortimer, J. T. and R. G. Simmons 1978. Adult socialization. *Annual Review of Sociology*, 4, 421–54

Moscovici, S. 1961. *La psychanalyse, son image et son public*. Paris: Presses Universitaires de France

1968. *Essai sur l'histoire humaine de la nature*. Paris: Presses Universitaires de France

1970. Préface. In D. Jodelet, J. Viet et P. Besnard (eds.), *La Psychologie sociale: une discipline en mouvement*. Paris: Mouton

1976. *Social influence and social change*. London: Academic Press

1981a. On social representations. In J. P. Forgas (ed.), *Social Cognition*. London: Academic Press

1981b. *L'Age des foules: un traité historique de psychologie des masses*. Paris: Fayard

1984a. The phenomenon of social representations. In R. M. Farr and S. Moscovici (eds.), *Social representations*. Cambridge: Cambridge University Press

1984b. *Psychologie sociale*. Paris: Presses Universitaires de France

Moscovici, S., G. Mugny and J. A. Pérez 1984–5. Les Effets pervers du déni (par la majorité) des opinions d'une minorité. *Bulletin de Psychologie*, 38, 803–12

Mugny, G. 1980. Introduction à l'étude expérimentale des rumeurs. *Bulletin de Recherche*, 20

1982. *The power of minorities*. London: Academic Press

(ed.) 1985a. *Psychologie social du développement cognitif*. Berne: Lang

1985b. La psychologie sociale génétique: une discipline en développement. In G. Mugny (ed.). *Psychologie sociale du développement cognitif*. Berne: Lang

1985c. L'intelligence, son développement, et leurs répresentations: présentation d'un programme de recherche, *Bulletin Suisse des Psychologues*, 6, 97–108

Mugny, G. and F. Carugati 1987. *Psicologia sociale dello sviluppo cognitivo*. Firenze: Giunti Barbera

Mugny, G., P. De Paolis and F. Carugati 1984. Social regulations in cognitive development. In W. Doise and A. Palmonari (eds.), *Social interaction in individual development*. Cambridge: Cambridge University Press

Mugny, G. and W. Doise 1978. Factores sociologicos y psicosociologicos del desarrollo cognitivo. *Anuario de Psicologia*, 18, 21–40

1979. Factores sociologicos y psicosociologicos en el desarollo cognitivo: una nueva ilustracion experimental. *Anuario de Psicologia*, 21, 5–25

1983. Le Marquage social dans le développement cognitif. *Cahiers de Psychologie Cognitive*, 3, 89–106

Mugny, G., C. Kaiser and S. Papastamou 1983. Influence minoritaire, identification et relations entre groupes: étude expérimentale autour d'une votation. *Cahiers de Psychologie Sociale*, 19, 1–30

Mugny, G., M. Lévy and W. Doise 1978. Conflit socio-cognitif et développement cognitif: l'effet de la présentation par un adulte de modèles 'progressifs' et de modèles 'régressifs' dans une épreuve de représentation spatiale. *Revue Suisse de Psychologie*, 37, 22–43

Mugny, G. and J. A. Pérez 1985. Influence minoritaire, conflit et identification: étude expérimentale autour d'une persuasion 'manquée' lors d'une votation. *Cahiers de Psychologie Sociale*, 6, 1–13

1986. *Le Déni et la raison. Psychologie de l'impact social des minorités*. Cousset: Delval

Mugny, G., A. N. Perret-Clermont and W. Doise 1981. Interpersonal co-ordinations and sociological differences in the construction of the intellect, in G. M. Stephenson and J. H. Davis (eds.), *Progress in applied social psychology*, vol. 1. London: Wiley

Neisser, U. 1979. The concept of intelligence. *Intelligence*, 3, 217–28

Osgood, C. E., G. J. Suci and P. H. Tannenbaum 1957. *The measurement of meaning*. Urbana: University of Illinois Press

Owen, M., M. A. Easterbrooks, L. Chase-Lansdale and W. Goldberg 1984. The relation between maternal employment status and the stability of attachments to mother and father. *Child Development*, 55, 1894–901

Perrenoud, P. 1982. L'évaluation est-elle créatrice des inégalités de réussite scolaire? Genève, *Cahiers du Service de la Recherche Sociologique*, 17

Perret, J. F. 1981. A quelles causes les difficultés en mathématiques sont-elles attribuées? Neuchâtel: Institut Romand de Recherches et de Documentation Pédagogiques

Perret-Clermont, A. N. 1980. *Social interaction and cognitive development in children*. London: Academic Press

Piaget, J. 1956. *La psychologie de l'intelligence*. Paris: Armand Colin

1965. *Etudes sociologiques*. Geneva: Librairie Droz

Piaget, J. and B. Inhelder 1948. *La Représentation de l'espace chez l'enfant*. Paris: Presses Universitaires de France

Piattelli-Palmarini, M. (ed.). 1979. *Théories du language, théories de l'apprentissage*. Paris: Editions du Seuil

Poeschl, G., W. Doise and G. Mugny 1986. Les Représentations sociales de l'intelligence et de son développement chez les jeunes de 15 à 22 ans. *Education et Recherche*, 7, 75–94

Ponzo, E. (ed.). 1977. *Il bambino semplificato o inesistente*. Roma: Bulzoni

Reiner, A. 1983. Yinbilliko: history of an alternative school. Unpublished doctoral thesis, Macquarie University

Roberts, G. C., J. H. Block and J. Block 1984. Continuity and change in parents' child-rearing practices. *Child Development*, 55, 586–97

Robinson, E. and P. Robinson 1981. Ways of reacting to communication failure in relation to the development of the child's understanding about verbal communication. *European Journal of Social Psychology*, 11, 189–208

Robinson, E., R. K. Silbereisen and A. Claar 1985. Le Développement de la communication. In G. Mugny (ed.), *Psychologie sociale du développement cognitif*. Berne: Lang

Rosch, E. 1977. Human categorisation. In N. Warren (ed.), *Studies in cross-cultural psychology*, vol. 1. London: Academic Press

Rosenthal, T. L. and B. J. Zimmerman 1978. *Social learning and cognition*. New York: Academic Press

Rostand, J. 1965. *L'Hérédité humaine*. (6th edition). Paris: Presses Universitaires de France

Rouquette, M. L. 1973. La Pensée sociale. In S. Moscovici (ed.), *Introduction à la psychologie sociale*, vol. 2. Paris: Larousse

1975. *Les Rumeurs*. Paris: Presses Universitaires de France

Salvat, H. 1976. *L'Intelligence: mythes et réalités*. Paris: Editions Sociales

Schubauer-Leoni, M. L. and A. N. Perret-Clermont 1985. Interactions sociales dans l'apprentissage de connaissances mathématiques chez l'enfant. In G. Mugny (ed.), *Psychologie sociale du développement cognitif*. Berne: Lang

Serpell, R. 1977. Estimates of intelligence, in a rural community of Eastern Zambia. In F. M. Okatacha (ed.), *Modern psychology and cultural adaptation*. Nairobi: Swahili Language Consultants and Publishers

Shipstone, K. and S. L. Burt 1973. Twenty-five years on: a replication of Flugel's (1947) work on lay 'popular views of intelligence and related topics'. *British Journal of Educational Psychology*, 43, 182–7

Siegler, R. S. and D. D. Richards 1982. The development of intelligence. In R. J. Sternberg (ed.), *Handbook of human intelligence*. New York: Cambridge University Press

Sigel, I. (ed.). 1985. *Parental belief systems*. Hillsdale, N.J.: Lawrence Erlbaum

Silbereisen, R. K. and A. Claar 1982. Stimulation of social cognition in parent-child interaction: do parents make use of appropriate interactions strategies? Colloque, 'Nouvelles perspectives dans l'étude expérimentale du développement social de l'intelligence', Geneva

Smedslund, J. 1966. Les Origines sociales de la décentration. In F. Bresson and M. de Montmolin (eds.), *Psychologie et épistémologie génétiques*. Thèmes piagétiens. Paris: Dunod

Staats, A. W. 1975. *Social behaviorism*. Homewood, Ill.: Dorsey Press

Sternberg, R. J. 1980. Factor theories of intelligence are all right almost. *Educational Researcher*, 9, 6–18

(ed.). 1982. *Handbook of human intelligence*. Cambridge: Cambridge University Press

Sternberg, R. J., B. E. Conway, J. L. Ketron and M. Bernstein 1981. People's conceptions of intelligence. *Journal of Personality and Social Psychology*, 41, 37–55

Stoetzel, J. 1943. *La Théorie des opinions*. Paris: Presses Universitaires de France
Stolz, L. M. 1967. *Influences on parent behavior*. Stanford: Stanford University Press
Strauss, S. 1972. Inducing cognitive development and learning: a review of short-term training experiments I. The organismic developmental approach. *Cognition*, 1, 329–57
Strauss, S. and J. Langer 1970. Operational thought inducement. *Child Development*, 41, 163–75
Tajfel, H. 1972. La Catégorisation sociale. In S. Moscovici (ed.), *Introduction à la psychologie sociale*. Paris: Larousse, vol. 1
Thommen, B. 1984. Social representations of intelligence. Colloque 'Représentations sociales de l'intelligence et de son développement'?, Geneva
Thuillier, P. 1984. La tentation de l'eugénisme. *La Recherche*, 15, 734–48
Tomkiewicz, R. 1984. In M. Gomez, QI = AM/AR × 100. *Autrement*, 57, 58–63
Tort, M. 1974. *Le Quotient intellectuel*. Paris: Maspero
Valsiner, J. 1984. Conceptualizing intelligence: from an internal static attribution to the study of the process structure of organism-environment relationships. *International Journal of Psychology*, 19, 363–89
Vandenplas-Holper, C. 1979. *Education et développement social chez l'enfant*. Paris: Presses Universitaires de France
Verolié, M. and M. Castello (eds.). 1984. Intelligence, intelligences. *Autrement*, 57 (special issue)
Von Cranach, M. 1982. The psychological study of goal-directed action: basic issues. In M. Von Cranach and R. Harré (eds.), *The analysis of action: recent theoretical and empirical advances*. Cambridge: Cambridge University Press
Vygotsky, L. S. 1962. *Thought and language*. Cambridge, Mass.: The M.I.T. Press
1978. *Mind in society: the development of higher psychological processes*. Cambridge (Mass.): Harvard University Press
Wallon, H. 1969. Henri Wallon, numéro spécial, *Enfance*
1976. L'étude psychologique et sociologique de l'enfant. *Enfance*, 105–16
Walper, S., K. P. Mulle, P. Noack and R. K. Silbereisen 1981. *Stimulation of social cognition in children: do parents use theoretically appropriate interaction strategies?* Sixth Biennial Meeting of the International Society for the Study of Behavioral Development, Toronto
Wechsler, D. 1974. *Manual for the Wechsler adult intelligence scale for children – Revised*. New York: Psychological Corporation
Whiting, B. B. 1974. Folk wisdom and child rearing. *Merril-Palmer Quarterly*, 20, 9–19
Wober, M. 1974. Towards an understanding of the Kiganda concept of intelligence. In J. W. Berry and P. R. Dasen (eds.), *Culture and cognition*. London: Methuen
Zavalloni, M. 1971. Cognitive processes and social identity through focused introspection. *European Journal of Social Psychology*, 1, 235–60
1973. L'Identité psychosociale, un concept à la recherche d'une science. In S. Moscovici (ed.), *Introduction à la psychologie sociale*, vol. 2. Paris: Larousse
Zavalloni, M. and C. Louis-Guérin 1984. *Identité social et conscience. Introduction à l'égo-écologie*. Montreal. Les Presses de l'Université de Montréal–Privat

Index